K. Suzanne Moorhouse, always happy with a Beardie at her side

I dedicate this book to all Bearded Collies,
past, present and future, in the hope
they lead a happy, content and fulfilled life
and give as much pleasure to their owners
as all my Beardies have given me.

Talking about . . .

'Beardies'

K. Suzanne Moorhouse

Willowmead, Kerswell Green, Nr. Kempsey, Worcs. WR5 3PE

First published 1990
Second impression 1993

ISBN 0-9521109-0-3

Jacket front: *Polhilsa Pulchritude of Willowmead (Pippin)*
Grand-daughter of Perfect Lady

Jacket back: *Ch. Willowmead Super Honey and her daughter*
Ch. Willowmead Perfect Lady

Photoset in 10 on 11 point New Century Schoolbook
Designed and produced by:
Rivers Media Services Limited, (Publishing Consultants),
Berrows Business Centre, Bath Street, Hereford. HR1 2HE
Printed in Great Britain by Redwood Press Limited, Melksham, Wiltshire

Contents

Acknowledgements

MY thanks are due to all the people who so kindly lent me their precious photographs and gave me the interesting and amusing stories about their beardies for the chapter on famous dogs of the breed, especially the ones who didn't need badgering to remind them.

To Major James Logan for his very comprehensive history of the breed.

To Maureen Reader who immediately agreed to do the majority of the typing of the manuscript for me, having to decipher my appalling handwriting.

To Anne Wilding who stepped in to write the Foreword, when Maureen was unable to do it, due to her mothers illness.

To John Stanbridge for all the excellent sketches he has done for the Standard, and last, but not least, to all my own Beardies, without whom this book could never have been written.

Photograph Acknowledgements

Chet Jezierski	1, 2, 6, 7, 12, 49, 71.	Pat Jones	164.
Evelyn Elliot	9, 95, 101.	Fred Randall	166.
Cynthia Pickering	10, 130, 130, 131, 131.	Mike & Janet Lewis	173, 176, 183, 184, 195, 198.
Anne Sauter	11, 36, 37, 38, 189.	Paul & Jean Keith	179.
Monty	29.	Maureen Betts	178.
Cooke	35, 36.	Beverley Cuddy	174.
Garth Nicholls	34, 39, 40, 67.	Don Maskill	172.
Rosie Schroeder	40.	Elsie Corderoy	170.
Dianne Hale	41, 176.	Shirley Holmes	185, 191.
Roger Carter	51, 52, 53, 53, 54, 54, 55, 56, 56, 57, 57, 57, 88, 88, 88, 89.	Jackie Tidmarsh	186.
		Trish Gilpin	188.
		Brenda White	192.
Justine Waldron	74.	Sue & Willie O'Brien	193, 200.
Mary McCormack	74.	Bryony Harcourt-Brown	196.
Pam Gaffney	93.	James Logan	218, 223, 228, 228.
Maureen Reader	108, 163.		
Anne Waldron	113.		
Pat Scott	129, 132.		
Barbara Iremonger	151, 152, 153, 153, 165, 221, 222, 225, 226.		
Joyce Collis	115, 156.		
Jenny Osborne	158.		
Jenni Wiggins	160.		
Lynne Evans	161.		

Colour Pages

Chet Jezierski, Anne Sauter, Tom Clarke, Brenda White, Elsie Corderoy, Jackie Tidmarsh, Jenny Osborne, Dianne Hale, Sue & Willie O'Brien, Althea Richardson, Mike & Janet Lewis, Cathie & John Whitaker, Cynthia Pickering, Pat Scott.

Foreword

IN my opinion the Bearded Collie is the closest to a shaggy mongrel that a pedigree dog can get which is why I was attracted to the breed many years ago. However unlike mongrels Beardies have traits all their own. Anyone who owns one or more of this delightful breed know what fun loving dogs they are, full of mischief and always ready for a game which make them ideal family pets.

My first Beardie, Ben, was a wilful character but without a trace of malice. His greatest pleasure was embarassing me in the showring, barking, pulling on the lead and rolling over for the judge. He would then spend the rest of the day sleeping on his bench looking as though butter wouldn't melt in his mouth. Oh how I wish this book had been available then as I could have learnt so much about what I was doing wrong.

Despite his antics at the shows I was bitten by the showing bug and decided I would like to purchase a foundation bitch. After studying the Beardies in the showring at that time I concluded I had to have a Willowmead. After several months wait Maggie, Willowmead Summer Wine, came to live with us. Whether it was her breeding or because I had learnt from my mistakes with Ben, Maggie was easy to train and show and went on to become my first champion. Since that day in 1976 when Maggie became part of the family Suzanne has always been there to answer any questions I had or help find a solution to any problem however small. She assisted with Ben's studwork and helped Maggie whelp her first litter while I had a stiff drink to get over the wonder of it all.

During the long chats we discussed the finer points of Beardies and I learnt a lot about the old dogs which to me were just names on pedigree forms. This book answers all the questions I had in those early days and provides much more besides. The section on the influential dogs in the breed will be an invaluable reference for the future and the amusing anecdotes by there owners really bring these Beardies to life. It's good to know that even the most famous Beardies have their mischievious moments.

That the author is eminently qualified to write a book about Beardies is beyond question. Beardies are in the family's blood as like her mother and grandmother Suzanne grew up with a Beardie as the family pet. She acquired her first registered Beardie, Ch. Willowmead Barberry of Bothkennar, in 1955 and has the oldest established Bearded Collie kennel in the world, 'Willowmead'. She was a founder member of the Bearded Collie Club and persuaded secretaries to give the breed classes at Championship Shows.

By writing this book the author shares her knowledge, expertise and love of the breed. It is both amusing, entertaining and packed with information about her experiences with the breed over the years.

I fully recommend this book to anyone who owns, or intends to own a Beaded Collie. Anyone who breeds a litter would be well advised to purchase copies of this book to give their puppy buyers.

Anne Wilding, Bendale Bearded Collies.

Introduction

SEVERAL times over the last twenty years, I have been asked to write a book about Beardies, one person even offered to edit it for me, but the answer has always been, I'm much too busy, just don't have time etc. Then when I was approached once more about two years ago I thought, well I have no intention of mating any of my bitches for at least twelve months so life will be comparatively quiet, why not have a go? I have always enjoyed writing, regularly sending twenty page letters home from school and essay writing was one of the subjects I preferred, so decided to give it a try.

I'm afraid I did not read any dog book I could get my hands on, as a friend of mine suggested, but just sat down and put my own thoughts, ideas and experiences, in I hope, a readable and understandable way. I tried to remember all the questions the many new puppy owners asked and answer them, greatly helped by a couple who had just bought their first show puppy from me and were extremely keen to learn everything they could, to rear and train their pride and joy.

I did not want to write about the various Beardie Kennels, as those are covered in every other Beardie book, so decided to do something on all the Tambora Points Trophy winners and the Bearded Collie Club best in show winners.

The one person that I knew had kept complete records of the breeds history is Major James Logan, and as I knew there was no way I could get all the data necessary, I asked Jim if he would help me with the history. I am delighted with the work he has sent me, and I'm sure everybody will find plenty there that is news to them too.

I have thoroughly enjoyed writing this book and hope that it will give pleasure as well as information to all that read it.

K. Suzanne Moorhouse.

General points to consider before buying a Beardie

THE Beardie is a medium sized dog that looks bigger than he actually is under his long shaggy coat. Bitches usually weigh between forty/fifty lbs. Dogs between forty-five/fifty-five lbs, so it's not too difficult when you have to carry them for any reason. The beardie has been bred for hundreds of years to work with sheep and cattle, which means he is a dog that has to work all day. No shepherd is interested in a dog that is tired after half an hour of running around, and today's beardie can still go all day, so he is not content to go for a sedate half hour stroll and sit quietly for the rest of the day. He needs long busy walks and as he has also had to use his brain to obey his masters wishes and sort out, as well as drive flocks, that brain is still there, if he is left all day, shut up in the house he still needs work. His busy body too will soon find things to do, I have heard of more than one house in disarray when the owners have been out all day.

I find beardies excellent guards too although they are normally dogs that love people. I do not have strangers round in the orchard at the back

A Beardie is an active dog - seen left: Britannia Sweet Libeardie and right: Bendale Sweeter than Wine

Britannia Ticket to Ride - at full gallop

of the house. Visitors come in through the front door, but on the odd occasion that someone has come round the back, the dogs are very protective of me and my property, some dogs more than others. One day, when I had the two or three that I knew were more inclined to guard indoors, as I had a friend coming, I called them in, and had left the ones out that I felt were no problem, the friend came up to the gate at the side of the house and put her hand over the gate to say "hello", she received quite a bite on one finger. I felt dreadful and bandaged her up, but as she said, she should not have put her hand over the gate. These dogs were only doing their duty and guarding the property, and I do feel much safer knowing that my dogs will protect me at the same time. When people come to the house the dogs are introduced to them in the lounge, they race in and say "hello" to everyone in complete delight, so if you prefer not to own a dog that has a definite instinct for protecting his property, it might be an idea to think of a different breed.

Temperament

Beardies also need plenty of exercise, again, when you think of the years of working sheep and the necessity of going all day, they need long interesting walks, not once a week but everyday. They are also dogs that need people. They love just to be with you, and will happily follow you everywhere, quietly behind you if you go out into the garden to work, lying by your side as you weed, or happily racing round. A small garden can rapidly turn into a quagmire of mud with the white beardie paws also quickly turning brown or mud coloured, with paws then having to be put into buckets of water before they come into the house, to save the furniture and carpets from also becoming mud covered.

Beardies are a very trainable breed, providing you do it in the right way. They are a very sensitive breed as opposed to a nervous one and if you ask a beardie to do something nicely and with kindness, he will do anything for you, whereas if you just shout and scream at him he will become totally confused and not be able to do anything right. You really have to find the balance between gentleness and firmness. All dogs are pack animals, and if you do not become pack leader, the intelligence of a beardie will very soon take over, to the detriment of all concerned, especially the dog. By firmness, I do not mean shouting or hitting the dog, but consistancy with commands and carrying through with all instructions. Beardies are great creatures of routine and will soon tell you if you have forgotten the time and its his usual walk at ten o'clock.

Choosing the Colour

Beardies are a most obliging breed for choosing a colour. There are five colours in the breed, and I defy anyone to be able to say what colour an adult will be when seen at eight weeks of age. The five basic colours are black, slate, blue, brown and fawn, all with or without white collie markings. I personally have never seen one without some white coat, but I understand it is possible. Blacks are born black and stay black throughout their life. Slates are born black, but go slate at any time after eight weeks of age or so. Blues are born a chinchilla grey and go usually a lighter shade of slate. Browns are born various shades from almost darkest chocolate to pale brown, and also change from sometimes as young as four weeks old. Fawns are born a pinkish mushroom brown, and go a lighter brown as adults. Beardies can continually change colour with every coat drop, dogs twice a year, i.e. spring and autumn, and bitches after every season, even into old age. The white markings are usually on the foreface going up to a blaze on the skull into a white collar, on the chest, front legs, and feet at the back with a white tip on the tail. Quite a lot of dogs do not have a white collar which is quite acceptable, although I personally prefer some white collar as it does give the impression of reach of neck for the show ring. Beardies also have the unusual trait of having eye colour to tone with coat colour so that a black dog has a dark brown eye, a slate dog also has a dark brown eye, a blue has a beautiful grey eye and browns a gold amber eye with fawns having a progressively lighter golden eye. A black dog with a light grey eye has been seen, but is strongly discouraged by breeders as it gives a very hard staring expression and the desired expression is soft and enquiring.

The coat colour changes are really dramatic. There you are with your jet black eight week old bundle of joy, with perhaps a slight greying pair of spectacles showing up and slowly everytime you brush him there is a slight change, at least so it seems, when you suddenly realise that at eight months old you cannot tell his white from his black, as he has changed to a pale silver all over. Then, slowly, at about fourteen months you see dark hairs coming in over the shoulders and quarters. These hairs steadily increase till they cover the whole of the back and you have a silver dog with white markings, which seem to steadily get darker, to the lovely shade of slate, so usual in beardies. The slate can be almost black to the palest of silver with all shades inbetween. It is the same with browns and blues. One brown bitch I had was really white all over at twelve months old. She had a full white collar and you just could not distinguish it from her brown at this stage. By three years old, she was the most beautiful gold brown colour, which she retained till she died. Quite a few dogs get steadily darker into old age, and occasionally one will start to go lighter again into the teen years and end up at about sixteen years or so nearly as light as a yearling. The other unusual feature of the bred is that pigment again follows coat and eye colour, so a black and slate have black noses and eye rims, whereas a blue has a bluish shade to his pigment, and browns have brown noses and fawns slightly lighter colours. I personally prefer the stronger colours and have never kept either a fawn or a blue, but know both are of equal merit. True blacks used to be pretty rare, but there do seem to be more around these days. I had my first one five years ago, and I just could not believe she would not fade out to a slate, but she is still jet black with thankfully a very good quality strong coarse coat. Most blacks are inclined to have very soft coats which is not desirable, as beardies should have coarse, weather resistant outer coats, with soft undercoats, as soft silky coats would never stand the harsh winter weather for the dog to work satisfactorily.

When the dog is at the yearling stage, it can be very difficult to distinguish between the slates and blues, and the browns and fawns. Sometimes the pigment on the blue is so strong and dark and the slate can be slightly washed out, which is not a good thing, so that when you are judging you just have to ask, as these days the eyes do not always give you the answer, which they should do if they are correct. With the brown and fawn, the best thing to tell them apart is that fawns usually do not fade out quite as much as browns, and the browns always keep the brown tips to their ears, whereas the fawns fade out completely. I usually find that with my browns their elbows usually stay brown too, but this does not always happen.

Male or Female?

There is often a difficult decision to be made as to which sex of dog to choose, when you decide to acquire a puppy. If you intend to start showing it can be quite an important thing to consider. The dogs usually carry a bigger coat than the bitches, don't drop coat so often, so will not have to be retired from the ring, whereas a bitch can often do a fairly dramatic coat drop after her season or after a litter. Your dog will only be used at stud if he can do a great deal of winning. Except for the occasional time, a bitch will not look so impressive in the showring, but could if she makes the grade of excellent quality, have some litters, providing she also produces good quality offspring, which applies to the stud dog too, of course. The most important thing, before you think of breeding from any dog, is the temperament suitable, are they happy, easy to live with dogs that are calm, obedient and sensible, loving and affectionate, as without these attributes, they should not be mated.

If you want a puppy as a friend, companion and guard, both sexes have advantages and disadvantages. I personally prefer dogs, they do not come into season at the wrong moment, usually just as you are about to go on holiday, they do not have the hang-ups and temperament mix-ups that can arise just before seasons, or false pregnancies just after seasons. I find they are equally, if not more loving than bitches, and usually better guards. A lot of people come with the idea firmly fixed that they want a bitch as they are more affectionate, are smaller and do not wander. If you never let your dog out to wander, and I strongly recommend you never do, as if he should cause an accident, these days you are liable for all damages he might be involved in, which could reach astronomical amounts. It could also involve you with neighbour disputes and perhaps unwanted puppies. I have never found my dogs show any inclination to wander, they are quite happy to stay close to the house and family. Bitches also are not necessarily smaller either, as I have had a dog the smallest puppy in a litter and a bitch the biggest. If you already have either a dog or a bitch you must definitely have another of the same sex, as to keep two entires in a house as family pets is virtually impossible, if you want to keep your sanity, and the happiness of the dogs. They get dreadfully frustrated if they know the bitch is in season in the next room, and the last thing you want is an unfortunate accident and again, unwanted puppies. The solution if you do prefer one of each sex, is to either spay the bitch or castrate the dog, then it can work to perfection. I personally prefer not to spay unless it is imperative for health reasons, as I find it gives bitches huge, very soft coats, which can take a great deal of grooming, as the softer the coat, the harder it is to keep free of tangles, but in some situations it is the preferable solution.

Another question I am regularly asked is, should two puppies be bought together, as people often think they will be company for each other and grow up together. I'm afraid the answer is a very definie NO. The two puppies will just want each other and have very little interest in their owner, usually get wilder in their games together, rip coat out all over the place and pay very little attention to any training you might be trying to give them. A typical situation is house training. Puppy A wets the carpet, you chastise and put puppy A outside for him to oblige there.

5

Puppy B smells the by now interesting smell and also marks the same spot, you again put puppy B outside, but puppy A can also smell that puppy B has wet and copies, housetraining lessons forgotton, so you end up at square one with usually two very upset puppies and nobody's temper improving. Do, by all means have two beardies, they adore each other and get on very well, but let at least twelve/eighteen months pass before you obtain the second one, and then the first one will usually readily help with training and you will find half your work done for you.

Puppy or Adult?

Another thing to take into consideration when you first think of a dog is, which is the right age to acquire him. I personally think a puppy has the edge on an older dog, if your circumstances permit, as with the saying "give me a child for a few months and he is mine for life", a lot of that also applies to dogs, those first lessons are the ones that really develop the character of the dog for the rest of his life. Puppyhood is also great fun, some of the antics that puppies get up to are a real joy to watch and join in with, and puppies grow up so quickly, it seems such a shame to miss these few short months of pleasure. There is always the situation sometimes when it is just not possible to have a very young dog about the house, then there are several alternatives to think about. You can

Puppy or Adult? - Pictured left to right: Desertstorm Blow'n the Wind, Britannia Sergeant Pepper, Britannia Ruby Tuesday

approach a breeder and see if they have something available, sometimes there can be a young dog that has been run on for the showring and not quite made the grade. It is as well to find out how much and what sort of training the dog has had as sadly a few large Kennels keep all their dogs in kennels and rarely, if ever, have them in the house, so there could be a real problem with house training and socialising the dog. Luckily in beardies, most breeders have just a few dogs and keep them in the house as pets, so of course, they would be fully trained and so make perfect pets, as show dogs have to be fully socialised and trained to accept grooming, other dogs, lead and car travel etc.

Beardie puppy playing in the snow

Another way to obtain an older dog is through the rescue schemes run

Baby puppy, Britannia Steel Wheels at 8 weeks and
Britannia Stars and Stripes at 4 months

by all the different clubs. There could be a problem with a dog off rescue as he could have been put on the scheme for various reasons, sometimes by foolish owners who do not understand the many and varied needs of an active, long coated breed, sold to them by people who have very little interest in how the puppy progresses, and not giving any after sales help, so the situation can go from bad to worse, and a small problem can develop into serious trouble, even to biting, and total misbehaviour, which can be very difficult to cure. There are a lot of dogs that come onto rescue although they are perfectly alright, as the main cause these days seems to be marriage break-up, so if you do prefer an older dog, rescue can be a thing to consider, providing you have the patience to wait for the dog to accustom himself to a completely different lifestyle and new environment, which a puppy would settle in to without a second thought. I have had three older dogs arrive at Willowmead at different times and all three were very insecure for a few days and needed masses of love and reassurance. They had all been in bad situations before I had them so that did not help, but all three were very devoted companions in a very short time, and there can be a great feeling of satisfaction that you have helped a dog who has had a pretty raw deal, and can give him a happy and fulfilled life.

Beardies, as a breed, get on very well indeed with other dogs and I have only come across a very few that are aggressive to any other dog. A bitch will grumble or snap if a dog will persistently pester her, but will if they meet as friends greet all other beardies, as they recognise their own kind at once, with delight and wagging tails. They usually greet all other breeds in like manner, not quite so effusively as to another beardie, but still with delight and are extremely hurt if the other dog does not reciprocate in like manner, or with total disbelief if the other dog should snap, as some of the terrier breeds are inclined to do.

Properly introduced, they get on very well indeed with the family cat especially with a young puppy, there is never any trouble, at least not from the beardie. Should you bring in an older dog that has been trained to chase cats, you could be in for much more trouble, so if you have a cat, I would suggest you ask the owner of any older dog you are thinking about if he is used to cats first, before you decide to take him home, as cat chasing is a very difficult habit to break. The same could apply to pet rabbits, guinea pigs or similar. A puppy will accept anything he meets in his new home and respect it, so long as you train him not to chase or tease. I used to have five cats at home when I started to breed dogs and all the dogs, including beardies and poodles, got on very well with the cats indeed. I do not have any cats now, as I prefer the birds, and all my beardies chase cats off if they discover any in the orchard. My sister has cats though, and when my dogs go visiting, they leave the cats strictly alone, almost being afraid of them, but it could be something to do with being in a strange house that makes them be well behaved, so I would not count on it being the same at home.

8

Beardies get on well together

Beardies are a fairly long lived breed, not like a great many giant
breeds such as Great Danes, Newfoundlands and such, where if you can
manage to keep them till eight years old you are lucky. I have heard of
two beardies living till they were nineteen years old. Romany, one of
mine was eighteen and his sister. Sweetheart, was seventeen when they
finally went, although most of mine have died between fourteen and
sixteen years old, so when you first think of a puppy, consider if you will
still be in the right circumstances in sixteen years time to still have a dog,
as far as is possible, of course. If you are likely to be posted abroad in
about five years time, you can certainly take the dog with you, but if it
should be a short term engagement, you will have to think of the six
months quarantine, before you can bring him home, and that could be
very expensive indeed. There does seem to be a dangerous year for
beardies though, and that is at eleven years old. I have heard of so many
of the breed dying at eleven years that it does cause some concern, but
providing they go through that year safely they do seem to go on till
fifteen or sixteen years quite happily.

Another thing that I am regularly asked by people thinking of a puppy
is, how are they with children. I am the second oldest of a family of five
children and was only three when Rory, my first beardie arrived. He
literally brought up four of us, as Sally, my youngest sister, was born
after he died, and he was the most marvellous friend, but my Mother
would never let us tease or pull him about. I remember once when I was
about six and was wandering around with a biscuit held in my hand

9

Walkies - even when you both
need a stick!

behind my back, when Rory quietly walked up and removed the biscuit from my hand and ate it. I burst into tears, telling my Mother, Rory had stolen it, only to be told if I wandered around holding the biscuit down, of course, he would take it. People must realise that the dog is a living, feeling animal and must have his rights about the house and with the family, and is not a stuffed toy for the children to maul about, then he will be the most perfect companion for everyone to get on with.

Beardies are very intelligent indeed and must never be teased, they can soon spot the difference between being played with and teased. Just to give another example of his working things out, with Rory again, he really loved you to throw a ball for him to fetch and return. As previously said, we were never allowed to tease, but a friends small boy thought it great fun to throw the ball for Rory. He did it three or four times, then pretended to throw it without actually letting the ball go. The child thought this great fun, because Rory rushed off for the first couple of times to look for the ball. He soon realised what the child was doing and the next time the child pretended to throw the ball, Rory just walked up to him and took the arm with the ball in it in his mouth and held it. The child promptly screamed and both Mothers came rusing out. My Mother told the child off for teasing, as she had been watching the whole performance, a salutory lesson for one child. I hope he never teased a dog again. Rory did not even leave the smallest mark on the childs arm, his hold was so gentle, but not every dog would be so careful, and if the dog had been chastised or hit after he had been teased, who is to say the next time he might have bitten hard, so it is as well to realise that beardies are exceptionally intelligent as well as loving dogs. I will never forget one person who said to me, "I will never have another beardie, they are just too intelligent a dog, for my taste"

Another point to take into consideration is the fact that they are a very sensitive dog as a breed, hating loud noises, possibly due to their extra acute hearing. If you stop to think, when he was a working dog up in the Scottish highlands, he had to go up a mountain to gather the sheep and listen for the faintest bleat from a sheep, possibly a great way off, without exceptional hearing, he would not have heard that sheep and would not have brought it down to his shepherd. Beardies really hate loud noises, such as low flying aircraft passing over flat out, as I frequently get over my cottage. They do get used to them, they have to, but I know they do not like it at all. The majority of them hate thunderstorms too, and I have seen the boldest, happiest beardie turn into a shivering jelly at the first clap of thunder. There are not many that find guns very appealing either. I was judging recently and some guns went off in the main show area, as the dog show was held in conjunction with an Agricultural Show. Most of my class of puppy dogs were really upset, and it did not help to assess movement when the puppy just wanted to leave as fast as possible. I have

even heard of beardies bolting if out and off the lead when guns go off fairly near, then it can be very difficult indeed to stop the dog, who is terrified. It is something to think about if you prefer an older dog and live near a rifle range or fields where the farmer puts bird scaring bangers on regularly. Your puppy will grow up and will be quite used to the noise, but an older beardie could have great difficulty in getting accustomed to it, if he has never met this problem before.

Beardies have very acute hearing - was that thunder?

Another question I am regularly asked is, how easy are beardies to train, as they are very intelligent, it can work both ways. I always say to people, ask your beardie to do something nicely, and he will do anything for you but if you shout at him he will get totally confused and you will just not get anywhere. Beardies try so hard to please, that sometimes they try too hard and people just get angry and say its a stupid dog. You cannot blame the dog if you have not been clear in your commands, believe me, beardies seem to know what you are thinking, never mind what you say to them. Some beardies can become very timid if not socialised from an early age, so plenty of stimulation and socialisation from the very first, is necessary.

Another point worthy of mention, is that of bitches coming into season. I have had a bitch come into season for the first time at six months, but never earlier and I usually find most of them start with their first season around twelve months of age. I have also only ever had two that cycled every six months, most of mine seem to be roundabout seven and a half to nine months inbetween seasons, and most are pretty regular in their timing, which does help when you are planning holidays. I have heard of two bitches that have been very late indeed with their first seasons, one was eighteen months and the other two and a half years. The owners had quite given up the thoughts of them ever coming into season, when they eventually did.

Occasionally, I have people enquire about buying a beardie, and when I ask if they are out at work all day and they say they are, then I will not sell, as I'm afraid beardies are not suitable to be left for long hours on a regular basis, as being very intelligent, they soon put their minds to finding something to do, and if there is nobody to train them otherwise, they will soon find an occupation that can turn out to be very destructive, as beardie teeth can go through kitchen cabinets extremely fast. Beardies are, first and foremost, people dogs, so really must have human companionship to be happy. There is nothing so sad as a beardie shut out, away from his master or mistress. They can also become rather noisy, a beardie being a huntaway dog who gathers his sheep by barking, and believe me, they never seem to get a sore throat from barking, so if he is left outside, he would just sit and bark all day, which would not make you very popular with the neighbours within near earshot, so please, if you are out at work all day, don't go and get a beardie.

Top left: Am. Ch. Willowmead Mid Winter Boy, Inset top right: Willowmead Man of the Moment, Centre: Pure Magic of Willowmead, Right: Ch. Willowmead Juno of Tambora, Bottom left: Ch. Willowmead Perfect Lady.

Standard of the Bearded Collie

THERE is one thing that needs to be studied before you purchase or even think of showing or breeding Beardies and that is the Standard. Every breed has a written Standard describing exactly how the dog should be constructed, the type and colour of coat and what sort of disposition the dog should have.

Bearded Collie Breed Standard

(Reproduced by kind permission of The Kennel Club)

GENERAL APPEARANCE: Lean active dog, longer than it is high in an approximate proportion of 5 to 4, measured from point of chest to point of buttock. Bitches may be slightly longer. Though strongly made, should show plenty of daylight under body and should not look too heavy. Bright, enquiring expression is a distinctive feature.

CHARACTERISTICS: Alert, lively, self-confident and active.

TEMPERAMENT: Steady, intelligent working dog, with no signs of nervousness or aggression.

HEAD & SKULL: Head in proportion to size. Skull broad, flat and square, distance between stop and oooiput being equal to width between orifices of ears. Muzzle strong and equal in length to distance between stop and occiput. Whole effect being that of a dog with strength of muzzle and plenty of brain room. Moderate stop. Nose large and square, generally black but normally following coat colour in blues and browns. Nose and lips of solid colour without spots or patches. Pigmentation of lips and eye rims follows nose colour.

EYES: Toning with coat colour, set widely apart and large, soft and affectionate, not protruding. Eyebrows arched up and forward but not so long as to obscure eyes.

EARS: Of medium size and drooping. When alert, ears lift at base, level with, but not above top of skull, increasing apparent breadth of skull.

MOUTH: Teeth large and white. Jaws strong with a perfect, regular and complete scissor bite preferred, i.e. upper teeth closely overlapping lower teeth and set square to the jaws. Level bite tolerated but undesirable.

NECK: Moderate length, muscular and slightly arched.

FOREQUARTERS: Shoulders sloping well back. Legs straight and vertical with good bone, covered with shaggy hair all round. Pasterns flexible without weakness.

BODY: Length of back comes from length of ribcage and not that of loin. Back level and ribs well sprung but not barrelled. Loin strong and chest deep, giving plenty of heart and lung room.

HINDQUARTERS: Well muscled with good second thighs, well bent stifles and low hocks. Lower leg falls at right angle to ground and, in normal stance, is just behind a line vertically below point of buttocks.

FEET: Oval in shape with soles well padded. Toes arched and close together, well covered with hair, including between pads.

TAIL: Set low, without kink or twist, and long enough for end of bone to reach at least point of hock. Carried low with an upward swirl at tip whilst standing or walking, may be extended at speed. Never carried over back. Covered with abundant hair.

GAIT/MOVEMENT: Supple, smooth and long reaching, covering ground with minimum of effort.

COAT: Double with soft, furry, and close undercoat. Outercoat flat, harsh, strong and shaggy, free from woolliness and curl, though slight wave permissible. Length and density of hair sufficient to provide a protective coat and to enhance shape of dog, but not enough to obscure natural lines of body. Coat must not be trimmed in any way. Bridge of nose sparsely covered with hair slightly longer on side just to cover lips. From cheeks, lower lips and under chin, coat increases in length towards chest, forming typical beard.

COLOUR: Slate grey, reddish fawn, black, blue, all shades of grey, brown and sandy with or without white markings. When white occurs it appears on foreface, as a blaze on skull, on tip of tail, on chest, legs and feet and, if round the collar, roots of white hair should not extend behind shoulder. White should not appear above hocks on outside of hind legs. Slight tan markings are acceptable on eyebrows, inside ears, on cheeks, under root of tail and on legs where white joins main colour.

SIZE: Ideal height: Dogs 53-56 cms (21-22ins); Bitches 51-53 cms (20-21ins). Overall quality and proportions should be considered before size but excessive variations from the ideal height should be discouraged.

FAULTS: Any departure from the foregoing points should be considered a fault and the seriousness with which the fault should be regarded should be in exact proportion to its degree.

NOTE: Male animals should have two apparently normal testicles fully descended into the scrotum.

I hope it might be helpful to go through each section of the Standard and try to explain it more fully.

The first part is under the heading "General Appearance". A lean active dog, longer than it is high in an approximate proportion of five to four, measured from the point of chest to point of buttock. Bitches may be slightly longer. Though strongly made, should show plenty of daylight under the body and should not look heavy. A bright enquiring expression

Totally wrong tail carriage - far too high and curled over the back

Acceptable tail carriage on the move

Correct reaching front movement - note again correct tail carriage
Ch. Willowmead Super Honey

Perfect side movement - note correct head and tail carriage
Willowmead Wish upon a Star

Lack of pigment - Butterfly nose

A white Beardie - This is not acceptable

Dog with plain markings

Dog with flashy markings

Blue and black 7 week old puppies

Black, brown and fawn 4 week old puppies

Blue Adult - Am. Ch. Bendale Special Lady

Slate Adult - Willowmead Silver Lace, 4 Res. C.C.s

Fawn Adult - Ch. Britannia Fawn Lady, owner Sondra Franc

Brown Adult - Ch. Willowmead Super Honey, aged 13 years

Black Adults. Left: Ch. Britannia Just Jeffrey, aged 6 years old, and right: Ch. Britannia Sweet Libeardie, aged 2 years

Willowmead Someone Special
A bright enquiring expression, also shows excellent stop

is a distinct feature of the breed. Lean does not mean thin. I find if you can just feel the ribs under a good covering of skin, but not the hip bones sticking up, that is about right. On some young dogs (under two years) it can be very difficult to get sufficient weight on as they can be very active and some can also be a bit picky about food, consequently, the weight is difficult to keep on them, but over two years if the dog is still very thin I would get a bit concerned and start looking for another reason for lack of body weight. At the same time do not get your beardie too fat, don't forget the breed should be lean and if you cannot feel the ribs at all, or he is straight from shoulder to tail with no waist, he needs to go on a diet and have lots more walks. Active, means just that, so if you don't like long walks and a dog that can play for hours, don't think of a beardie.

The next bit is self explanatory, so we will go on to 'strongly made' which really covers the whole dog. When you look at a beardie, he should look as if he has plenty of substance, not cloddy, such as a Newfoundland, not delicate such as a Whippet and we have all three types in the breed, so try and develop an eye to recognise the happy medium. Should show plenty of daylight under the body really refers to length of coat and I'm afraid the popular type of show coat these days blatently ignores this bit of the standard, as dogs are forever winning with coats almost trailing on the floor, with definitely no daylight to be seen under the body. See

Correct Top line

Dipped Top line

photographs for correct coat length. Bitch's can carry longer coats than dogs due to their shape, but it still should not be too long.

"Bright enquiring expression" is a definite must and can only be retained with love. A beardie that is not loved turns in to himself and looks so sad it is heartbreaking, his whole face goes dead and the eyes just go blank. Love your beardie, show him his favourite toy, a special tit-bit and you will instantly see his true bright enquiring expressive eyes.

"Characteristics", alert, lively, self-confident and active are all self explanatory, with emphasis on active. After watching my lot racing round today, just galloping for the sheer joy of being chased by each other their good health and love of life is evident, so please do make sure you have the facilities and the inclination for a very active dog.

"Temperament", steady, intelligent working dog with no signs of nervousness or aggression. Beardies are first and foremost working dogs. They have been bred for centuries to work all day and still have this ability which again lends emphasis on the active bit, and are very, very intelligent seeming to know what you are thinking, never mind saying, something to them. They can also tell the time and know just what you should do at any time during the day and soon tell you too. Beardies should not be nervous. This is not the same as sensitive which they most definitely are. Ask a Beardie nicely to do something for you and he will do anything you ask, but get angry, shout and scream and he will do nothing for you at all, just get upset and confused. Aggression, certainly has no part in a beardies make up and must be very strongly condemned. Any dog that shows any sign of aggression should never be bred from.

"Head and Skull", head in proportion to size, skull broad, flat and square, distance between stop and occiput being equal to width between

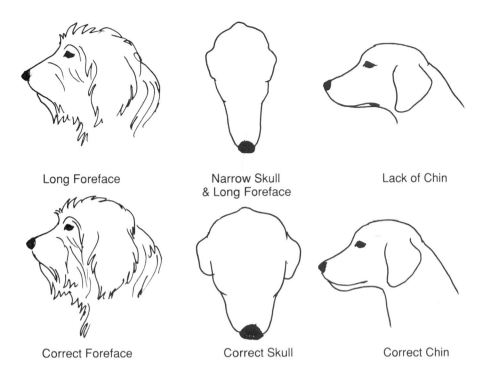

Long Foreface	Narrow Skull & Long Foreface	Lack of Chin
Correct Foreface	Correct Skull	Correct Chin

orifices of ears. Muzzle must be strong and equal in length to distance between stop and occiput, the whole effect being that of a dog with strength of muzzle and plenty of brain room. Moderate stop, nose large and square generally black, but normally following coat colour in blues and browns. Nose and lips of solid colour without spots or patches. Pigmentation of lips and eye rims follows nose colour. I feel great attention should be paid to the head being in proportion to the rest of the dog. There are quite a few dogs around that have heads too small for the size of body they have and it does give an odd imbalanced look to the dog as a whole. It is more common than too large a head in beardies.

Moderate stop can mean different things to different people. I like to feel a fairly distinct rise and in baby puppies is very obvious if they are going to have a good stop, so if a baby puppy does not have a really good stop, only a slight rise, it will be almost non-existent as an adult. A good stop gives a much nicer expression and usually goes with a good broad skull and strong foreface. I do like strong pigmentation, although a pale washed out nose leather and eye rims can sometimes indicate light coat colours in the adult dog.

"Eyes" toning with coat colour, set widely apart and large soft and affectionate, not protruding. Eyebrows arched up and forward, but not so long as to obscure the eyes. The colour of beardie eyes is a real mixed bag. For a black dog the eye should be a very dark brown, indeed, a dark slate should also have a dark brown eye, but not quite as dark as the black beardie. A light slate should have a correspondingly mid brown eye and a blue dog has a grey or slightly lighter grey to mink coloured eye. I have seen a white (not wall-eye) in a blue dog but found it very objectionable. The dark brown have a dark amber eye, this being totally different to the brown eye of a slate dog, and the lighter browns have an eye with more yellow in it. The fawns have a progressively lighter and more yellow eye than the browns to match their paler adult coat colour. Sadly light coloured eyes are creeping into the breed in all coat colours and the lighter the eye the harder the expression.

"Ears" of medium size and drooping. When alert ears lift at base level with, but not above top of skull, increasing apparent breadth of skull. A beardie should not have long pendulous ears when pulled down and measured against the foreface. I don't like to find the ears going any longer than just beyond the eye, when pulled forward towards the end of the muzzle. Some ears lie flat to the head and some, especially the smaller ears have a fold down the middle. These ears are far more mobile than the flat ear and have more lift when the dog is alert.

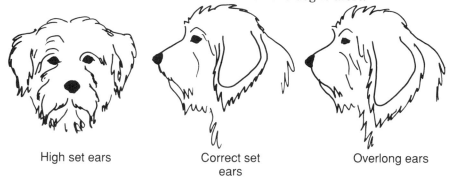

| High set ears | Correct set ears | Overlong ears |

"Mouth", teeth large and white, jaws strong with a perfect, regular and complete scissor bite preferred, i.e., upper teeth closely overlapping lower teeth and set square to the jaws. Level bite tolerated but undesirable. Beardie jaws are a law into themselves, something I have never heard of in any other breed. From the first signs of teeth appearing in puppy mouths, the top and bottom jaws can grow at different rates, from vastly overshot to slightly undershot and ending up as a perfect scissor bite, usually by six months, but it can be any thing up to two years before it is all correct. I must say, I do prefer to have a perfect bite all the way through teething, but certainly do not worry if it all moves about throughout puppyhood. The worst problem with beardie mouths is overshot, rather than undershot, in fact, I have only heard of a few undershot dogs but as Mrs Willison founded the Bothkennar beardies with two of her six original dogs being overshot, it is ever likely that we

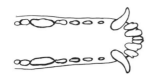 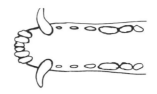

Bottom Jaw
Total 22 teeth. 6 incisors, 2 canines,
8 premolars, 6 molars.

Top Jaw
Total 20 teeth. 6 incisors, 2 canines,
6 premolars, 6 molars.

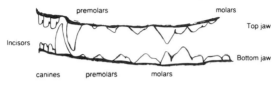

shall get a fair proportion of overshot dogs still occuring in the breed.

"Neck", moderate length, muscular and slightly arched. I feel the word *moderate* needs to be emphasised, as necks seem to be getting longer and longer, and consequently weaker and thinner. I do like a nice reach of neck but the whole shape of the dog is altered with long giraffe type look alikes and the extra long necks usually lose the slight arch which is so attractive.

Neck too long   Neck too short

"Forequarters", shoulders sloping well back, legs straight and vertical with good bone covered with shaggy hair all round. Pasterns flexible without weakness. The upper arm is not mentioned, but great care should be taken to check that this also is well angulated to give the required long reachy front movement. An upright upper arm usually means short stepping movement. Beardies should have good bone but not too heavy, which can make them look cloddy.

| Ballerina front | Close front | Correct front |

"Body", length of back comes from length of ribcage and not that of loin, back level and ribs well sprung but not barrelled. Loin strong and chest deep, giving plenty of heart and lung room. Particular attention should be paid to the length of loin, as overlong loins are proving the rule instead of the exception these days. Beardies have a very unusually shaped rib, being more oval with a narrowing bottom part. The chest should be deep enough to be below the elbows by a least an inch but never above the elbow. This is particularly obvious in young puppies.

"Hindquarters", well muscled with good second thighs, well bent stifles and low hocks. Lower leg falls at right angle to ground, and in normal stance, is just behind a line vertically below point of buttocks. Do watch out for over angulation, some beardies can be vastly overangulated, and some owners also set up the dogs far too wide behind. The rear legs should be more or less the same as the front legs as regards width when standing naturally. Also undesirable is the almost straight rear leg with no angulation. This sort of construction will prevent the dog moving

| Cow hocks | Correct rear |

correctly and lose the rear drive. He would certainly not be able to work all day, getting tired far too early to be of any use to a shepherd.

"Feet", oval in shape with soles well padded, toes arched and close together, well covered with hair, including between the pads. Please don't trim the hair between the pads, which is something I have been asked about on several occasions.

"Tail", set low, without kink or twist and long enough for end of bone to reach at least point of hock, carried low with an upward swirl whilst standing or walking; may be extended at speed, but never carried over the back and covered with abundant hair. Any stud dog will always put his tail up when he sees a bitch in season and I do wish people would remember that a dog may carry his tail extended at speed and not condemn him for it in the showring.

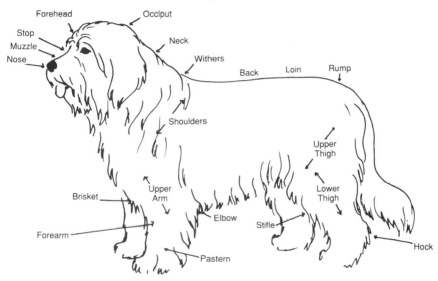

"Coat", double, with soft furry and close fitting undercoat. Outer coat flat, harsh, strong and shaggy, free from woolliness and curl, although a slight wave is permissible. Length and density of hair sufficient to provide a protective coat and to enhance shape of dog, but not enough to obscure natural lines of body. Coat must not be trimmed in any way. Bridge of nose sparsely covered with hair, although slightly longer on side just to cover lips. From cheeks, lower lips and under chin, coat increases in length towards chest, forming typical beard. There are quite a few beardies that have fuzzy coats reminiscent of Old English coats, luckily, not so many these days, but something that quite a few teenagers go through after they lose their puppy coats and prior to growing the correct adult coat at around three years of age. Coats can also get very heavy on

Over-long coat and falling away at the rear

the head at the same stage, but please do not resort to eye plucking or trimming if you intend to show, as our standard pacifically states "no trimming".

"Colour", slate grey, reddish fawn, black, blue, all shades of grey brown and sandy, with or without white markings. When white occurs it appears on foreface, as a blaze on skull, on tip of tail, on chest, legs and feet, and if round the collar, roots of white hair should not extend behind shoulder. White tan markings are acceptable on eyebrows, inside ears, on cheeks, under root of tail and on legs where white joins the main colour. In the tricolour dogs the tan markings can go almost white. I have only seen a very few dogs where the tan stays dark, it nearly always fades to almost white and judges need to be careful not to condemn a dog for white being in the wrong places, when, in reality it is tan markings. In a dog with full white markings i.e. full collar, white front legs up to body and white right up to the hocks, the white invariably goes up the stifle to the body also. This is perfectly correct. If the dog has white feet only on the rear, the white might not go up the legs at all, or might only go up to the body inside the leg, so is not visible from the side view. Although I feel the white markings give the dog a pleasing appearance, a plain dog can be of equal merit constructionally and must not be penalised for lack of white. In fact, if the plain dog is of better quality, he should always win over a flashy dog who is not so well made.

"Size", ideal height: dogs 53-56 cms (21-22 inches), bitches 51-53 cms (20-21 inches). Overall quality and proportions should be considered before size, but excessive variations from the ideal height should be discouraged. I am seriously concerned about the height that seems to be creeping into beardies at the moment. They are really getting bigger and bigger. I have a dog that is just under 22 inches that I am showing at present and he is being called small, as there are so many huge dogs in his classes. They must be 24 inches. I would most seriously penalise any dog over or under one inch out of the standard. If things such as size slowly are accepted, the oversize becomes the norm and another inch is added on, then we will end up with 26/27 inch beardies, something I would certainly not wish to see.

"Faults", any departure from the foregoing points should be considered a fault and the seriousness with which the fault is regarded should be in exact proportion to its degree. I find faults a somewhat controversial subject and feel the best way to consider faults is to what degree would the fault hamper the dog's working ability, for we must always remember the Bearded Collie is a working sheepdog not a lap dog. Consequently, if a bit of pigment is not quite filled in on a puppy, that would not affect his ability to work, but it is still a fault, and in an older dog certainly not desirable, but I would not totally condemn him. Cow hocks or ballerina fronts would definitely cause problems in a working dog, so if I was judging, the well made dog with the butterfly nose would go above the badly constructed one.

Note: male animals should have two apparently normal testicles fully decended into the scrotum.

Gait/Movement

Supple, smooth and long reaching, covering ground with minimum effort. A Beardie moving correctly is a joy to behold. He should float round the ring without the least sign of effort, giving the impression that he will never tire. The front legs should extend well forward, with the

| Correct | Narrow | Wide | Out at Elbow | Crossing | Crabbing |

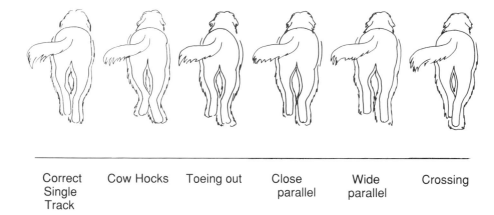

| Correct Single Track | Cow Hocks | Toeing out | Close parallel | Wide parallel | Crossing |

rear driving well from behind. He should never short step or hackney, lifting the feet high in a short stepping movement.

As his speed increases, so his stride lengthens, topline must always stay level at all speeds. He should neither toe in or toe out, front or rear, both wasted effort, which will tire him.

Hocks should move perfectly straight without any looseness, something which is seen very regularly in a great many dogs these days, as is also an almost circular movement in the front legs, both of which come from incorrect assembly of the dog's construction.

The tail can be carried either low, but not necessarily, or extended as he increases speed, to a level with his back, never curled up over the back as this gives a totally unbalanced impression of the picture of fluid movement.

Hackney action   Over angulated rear

Different Colours

The colours in Beardies make a fascinating study. In the original standards published in the late eighteenth century and early nineteenth century stated all Beardies, immaterial of which colour coat they had, should have darker eyes and black noses. I have seen really good sandy browns with jet black noses, although not registered dogs, they were quite definitely Beardies. But since Mrs Willison started with Jeannie as a brown, and she had a brown nose, all registered browns have brown noses. I have never heard of, or seen, the black nose in other than those dogs, but maybe it could re-appear again one day. It would now be considered a fault, as the standard definitely states pigment must follow coat colour.

There are five different colours in Beardies. Black, Slate, Blue, Brown and Fawn. Black and slate are both born black, with the slate changing colour at any time from a few weeks, to a few months, to even years old. Slate can be any shade of grey from almost black to palest silver. Blacks are born black and stay jet black, and are very rare. Most people who claim to have blacks are usually the owners of very dark slates. I am not keen on jet blacks myself, as I feel they are too similar to Border Collies but they can certainly look very striking with full white markings. Blues are born a type of chinchilla grey and usually have a quite different type of coat at six/eight weeks to the blacks. There is definitely no mistaking a blue puppy for a black, and I am somewhat appalled by claims of navy blue puppies being registered as blues, when they are merely slates. It can mess up breeders plans if a dog is registered as the wrong colour.

The browns can also be called sandy or reddish fawn, but for simplicity I will stay with brown. They can be either light or dark brown with all shades inbetween. When the puppy is still wet at birth, they can be so dark that it is virtually impossible to distinguish them from blacks but as they dry out you can see the brown showing up. I have had puppies as dark as this several times and they usually stay very dark brown as adults. Fawns are born a pinkish or mushroom colour and as blue to black there is no mistaking a fawn puppy. They also, as with some blues, quite often have a different type of coat to the browns. I will now only talk of the colours as black, blue etc. at birth, so as not to confuse the issue.

Beardies seem to be the only breed where the pigment and eye colour matches the birth colour, so a black should have a dark brown eye and the darker their coat, the darker the eye colour. If your Beardie has a pale silver coat he can also have a progressively lighter brown eye. A blue has a blue grey eye and I have seen an almost white eye in blues which I do not like, as I feel it gives a very hard expression. Although it would be a very serious fault in a black, it is far more acceptable in a blue. A brown has a lovely amber eye, a completely different colour to a black's eye and a fawn has more of a dilute amber eye, to match the lighter coat colour.

Blacks should have black pigment, nose, lips and eye rims. Browns, brown nose etc. and blues have grey noses, sometimes, so dark, that it is difficult to tell them from blacks. Fawns have lighter brown noses, lips and eye rims.

When you are breeding, black is the dominant colour of all the four and if you mate a dominant black to any other colour you will only have black puppies even if you mate him to a dominant brown you will still have all black puppies, as brown is recessive to black. In my line I have had quite a few dominant black dogs, one of which was Crofter. He once had a brown bitch belonging to Trudy Wheeler for mating and Trudy said she would have loved to have some black puppies from her bitch, but she was a dominant brown. She said this as they were tied and I informed her that providing the mating proved fruitful she was about to have her wish fulfilled, as Crofter was, like his father, and quite a few of his offspring, a dominant black. She did, of course, have seven black puppies, but every other litter she had were all brown, as she was not mated to dominant blacks before or after. Not all black dogs are dominant blacks. They are, in fact, fairly rare, as most Beardie colours are so mixed that the majority are factored for two or more colours. I find that the black/blue only are fairly common but you can get dogs that are factored for all four colours, which make the litter very interesting, providing you can find a dog and bitch that are both factored for all four colours. If one parent is only factored for one, two or three colours you will not get them from that breeding, as both parents have to carry genes for all four colours to get them. Also if you mate two browns together you will only have browns and fawns, not any blacks or blues. Plus if you mate two blues together, you will only have blues and fawns as both colours are dilute.

See photographs in colour pages.

How to obtain your Prefix

I think it would be helpful to mention about the British system of Prefix and Affix. When I first decided to start breeding dogs in 1953 I thought I would like my own kennel name. In those days, you applied, as now, to the Kennel Club for your choice of name. You have to send six names in, to see if they are available, on a form you acquire from the Kennel Club. All the first six I chose had been granted already, so I sent in a further six. Only two of these were available and the first one was Willowmead, which I was subsequently granted. In those days you could use your name as either an affix or prefix, in both the puppies you either bred or bought in. I decided to register all my black or blue born puppies with Willowmead as an affix, and all my browns or fawns with Willowmead as a prefix, so anyone reading the pedigree of a Willowmead bred Beardie would know that if the name such as Ch. Willowmead Super Honey (prefix) was born brown (or fawn) and Pure Magic of Willowmead (affix) was born black (or blue). This worked very well until the Kennel Club decided that all prefix's must be just that, and if you bred the dog you could only use your name as a prefix and if you bought in a dog you could use your name only as an affix. It is a very sensible idea, as anyone can tell who bred the dog and who bought it in afterwards, but it did rather mess up my system. From 1977 all my dogs have been registered with Willowmead as a prefix.

There is one exception to that rule, and this is if you have bred both parents, as in the case of Pippin, I bred her dam, Willowmead True Delight and sold her as a puppy. True Delight was mated to Ch. Willowmead Red Admiral and I had Pippin, the bitch from the litter. Her breeder registered Pippin as Polhilsa Pulchritude, but as I had bred both parents I could have registered her as Willowmead Pulchritude. I did not, as her breeder was keen to do the registration, so I just added "of Willowmead" on the end which makes it clear that Mary McCormack bred the bitch and I subsequently owned her.

Establishing the Willowmead Line

I have sometimes been asked how to establish a line. I can only tell people how I have established my own line, the Willowmead Bearded Collies, so perhaps it might be of some help.

Rory, 1944

I have, I suppose, inherited my love of Beardies, as my mother had one as a child and my grandmother also had one as a child, further back than that I cannot go. My first beardie was called Rory. He didn't have a pedigree, at least not one we ever saw, but as he was born in 1938, was he one of Mrs Cameron Millers? Sadly he died in 1947, and we all wanted another Rory, but as we lived in the Midlands in Warwickshire, there were no other beardies that we had seen in the area, so in May of 1947, we took a touring trip of Scotland. We only saw two beardies on that trip, even though we travelled as far as Fort William, well up into Scotland. The two beardies were with a farmer and his horse and cart, one sitting up beside him with the other running behind, both were slate and white. We stopped the car to ask the farmer if he either knew of any beardies available for sale, or if he would part with one of his dogs. His reply was "any amount of gold would not buy his dogs" and sadly he did not know of any puppies available, so that ended our quest for the time being.

In the meantime, I grew up, left school and started my own kennels of miniature poodles. In the Dog Annuals of 1954 I saw a half page advertisment with a photo of a whole row of beardies held by Rosemary, Mrs Willisons kennelmaid. At last, Rory dogs were being bred, and so hopefully for sale. I immediately contacted Mrs Willison about a bitch puppy. As there were so few bitches being born, I had to wait till the following June to get my puppy, Barberry of Bothkennar. I promptly added my prefix, so she became Willowmead Barberry of Bothkennar. The first show I attended with her was a sanction show held by the London Provincial Collie Club in January 1956 in St Mary's Church Hall, Marylebone, London. Mrs Willison had managed to have classes put on at most of the London Collie Club shows and it was a great thrill to attend and meet all the other people who had beardies, about a dozen of us, all told. The next show I went to was Crufts. In those days you did not have to qualify to go to Crufts. We were in the non-classified section, which is where we stayed until 1958. All the bitches bought from Mrs Willison were on breeding terms, due to the very few dogs and bitches available, so in 1956 Barberry was taken down to Mrs Willison to be mated. She wanted to use Bannock on Barberry but I did not like him, and neither did Barberry and she would not stand properly and he was not very keen either. I asked if we could try Britt and Mrs Willison was horrified, saying he was a maiden dog and she a maiden bitch. I suggested at least we could try and see what happened. Barberry loved Britt at first sight and he proved a very efficient stud dog. We had a very fast mating resulting in a rapid tie and nine weeks later, a litter of ten puppies. These days I would never let a maiden bitch, especially one so young, rear a litter of ten puppies, but due to the breeding terms arrangement (I have never bought a dog on terms since) and the fact that we were desperate for registrations to get the magic number of one hundred and fifty dogs registered in three years to apply for championship status, I let her rear all ten puppies.

Unfortunately, she followed the prevailing style and had eight dogs and two bitches. Mrs Willison came up and chose her two dogs. I luckily managed to keep the one I wanted, who was registered as Will O'Wisp of Willowmead, and then came the very difficult task of selling the rest of the litter. Both bitches were seven months before they left and the last dog went at ten months and half the litter were given away as pets to friends, the best price I got was ten pounds for the ten month old dog. One of the bitches went to Holland and was one of the very first beardies to go abroad. Mrs Willison had exported one or two before, but Lone Charm

Ch. Willowmead Barberry of Bothkennar, 1960

Will O'Wisp of Willowmead, 1958

was the first of the Willowmeads to leave the English shores. I had one more litter to have from Barberry to complete the breeding terms and this time Mrs Willison decided on Bobby of Bothkennar as the sire. The result was seven puppies and, at last, more bitches, prices had gone up too. We were asking ten pounds for all the puppies now and I sold all of them except the bitch I decided to keep for myself. She was named Merrymaker and was born in 1957.

In the show world I arranged with both the Birmingham Ch. Shows and the Midland Collie Club to put classes on for Beardies. The Secretaries were quite happy to put any classes on that you asked for, providing you guaranteed the classification one hundred percent, so we would usually have three to five classes, and I never had to pay out on any of my guarantees. Blackpool show also were happy to put classes on for beardies, as I was showing my poodles all over the country at the championship shows naturally the beardies came too in the non-classified classes. We regularly won best non-classified with one or other of the dogs and were usually to be seen in the best in show ring, which certainly helped to get the breed known. There was no group system in those days, all best of breeds went into the best in show ring together for Best and Reserve in show.

As I was very pleased with the type of beardie I now had, I decided to fix it by mating Will O'Wisp to Merrymaker as a half brother/half sister mating. Will O'Wisp was a medium sized dog with a lovely broad flat head, slightly long in foreface, but with a good dark eye. He had a very straight coat which, like his sire Britt, never put on a great deal of length, and was very easy indeed to care for. His movement was a joy to watch, very sound, driving and true. He did carry his tail up a bit, more than is popular today, but never over his back. My brother, Michael, used to handle him quite often in the showring, and I will never forget once, when we were at a championship show with Tom Corbett, one of our older top all-rounders judging, Michael took Will O'Wisp up to the top of the straight up and down, he turned to come back and as he did, tapped Will O'Wisp's tail down. As he arrived back at the judge, Mr Corbett told him never to touch a dogs tail in the ring again. A salutary lesson I have never forgotten. Merrymaker was a pretty bitch with again a nice head, she didn't have the longer foreface of Will O'Wisp and never carried her tail up. Her coat was not as good as his, with more of a wave in it. She was also nice and sound, but as her sire was Bobby of Bothkennar, I was careful with checking her offspring, as he used to move a little close behind.

I felt as there was no inbreeding whatsoever in the pedigree, at least we had no knowledge of it, as most of the pedigree's were blank spaces or filled in with the popular work "unknown" or a "trained worker". From this mating I kept a brown dog called Audacity and sold a brown bitch called My Honey to Mary Partridge of Wishanger beardies. Mary had also bought Barberry's litter brother, "Barley", from Mrs Willison.

30

A Slate dog - 6 months old - Willowmead Wish upon a Star

12 months old - Willowmead Wish upon a Star

2 years old - Willowmead Wish upon a Star

A Brown dog - 7 weeks old - Am. Ch. Willowmead Red Ruairidh

12 months old - Am. Ch. Willowmead Red Ruairidh

4 years old - Am. Ch. Willowmead Red Ruairidh

Some lovely head studies
Left: A Black dog
Ch. Britannia Just Jeffrey
at 6 years

Right: A Blue dog
Nick Sauter
from the Willowmead kennels

Left: A Brown dog,
Am. Ch. Willowmead
Mid Winter Boy

Right: A Slate dog
Ch. Black Velvet
of Willowmead

A Brown bitch - 10 months old - Ch. Willowmead Perfect Lady

14 months old - Ch. Willowmead Perfect Lady

Three years old - Ch. Willowmead Perfect Lady

A Black puppy - Ch. Willowmead Plain and Fancy

Right: A Brown puppy
Am. Ch. Willowmead Red Ruairidh

Left: A Black puppy
Britannia Stars and Stripes

A Blue puppy - Nick Sauter

Audacity was a lovely colour and had a very straight coat, long reachy movement, won best of breed at eight months old and had a habit of chewing all the coat off his own legs, his mothers and fathers, and any of my other beardie's legs he could get his teeth into, so regrettably I decided he would have to go and found him a very good home to work sheep, keeping him so busy that he didn't have time to chew, or if he did, the fact he had short haired legs would be an advantage, rather than the disadvantage it was in the showring.

In the meantime, the number of beardies were steadily increasing at each show and we were getting more classes in consequence. I remember we were walking into a show once with the usual four dogs we had entered, when I was delighted to hear a voice behind me say "its nice to see bearded collies being shown again". It was Mr Warner-Hill, a very well-known and respected judge, and a real event to at last find a judge who actually recognised the breed. We went to so many open and sanction shows where you just knew the judge was wondering how we had managed to enter a mongrel, but slowly, more people started to realise it really was a breed, and due to the fact all the dogs were so sound, we regularly won, which certainly encouraged us to continue. All the collie clubs put classes on for us, so we were getting a fair amount of beardie classes to compete in and we thought nothing of travelling from one end of the country to the other, if they scheduled a class for beardies only. I was doing well with my dogs and the best year I ever had was in 1958 when we took every best of breed and several best of opposite sex too at every show where beardies were classified, with one or other of the dogs, Barberry, Will O'Wisp and Merrymaker, including Crufts, a record I doubt if any one will ever be able to beat.

We also had managed to register the magic one hundred and fifty dogs in three years so qualified for C.C.'s. The first year we had C.C's awarded was 1959, so I decided to go to East Africa to see my sister who had gone out the year before to get married. I only managed to get to Crufts that year as I was out of the country for five months from April to the end of September, so missed all the other three shows with C.C's on offer. I don't think I would go away now if I had stopped to think, but champions didn't seem very important to me in those days.

In the meantime, as a litter sister of Merrymaker, Moonmaiden, who had been sold to some people in Birmingham had come back to me, and I consequently sold her to Mrs Amice Pitt of King Charles fame. Mrs Pitt had moved up to a cottage on a big shoot in Dumfries and felt she would like a bigger dog than the cavaliers and pugs she had, as she lived in a very isolated spot. She did not want a puppy so I offered her Moonmaiden on breeding terms. Mrs Pitt found a very nice beardie that lived near to her that was a very good worker indeed and asked if she could use him on Moonmaiden rather than go back to a dog in the show world. I was delighted, as I wanted to reintroduce the working ability into my line. I consequently collected two puppies, a dog and a bitch, called Romany,

Merrymaker of Willowmead, 1959

Sweetheart of Willowmead, 1960

registered as Gypsy and Sweetheart. Sweetheart was a strong dark slate with the best shoulders I have seen in a beardie ever. Romany was a very strongly marked tricolour. Both had excellent bone and both moved really well, with lovely heads and dark eyes. I showed both with considerable success for about twelve months, then due to family commitments in 1961 I had to stop all my showing, so missed the fact that Mrs Willison was having to disband her kennels. Sweetheart, Romany and Merrymaker were found new homes. My father took Will O'Wisp, so he was never shown beyond his two C.C.'s. Barberry had won four C.C.'s so had obtained her championship. Sweetheart had been sold on breeding terms so, as I was not able to get her to another dog, I used Will O'Wisp. It proved a very nice litter and I retained Ruairidh. His temperament was the most perfect I have ever had since I had started with my show beardies. He was a good sized dog, beautiful head and with his mother's excellent shoulder. He was only shown twice, once a friend took him to Crufts where he did nothing and I took him to one show in Birmingham where he won all through his classes and the C.C.

By this time, Barberry had died, so I was left with only Ruairidh. In 1965 Diane Hale asked me if she could use Ruairidh at stud on her bitch Bobby's Girl of Bothkennar, a daughter of Bobby. The pedigree was very interesting and I was very pleased with the three puppies that it produced, Ch. Adorable, who was BOB at Crufts, Anne-Marie who had 10 Res. C.C's and a dog who went as a pet, but could easily have been

Ch. Broadholme Cindy Sue of Willowmead

shown. Diane used Ruairidh on Bobby's Girl again in 1967. This time there were eight puppies. I went to see them at six weeks and chose the pick dog and bitch for her and said they were a very nice litter again. Two weeks later Ruairidh, who was only five years old was killed by a car. I was desperate to get in touch with Diane to see if she had any puppies left. She still had a pet dog and the pick bitch. I collected the dog as I wanted to replace Ruairidh, but I'm afraid that within twenty four hours had taken him back, as he was nothing like my beardies at all. He was his mothers' son and nothing like his father at all, so I collected Cindy-Sue. She was everything I wanted, did all the same things that her father had done, even to putting all her toys under the same tree as he had always done.

I had not intended ever going back into the showring, but Diane begged me to show Cindy-Sue, now called Barberry after her famous forebear, as entries were so bad at shows, we were in danger of loosing our classes, so I relented and entered her at a collie club open show. She was eight months old and went best of breed. She then went to a championship show and won her class again, went to her next championship show and won bitch C.C. dropped her coat, so stayed at home for a few months, went to her next five shows where she won C.C. and usually best of breed, and at just under two years old, being a

Braelyn Broadholme Crofter

34

champion at eighteen months was retired from the showring. Cindy-Sue inherited a lovely straight coat and her fathers lovely floating movement, with her Grandmothers excellent shoulder. I had wanted to mate her to Ch. Osmart Bonnie Blue Braid and took her up to Mrs Osbornes, unfortunately Braid did not seem able to do the mating, so in desperation, I agreed to use Yager Aplomb, a brown dog Mrs Osborne had there, who mated her with no trouble. I retained a brown bitch, Wild Honey and Barbara Iremonger had picked a dog, Magic Moments, and he was her foundation dog for the Sunbree kennels. I later sold Wild Honey to Finland and have regretted it ever since.

The people who had bought Crofter, the pick dog of Barberry's litter found they were unable to keep him, so he ended up with me. Crofter proved to be a very versatile sire. He produced the first registered search and rescue dog in Scotland, the first qualified guide dog for the blind from a mating to one of Mrs Fosters Bredon bitches, he had International champion, champion and obedience champion children. Several of his offspring worked sheep and cattle for their farmer owners and Crofter himself won one C.C. and two reserve C.C's. He was a good sized dog with a long straight coat that he never lost, had super reach and drive and was one of the most courageous dogs I have ever known. Crofter was mated to a bitch called Breckdale Cala Sona River Danube who was a daughter of Alastair of Willowmead, a son of my original Barberry.

Ch. Willowmead Super Honey

35

Breckdale Pretty Maid, 1975, 1 C.C., 4 Res. C.C.s

Ch. Black Velvet of Willowmead

36

Cindy-Sue went back to Braid to try and see if we could get her mated to him again, but still no luck, so I took her straight away to my second choice, Ch. Wishanger Cairnbhan, where again, she was mated easily, and produced nine puppies. From this litter I retained a brown bitch, Willowmead Super Honey to replace Wild Honey from the first mating. Cairnbhan was a son of My Honey, so went directly back to Merrymaker and Will O'Wisp. Super Honey had a beautiful head and expression, a really rich sandy coat with the slight highland wave, still retaining the super shoulders and floating movement of Ruairidh and Sweetheart.

I was now developing two lines, one from Crofter and one from Cindy-Sue. Breckdale Pretty Maid, Crofters daughter was mated to Edenborough Soaring High, full brother to Ch. Edenborough Blue Bracken and produced Ch.'s Black Magic and Black Velvet and later to Braid who had no trouble mating her, and produced Ch. Dutch Bonnet. She also produced many overseas champions. Pretty Maid only managed to win one C.C. and four reserve C.C.'s, as she was being campaigned at the same time as Ch. Willowmead Mignonette of Orora, a full sister to Super Honey, who was top beardie, so poor Pretty Maid had to be content with reserve C.C.'s.

Super Honey, went for her first litter to Ch. Edenborough Blue

Ch. Willowmead Perfect Lady

37

Bracken as I had been so pleased with the type I had had with Pretty Maid to Soaring High. From that litter I retained a brown bitch, Willowmead Perfect Lady. Lady is about the best bitch I have ever bred. She was beautifully made, with Honey's head, the same shoulder and front and floating movement still coming down true, gorgeous dark eyes and a beautiful straight, easy care, coat. She won bitch C.C. at Crufts for three consecutive years, a record she still holds. Black Magic won dog C.C. at two of those three Crufts too, so out of the six C.C.'s, five were won by Willowmead bred dogs.

In the meantime, I had bought in a bitch bred by Jackie Tidmarsh called Juno. She was a daughter of Braid and Jackie's bitch Ch. Edwelweiss who, as a daughter of Cairnbhan, had Willowmead very close behind. Merrymaker and Will O'Wisp were also behind Edelweiss's dam, so I felt she fitted in very well with my breeding plans.

Honey then went to Ch. Brambledale Balthazar, a son of Braid, and I retained a dark slate dog puppy, who was called Pure Magic. I think he must have been one of the unluckiest of dogs, due to the fact that he would worry himself so much about bitches in season, he would refuse all food for weeks and consequently drop his coat. I would just get him looking nice, when the bitches would start coming into season again and

Ch. Willowmead Juno of Tambora

38

he would go off his food with the net result that he would drop coat again, so he ended up with two C.C.'s and three reserve C.C.'s. He also managed to win a championship show working group, but never that last elusive third C.C. Magic had the most delightful disposition, really excelled in movement and again what was now starting to be known as the Willowmead head. He was mated to Juno after she had been mated to Crofter previously which produced Ch. Willowmead Summer Wine amongst many overseas champions, and produced Touch of Magic who stayed and Ch. Willowmead Star Attraction, who was top puppy with Touch of Magic reserve top puppy. Star Attraction went on to top junior, and then top dog, while Touch of Magic missed reserve top junior by just one point.

Pure Magic of Willowmead

Perfect Lady was mated to Ch. Benedict Morning Mist, again, a son of Braid, and a brown dog Am. Ch. Willowmead Red Ruairidh was retained. Red Ruairidh was mated to Winter Memory and I found that combination worked really well and produced very even litters. The one retained from this breeding was Ch. Willowmead Red Admiral, a dark brown dog.

Going back to Super Honey,

Willowmead Touch of Magic

she was mated to Ch. Kimrand Simond and I retained a slate tricolour bitch, Silver Lace, who won four reserve C.C.'s but being a fairly plain bitch in markings did not manage her championship. Lace had Blue Bracken as great grandfather, so I mated her to Ch. Swinford Sky Rocket who also had Blue Bracken as his great grandfather. This proved a very nice mating too, a daughter went to Cornwall and she was mated back to Red Admiral and I went and collected a brown bitch, Polhilsa

39

Am. Ch. Willowmead Red Ruairidh

Willowmead Winter Memory

Willowmead Silver Lace, 4 Res. C.C.s

Pulchritude of Willowmead. Another litter from Lace was to Ch. Briaridge Lyrical Lord, who, on his sires side goes back to Cairnbhan and on his dams side to Cindy Sue. I kept a bitch, Plain and Fancy from that breeding and she is now a champion. Plain and Fancy was mated to Star Attraction and produced one of the best litters I have seen for a long time. All the litter were so similar it was very hard to choose between them. I kept a dog, Willowmead Wish Upon a Star who won best puppy (Our Dogs Trophy) and his Junior Warrant. His sister Willowmead a Star is Born is

Polhilsa Pulchritude of Willowmead

now a champion. Wish Upon a Star is so similar to his grandsire, Pure Magic in make and shape to almost be uncanny and still has the Willowmead head and floating movement.

Ch. Willowmead Plain and Fancy

Willowmead Wish upon a Star, J.W., Res. C.C.

Willowmead Man of the Moment, 4 Res. C.C.s

Touch of Magic was mated to Charncroft Captain Cook at Whistbrae and had Willowmead Man of the Moment, and in a second litter Willowmead Touch of Class, a bitch. Man of the Moment has a very straight coat of a lovely light slate colour. Touch of Class is a jet black bitch, the very first one I have ever bred. She has a good quality coat, not the usual soft fluffy coat associated with the normal black beardie, and with full white markings is very showy. Man of the Moment has four reserve C.C.'s. Both are slightly lighter in bone than I am used to and have a different type of head. Both are delightful animals to own and are very easy to live with. Touch of Class has one C.C. so far.

This is where we have arrived in 1990 with the Willowmead beardies, I have tried to retain all the good things I inherited from Mrs Willison's careful breeding when she re-established the breed and improve on some of the faults, which inevitably showed up, at the same time breeding a type that I hope is recognisably Willowmead, and as near as I can get to the standard of the bearded collie.

Willowmead Touch of Class, 1 C.C.

Touch a Dream and Touch a Star offspring of Willowmead Touch of Class

How to care for your Baby Beardie

Collecting from the Breeder and Training

WHEN the puppy is about seven to eight weeks old, its the time to let him go to his new home. I used to always keep all my puppies until at least eight weeks, but with one litter I had accepted a judging engagement abroad and the bitch had been mated before I realised that the puppies would not be eight weeks old and I would have to be in a different country. Having read that puppies are perfectly able to cope with the stress of a new home by seven weeks, I decided that now was the time to find out how true this was and all the litter of six puppies were collected on the day they were seven weeks of age. They all settled down beautifully and accepted their new homes far better than at the older age of nine or ten weeks. I do still prefer that the puppy is about seven and a half weeks old before he goes and if there are young children in the house, definitely keep him till eight weeks, simply because he is bigger and not so likely to be picked up by youngsters.

So the puppy is collected with his brush, comb, bed, lead and collar, insurance, doggy blanket and all relevant paper work, such as pedigree, diet sheet and leaflets full of doggy tips and hints, all of which will have been fully explained beforehand, and his new family pile back into the car and leave for home. I would suggest that some kitchen roll and a towel are bought in case of travel sickness and that he travels on the knee of the person sitting in the passenger seat in the front of the car. It is very important that the first trip in the car should be a happy experience to help give him confidence for the future and the nearer the front of the car, the less sway and so the less chance of travel sickness, and in the comforting arms of his new owner to soothe any fears of the strange new experience with people he does not as yet know, will help him to settle and enjoy it, thereby there being less stress to cause travel sickness. I also suggest that you go straight home as the puppy is not innoculated so cannot be put out, even in a field, to relieve himself, as there could have been a dog with distemper playing in that field half an hour before and you have no way of telling this, so even long journeys are best accomplished, as much as possible, in one hop.

As soon as you arrive at your destination, take the puppy out into a securely fenced back garden, put him down where you wish him to go, for hopefully the rest of his life, and give him the words you intend to use for

Dog puppies at six weeks old - Sire: Willowmead Wish upon a Star,
dam: Polhilsa Pulchritude of Willowmead

him to relieve himself. I always say "go be a good boy, or girl" if you have a bitch, and as by that time he will probably be ready to go, he should immediately squat. The second he does as you have asked him, praise him greatly, so that he understands that is what you want him to do. He can then go into the house to learn about his new home. I usually do not feed puppies for about half an hour after a journey, to let their tummies settle, and he can use that time exploring and finding out just where everything is. If there is already a dog in the household, I usually recommend that the older dog comes with the family to collect the new addition, as they can meet then on neutral ground, i.e. the car, and usually the older dog, after having a quick sniff, settles down in his usual place in the back, and is quite used to the smell of the new puppy while you drive home and is much more ready to accept his new companion.

After you have been home for about half an hour it is now time to feed the puppy, so that he really feels settled in. My puppies usually eat up very well, and its nearly always a case of nose into the dish, gobble, gobble, gone, and all my adults eat just the same and stay like it throughout their lives, which I find very useful, bearing in mind the old saying, that a hungry dog is a healthy dog, so if at any time they do not polish off their dinners, I know there is a good reason for it and they could be starting some illness, so can take appropriate measures before it becomes serious.

As you will see from the diet sheet (see pages 99-100), puppies need many and regular meals and great attention should be paid to the correct amounts to feed the puppy, bearing in mind that all dogs are individuals, and some need more food than others, so a diet sheet can only be a guide. I have fed this way and do find it is pretty accurate for their needs, apart from the fact that sometimes I need to increase by slightly more than the one ounce per week at between three and four months of age, as that is when the greatest growth spurt is going on. I usually feed milk up to approximately six months, but have found with several dogs that they go off milk around four and a half to five months, or if you should have regular loose stools, it could be the milk causing it, as adult dogs cannot digest milk, it is a complete waste of time to give it to them. I do find with beardies that it causes plenty of tummy upsets and diarrhoea, and with their long coats continual trouser washing can be quite a chore. I have regularly been told: "but he loves milk", to which I reply "a drug addict loves his drugs", but neither do them any good, so its best left out of the diet altogether. I usually recommend the puppy is left in the kitchen at night, at least till he is housetrained. When he is fully clean, it is up to his new owners wishes where he spends the night. I suggest paper is put down just outside his bed, as my puppies are reared on fur fabric in their bed and paper on the floor of the kennel, so are used to going on the paper, and usually will oblige in their new homes. Each night, put the paper a little nearer the door, and it is not unusual for the puppy to be clean in a couple of weeks, overnight. Some people have said they have not even had a single "job" at night right from the first night, but that is rather unusual. I also recommend that in the morning, rather than going into the bathroom first, then going down to the puppy, that you go down the second you get out of bed and let him out straight away, for the first few days, carrying him to the correct spot and saying "go be a good boy", waiting until he does, then the usual massive praising as soon as he does, and he can very soon be popped out and will know what to do, without you standing there. Not too amusing if it is pouring with rain or even worse snowing. After he has been good

9 week old puppy, a daughter of Willowmead Wish upon a Star

47

outside, everybody can come back into the house and have breakfast.

With my diet sheet I do not put times, as the puppy must fit in with his family's lifestyle. If you find it easiest to feed at 7 am then 12 noon you obviously get up earlier than I do. I find 8.30 am, 12.30 pm, 4 pm milk drink, 5.30 pm and 9.30 pm are the times I like to feed, as that breaks the day up fairly equally for his food, but as long as its fairly evenly distributed, use the times that suit you best, and so long as he gets the correct amount, that is the most important thing.

Going back to thoughts on house training, puppies need to go out very regularly, always as soon as they wake up from sleep, but do not grab him and rush him outside, pick him up gently and carry him carefully out to his spot, and always give lots of praise as soon as he obliges. If you leave it for some time he will not understand that you are praising him for relieving himself, for as soon as its done, he will forget and go off to do something else, so you must stay there and make a great fuss so he knows you are pleased that he has done it outside. Should an accident occur inside, never, never, rub his nose in it. It is your fault for not watching him carefully enough, and you could damage the very delicate area of his nose and scenting ability for later in life. He will also need to go out about every half an hour whilst playing, and after food, to pass a motion as well. Do not grab him straight up after he has finished doing his job, unless the weather is too bad, as after his praise and cuddle, its nice to go round the garden a bit and have a small play. If you should be lucky enough to have

Willowmead Touch of Class at 10 weeks old

nice warm sunny weather for a bit when you first collect your puppy, it can be made much easier by being able to leave the kitchen door open, and you will find, as beardies are very clean dogs, naturally, that he will usually, in a couple of days, realise that he should go out and trot outside himself.

It is a good idea to take him to his correct spot, otherwise you could find you have the problem that I had with one puppy, a few years ago. I have a small area just outside my back door, before you get into the garden. This area is slabbed, and when the garden is too muddy, I have a gate that I can close and keep the dogs dry. This puppy, as the gate was closed for a few days after he came into the house, would trot out and spend a penny just outside the back door, where it

Puppies of 8 weeks, 4 months and 10 months

would leave a wet patch, which of course, all the other dogs would trot through and straight into the kitchen with smelly paws, as the puppy seemed to need to go out every ten minutes or so. I very rapidly started to carry him out to the garden, even though he was very good and never did anything, even once, in the house. He was almost more of a problem, especially with other dogs continually going in and out, so a little time spent teaching him the correct place in the garden, and to go sufficiently far away, was time well spent.

When you have settled the puppy in, on arrival home, its a good idea to give a few minutes thought to how you wish to go on with him. Whatever you teach him now, as a very young puppy, is what will stay with him for the rest of his life. I know that at eight weeks he is a very small, beautifully clean little body, and looks lovely on the settee, but you must remember that a 50lb. very long coated hairy dog that has just been for a long walk over muddy fields, doesn't look so appealing on the best settee, neither does the settee or your clothes, so if you do not want him on the furniture never allow him to get on chairs or similar, right from the start. So long as you never put him up, there is not a lot of likelihood that he will start to get up himself. Also if you do not want him to jump up you in greeting, never allow him to jump up from the start and he will always stay down. It is very cruel to encourage him to jump up as a puppy, then to expect him to suddenly stop, just because you have discovered that he is now growing pretty big, has dirty paws and you have your best clothes on, because you are going out somewhere special. Dogs cannot understand a sudden change from one thing to the opposite and the secret of successful and happy training is consistency.

I do not let my dogs go upstairs, as I think it would be too dangerous with my open staircase to have several dogs rushing up and down, with the possibility of someone being knocked off the stairs, resulting in broken legs or similar, a chance I am not prepared to risk, so if you prefer not to let the dog upstairs, never let him go up and then he will not try. The puppy will not know about stairs when he first arrives, and if you do not mind him being upstairs, you will have to teach him how to get up and down. They usually manage to get upstairs without much trouble, its coming down that somewhat appalls the baby puppy, so I usually carry them down to the last step, pop him down on it and with only one step to come down, that's easy. The next time make it two steps to come down, then three, then four and afterwards he soon makes short work of going down with no trouble. As I do not have the dogs upstairs at home, I teach them to go up and down in my local multi-storey car park, where it is also useful to go into the lift, so thereby, accustoming the puppy to a small, shut in box, that goes up and down, just another of lifes odd situations, which he must begin to accept.

He will also need to go in the car for regular short trips to prevent travel sickness developing or to cure it if he has the tendency from the word go. Do not feed the puppy for a couple of hours before you put him in the car and if he is very sick, remove the water dish for an hour before his trip too. Just go short, gentle trips, no racing off, with fast cornering to throw him all over the car. Drive carefully and steadily, and preferably for only about ten minutes or so to start with. I always take my puppies into town and carry them round for half an hour so they can see all the noise and people, as well as traffic, hustle and bustle, from the safety of my arms, till they are fully innoculated. As soon as he is clear of his innoculations, he is then carried into town, put down in a precinct, and always trots back to the car himself, lead training accomplished.

Grooming

You need to start grooming your beardie as soon as you bring him home at eight weeks, as covered in Chapter Three. I always start the baby puppies, on the table, so he will be quite used to being up on a table before he leaves me. I usually use a card table, and always suggest to people that they try and acquire one, or something similar, before they collect the new addition to the family. There are purpose built dog grooming tables sold these days, obtainable from most big shows or by catalogue from the dog grooming specialists. These are really ideal in a lot of ways as they are so much more substantial than a card table, and

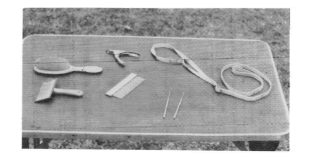

Tools, Mason Pearson
brush slicker brush, nail
clippers, teeth scalers,
comb and show slip

will not rock and upset a baby puppy. They also have proper rubber matted tops to prevent any slipping.

The brush I always recommend for care of a beardie coat is a Mason Pearson all nylon bristles with a rubber cushion, with a nylon and bristle mixture for the show dogs whites, when they go to shows. The whitener used for shows usually produces static in the coat, and the bristle in the combination helps to prevent the static build up. The other piece of equipment that is of equal importance is a steel comb. I always used a comb of about ten inches long with the teeth as far apart as I can find, and also with long teeth rather than short. You do not want a close toothed comb, as it will pull out far too much coat. I usually get a combination comb for the pet puppies, with one side having long, widely spaced teeth and the other having closer spacing between the teeth. These are very useful combs as, should you get a few small mats behind the ears or in the elbows, the close tooth side is very useful just to remove these mats.

Another tool for your doggy bag is a toothbrush and toothpaste. A small soft childs toothbrush is the best and most good pet shops these days sell dog toothpaste. Do not use human toothpaste on a dogs teeth. They do not like the flavour, whereas dog toothpaste has a flavour such as beef or liver which they like and enjoy, so makes teeth cleaning a treat, rather than a chore. I would suggest you start cleaning his teeth as soon as the adult teeth are well through at about six months. Do not start whilst he is still in the middle of losing teeth, as the gums can become very sore sometimes, and he will not appreciate having sore gums scrubbed by a toothbrush. If you make it a routine everytime you have finished his brush and comb, twice a week, he will always have good teeth and can save you a great deal of money in old age, by not having to go to the Vet for regular scaling and cleaning, plus all the ills that can develop from a poisoned system from tartar build up on teeth, or infected gums.

To go back to grooming, the first time you put your puppy on the table to groom him, just gently brush for a couple of minutes, praise him greatly, give a tit bit and put him down from the table. For the first couple of weeks, I would suggest you do it every day, after that twice a week should do. Every time he goes on the table, spend a little more time with

Puppy on table

the brushing, and after a few days gently comb a little too. Some puppies just want to wriggle and play all the time, trying to bite the brush or comb.

I have found if I give them a dog chew or something similar, they are busy with that, and I can get on with the brushing easily, and it all goes off without any hassle. It can be an advantage too, at this stage, to train the puppy to lie down whilst he is being brushed, although I prefer to groom my dogs standing on the table. Some naturally lie down, and if they insist I am perfectly happy to let them do so, but even if they do not want to lie down, it is better to train them to do so if you desire them to, as when you need to trim off tummies, or clear out elbows from knots, it is only possible when they are lying down, and starting as babies, they learn to accept it easily, whereas an older dog can protest at such a new situation.

To groom an adult beardie, I put him on the table, and to get him there I train him first to put his front paws on the table, by patting the table, you can then by putting your hands under each back leg just under the buttocks, with a quick flip and lift, he is on the table, with no effort on your part. If you pick him up bodily and place him on the table, some dogs can weigh up to sixty pounds, and that is quite a lot of dog to pick up, whereas with his help, he is on very easily with hardly any effort on your part. I do not encourage the dogs to jump on the table, although they are perfectly able to do this, as mine used to all jump up, but one day I had two bitches both jump on to the table together, one from each side. Luckily I was there and caught them both and put one back down on the floor, but it could have been a nasty accident, and there and then, I stopped all jumping on the table.

I always start to groom with the back end of the dog, taking the brush, I pick up a back leg and holding his paw brush it upwards very vigorously. I then comb it through. If it is properly brushed the comb will slide through easily. If it should jam in a knot, re-brush again to try and clear it. Should it be too much of a hard knot, gently pull it apart with you finger and thumb, re-brush, then comb it out. As soon as you have brushed upwards for the foot area then brush it back downwards, holding the long coat up with your left hand, brush downwards in definite firm strokes, always having a line, so that you can see the dogs skin. This is called line brushing, as you always have a definite line of brushed coat. Do this steadily all the way up to the top of the leg, going over the back of the dog to the backbone, brushing for several strokes, then combing through, to make sure you are right through all the coat with no knots being missed.

Paws on the table

Lift with hands under the buttocks, flip up

Go back to the foot again and now start brushing up the leg in the same way, but on the front of the leg. Go right up to where the leg joins the body, go down to the foot again and this time brush inside the leg, right up to the dogs tummy, again down to the foot and brush up the back of the leg, paying particular attention to the long trousers under the tail, brushing up to the top of the base of the tail. Next move to the sides of the dog. Go right under the stomach and rib cage and holding the coat back and up

53

Groom from rear end first, line brushing

with your left hand, brush vigorously as far to the opposite side as you can manage, going slowly up all the middle section right up to the backbone.

Next do a front leg. I usually sit the dog down to do his front legs, so when he is sitting comfortably, pick up the paw and brush vigorously upwards from the base of the foot. When you are quite sure there are no knots on the paw, again brush the front of the leg, up to the chest, then brush inside paying plenty of attention to inside the armpits, always a good spot for knots, then the back of the leg, checking the elbow area for either knots or hard skin. Then brush the outside and continue up the shoulder to the withers. Next brush up the front of the shoulder from the top of the front of the leg, up to the neck and over to the base of the skull. Then do the same on the other side, starting with the hind leg and working forwards, middle section, then front.

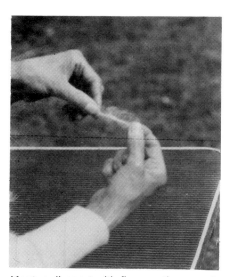
Knot, pull apart with fingers, then comb

Next do the chest, working from

Grooming front legs

between the front legs and brushing up to right under the chin, spending plenty of time under the chin, as this can get very matted if left, and is a very tender area if allowed to get tangled. Next do the face. Start brushing the coat away from the eyes right at the nose and with plenty of combing almost after every couple of brush strokes comb through. Carry on back towards the ears, then groom the ears. I usually like to start with the inside of the ear, brushing and combing very thoroughly, then do the outside, paying particular attention again to the underneath, as this is the worst place for tangles, and finish the head by brushing the top, finishing it off by brushing it backwards away from the eyes. Brush the coat downwards from the bridge of the nose and the hair under the chin forward. Stand the dog up again and brush his tail carefully, checking the underneath for knots. Check his eyes do not have any bits in or dirt in the corners, and finally sleek down all the coat and put the dog down on the floor for a shake.

If you find your dog prefers to lie down on the table for grooming, you can groom in just the same way, except that the dog is lying on his side. It is easier to groom his tummy lying down, and also under the elbows, so if you can train your dog to do both, lie down and stand up, you can have the best of both worlds. I do find that it is advisable to trim the tummy of both dogs and bitches, especially dogs, as if the hair is allowed to grow long it can get very smelly, and if you start early, puppies accept the scissors happily, whereas if you suddenly start on an older dog they are not sure what is going on and can suddenly jump up just as you are cutting a bit of coat off and could get caught with the scissors. Another spot I always keep trimmed is round the anus under the tail, also if necessary, the little tiny knots that seem to arrive in just a couple of days under the armpits where it is very tender to pull them out with the comb, so I usually trim those off too. The only other spot I will trim is the little knots that get between the toes, especially in muddy weather. All these places will not spoil the look of the dog in the least and cannot be seen to have been trimmed.

Holding dog to lie down, followed by a sequence of gently putting him down on his side

When your puppy is about twelve months old, you could put a bit to talcum powder in his ears and then very gently ease out a few of the hairs growing in them. Do this about once a fortnight, only a few hairs each time and always with talcum powder in first. He will soon accept you cleaning his ears of wool happily, so long as you do it very gently at first and only a few hairs at a time. Some people start to pull it out far too early and try and clear the ear completely in one go, ending up with a screaming puppy that has been badly hurt and frightened, and makes it very difficult to ever get near his ears again. You can also sometimes see either brown or yellowish colouring inside the ear flaps. Check whether he has been either digging or lying in a spot where he could have picked up dirt there. Have a good sniff deep into the ear canal and if there is the slightest smell, it is probably some ear problem starting, as this is wax from the ear, caused

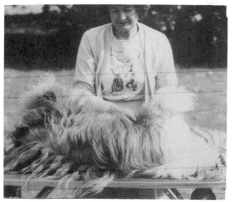

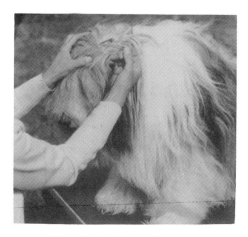

Cleaning hair from the ears

by a problem and is the first sign, even before scratching, of the ear, in fact, if I have seen any dirt or discolouration on the ear flap it has always been the start of trouble. I always keep ear medication in, and apply it straight away, so clear up any trouble before it even starts to get a hold. Cats can be a problem with causing trouble in dogs ears. The ear mites from the cat really seem to love dogs ears too, but since I have not had any cats, the ear problems with the dogs have been minimal. Do not leave ear troubles thinking they will go away, if ignored, once the canker gets a good hold, it can be almost impossible to clear up, and can easily get so bad it will necessitate an operation to open the ear canal, or even if it gets too serious, can lead to the dog having to be put to sleep to avoid further suffering. I have seen dogs with ears so bad that the dog holds his head permanently on one side to try and alleviate the pain. The smell is so bad that you can smell it as soon as you go into the same room and the poor dog is in agony. I can really sympathise, as I used to have dreadful earache as a small girl and would never wish it upon any poor animal.

Another thing to check whilst grooming is the dogs nails. Should the dog walk correctly and he is getting plenty of exercise, he should wear down his nails to short neat little claws, but unfortunately, a great many dogs walk in a lazy way, more on the back of the pad, so consequently they do not wear down their claws and these can grow very long. If you can hear the claws click as the dog walks, his nails are to long. There are some very good nail clippers on the market. I prefer the ones called the guillotine type and find they do a quicker, neater cut and the dog does not mind so much as with the plier type of model. If you look at your dogs claws carefully, you will see on the white nails a part nearest to the foot that is pink. That is the "quick" and you do not want to cut this, so just nip off the end, or white only bit. If you should cut the quick, first the dog will yell and pull his paw back very sharply and it will then bleed. If badly cut it will bleed copiously, and can go on for hours, so do take just a very small bit until you are confident that you will not cut the quick. It is more difficult with the black claws because you cannot see where the quick goes, so look carefully at a white claw first and see how far you need to cut on that claw, then cut more or less the same on the black claw, erring on the safer side, by cutting slightly less if necessary.

A lot of people say you will only get your dogs claws short if you give them lots of road work, but for the last twenty five years I have not done any road work with any of my dogs as I live right off any road and all the dogs run free on grass for several hours each day, and all have very short claws. I have never had to cut any of my beardies claws ever, except for the odd dew claw growing a little long, so providing you give plenty of free running you should have nice short claws. I also think a short claw is hereditary, in as much as I always pick the same shape and make of dog, so they move in the same way, hence wear their claws short.

Another thing to look for when grooming is your dogs anal glands. These are two glands just inside the anus. You cannot see them but can certainly feel them when they are over full, so can your dog and quite a

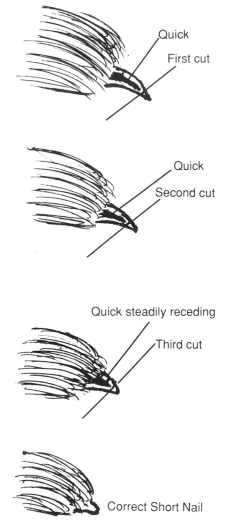

Quick
First cut

Quick
Second cut

Quick steadily receding
Third cut

Correct Short Nail

few beardies do seem to suffer from anal glands overfilling. The original purpose of the anal glands was to lubricate the back passage, when the dog was eating all and everything when wild, or as a scavenger, long before he was fed prepared food out of tins or similar, as most have their food dished up to them now. If the glands overfill and the dog does not empty them himself, it can easily, and regularly does, turn into an anal abcess, which will burst and spew out a mess of blood and gunge, much to the dogs distress and pain, and usually necessitates a visit to the vet for anti-biotics to clear it all up. Also, if it has once abcessed, it can do so again as a regular thing, which can end up as an operation to remove the anal glands altogether, so to prevent things getting this bad, should you notice your dog scooting along, dragging his rear end on the ground, or continually licking under his tail round the anus area, pop him on the table and feel gently on either side of the anus with your finger and thumb. If it should feel full or slightly swollen, rather than quite flat, get some cotton wool, a thin bit, otherwise you cannot feel, personally, I prefer a double thickness of kitchen roll, and put it to cover the area completely and press firmly each side of the anus with your finger and thumb, slightly underneath, rather than on top of the anus. The gunge can come shooting out, and should be liquid rather than porridge like, which means it is going towards an abcess if it goes thick, so press gently but firmly until there is no more liquid coming out. Then I suggest plenty of talcum powder puffed on liberally, as regretably, cleaning the anal glands is a very nasty, smelly job. I was doing it once for a friend in her living room and the gunge shot out with such force it shot straight across the room and decorated the television. We had to quickly rush round after finishing the dog, with some strong smelling disinfectant to clean the television up before it set on the thing. Dogs will sometimes evacuate their glands if upset or frightened. I used to have one that always did it as soon as she was put on the table at the vets, so was not terribly popular there, nor with me when I put her in the car to drive her home as she still smelled horrid.

Bathing

Beardies do occasionally need an all over bath, not every week, as some misguided owners have asked me. Bathing too regularly removes all the natural oils present in a healthy coat which keep the coat clean and shining. Even if the dog has been a long walk through muddy fields and looks terrible when he arrives home, you will usually find that when he has dried off, all the mud falls out of his coat, and especially if helped with a quick brush, he will look quite clean and respectable again, but if all the natural oils are washed out by too regular bathing, the coat will mat very easily and prove very difficult to keep clean.

Not all beardies hate their bath - Willowmead Music of the Night

Sometimes, an all over bath is necessary, so here is the way I prefer to do it. Always start with a very good groom. This is imperative, as should you put a dog into water that has any matts in his coat, the water completely changes the matts into solid felts, and it is totally impossible to part them with your fingers or comb them out. The only thing you can do is cut them out altogether, so if you intend to show the dog, you could have to wait around twelve months before that coat has re-grown properly. This also applies to pet dogs, as it is so much easier to comb out a small matt before you start.

After he is all nicely groomed and completely matt free, then prepare the bath. I really do not think you can do a proper job, and if you are going to the trouble of bathing him, you might as well do it properly, in a small bath or with buckets of water, so obtain a non-slip bath mat and place it in the bottom of your own bath. Get several large towels ready to hand and a good quality dog shampoo. Do not use a human shampoo as the dogs skin Ph is different from a human one and can cause intense irritation to a dog.

I once saw a miniature poodle who suffered for a couple of years with the most appalling skin trouble, all her tummy and back legs were red raw, all caused by her mistress using a human shampoo on her every six weeks. As soon as she changed to a good dog shampoo, the condition and the massive vets fees disappeared almost overnight.

There are dozens of different doggy shampoo's on the market these days, for every type of skin and skin condition imaginable, scaley skin, flea and parasite problems, itchy skin disorders, every colour coat from black to white with blue, brown and silver etc. inbetween, colour enhancers, colour densifiers and everything else you can wish for, so go along to a good pet shop and have a browse to see which will suit your dog best, before you decide to bath him, so you can be prepared in advance.

I usually just use a normal insecticidal shampoo made by the firm Mrs Willison's husband worked for, with her original Jeannie as the emblem for many years. Sadly this has now been changed to an ordinary drawing, but the shampoo is still equally as good. It also seems to bring up the whites of the beardie beautifully, and a dog with shining whites does look nice. I then mix the shampoo in a small plastic mug, as it is very concentrated and I would never put the neat shampoo directly on to the dogs coat, otherwise you will spend simply ages trying to rinse it out, then have a pint plastic jug for wetting the dog. If you have a shower attachment it can speed things up quite a bit, but if you don't it is not imperative. Then put the water in the bath about six to nine inches deep and only tepid. Dogs must not be bathed in hot water, and although they might enjoy swimming in cold rivers they don't like cold baths. You now have everything prepared so go and collect your dog. I usually put mine on a lead, as when they realise they are going into the bathroom, its brakes on all round and they usually go into rapid reverse, so at least you have some control with the lead. I did have one, once, who would trot in on his own and hop into the bath unassisted and stood there as good as gold, even on one occasion when I had to answer the phone, but he is still the only one that was so obliging, all the rest are definitely not keen.

Place several small wedges of cotton wool where you can reach them from your bath and before you put the dog into it, press a wedge of cotton wool firmly into each ear. The spares are kept handy if he should shake one out whilst standing in the water, and you can then replace it at once with a dry piece. Do not worry that they will get stuck down the ear, either the dog will soon shake them out as soon as he is finished, or you can remove them easily with your finger and thumb.

Pop the dog into the bath, making sure he stands on the bath mat, so will not slip, and pour some water over his back with the jug, as soon as he is settled and understands that its nice and warm and doesn't hurt. If you have a shower, check that the temperature is correct, tepid, and start to shower his back and back legs first, moving forward to this shoulders and front legs. Do not put the shower on his head, leave that quite dry for the time being. When he is fully wet, pick up your mug of mixed shampoo, pour it over his back and soap up well, then wash his hind legs. Don't forget to pick up his feet out of the water and soap up well too. Move forward and wash his front end, shoulders, front legs and chest, then wash his tail. Now very gently, pour some water over his head, face and ears, making sure you do not get water in his eyes or ears. If you find you are inclined to get some water in his eyes, with care you should not, but some dogs are not quite so well behaved as others. It is a good idea to get a special shampoo especially for the head, which is prepared not to sting the eyes. You now have a fully soaped dog, so commence with the jug to rinse off his head.

Make sure all the soap is completely out of the coat, and he is squeaky clean. You can continue with the shower to rinse off the rest of the body, if you do not have a shower attachment, rinse him as fully as possible with the water in the bath, then drain the water out and refill with some fresh, and rinse fully again to make sure all the shampoo is completely out of the coat. Let all the water drain out of the bath, squeeze as much excess water as possible out of his coat and cover with a large towel, lifting him out of the bath, to stand on another towel, where he can shake under the towel you have placed over him, so that you don't get soaked too. You can then vigorously towel him dry all over. You can easily use four or five large towels to get him damp dry, and if it is a nice warm sunny day, he can go outside to finish drying off. I find if, just before he is completely dry you pop him on his grooming table and brush lightly through his coat, it opens it up and helps to dry him quickly. If you have to bath in the winter months, make sure you do it as early in the day as possible, as you do not want to leave a damp dog overnight. I have never used a hairdryer on a adult dog, but have dried small puppies in the winter with one if I have had to bath them for any reason, although its been a rare occurence indeed, as I find my puppies usually keep so clean, it is totally unnecessary.

Puppies Growing Up

Feeding & Teething

BY the time your puppy is six months old, I usually find that I can go on to his adult rations, which is breakfast and dinner. I always feed every adult dog twice a day, as I feel that to go twenty four hours inbetween meals is far too long. Also, if your dog is a poor doer he will find it very difficult to take in a sufficient amount of food in one meal to keep up to his correct weight, whereas, if he is fed twice a day, he will do much better and will be able to eat just that little bit more to maintain his desired weight.

Puppies of six months are still growing a lot. I know different lines will shoot up to more or less their full height by six months, but they still have a lot of filling out and muscle mass to make, so even if your puppy looks fully grown, he certainly is not and will need extra rations for quite some time yet. My line is still very small, almost invariably, at six months old, although there is always the odd one out that will grow quickly of course, but the majority at six months are still small and grow on steadily till twelve months or so. I have even seen a bitch, a daughter of one of my breeding, grow nearly an inch after she was eighteen months, so it can be a very indefinite thing. So, bearing in mind that most of mine are small, I still feed a lot of food until about nine months, slowly cutting it down from about eight months, so much depends on the make and shape of your puppy, and how active he is.

One guide I have always used, and find it never fails, is to watch carefully as your puppy eats. Normally, he will be ready and eager for each meal and polish it off very rapidly. As soon as you notice he has slowed down a bit and perhaps leaves a few crumbs in his dish, decrease the amount immediately, usually one ounce off each meal will soon have him back eating everything up fast. Do not be tempted to try and make him eat it all up, or change his diet, thinking he might need something different to tempt him. I know its hard not to do this, but you will only overfeed him and he will only go off his food completely, or start to pick at his dinner causing more worry. I have worried too, thinking that I must keep weight on because the puppy is going into the show ring and I do not want skinny puppies, but it just does not work and they go right off their food, then really loose weight, and if an eight/nine month old puppy really loses weight, it is almost impossible to get him back into any sort of good condition until he is about two years old, so being careful, watching him eat and cutting down rapidly, can most certainly pay dividends.

You might have some problems too, with puppies eating whilst they are teething. I must say I have never had one have any trouble that way, but have heard of it from several other breeders. The poor little soul has very sore gums, which you can soon spot by looking at them, and seeing the gums all red and swollen. Should your puppy go off his food then, don't press him, just let his natural good health and appetite return and take over and he will soon be eating happily again. Beardies start teething quite early, sometimes just before four months old. They suddenly seem to start chewing on any and everything. We used to have a big refectory table in the kitchen and all the legs and feet had half gone from Beardie teeth. Skirting boards also seem to make good teeth removers, but I'm afraid I do not encourage this if I can catch the culprit. I find bones, large marrow ones only, fresh outside or sterilised in the house, are the best answer to teething troubles, and the dogs seem to love the dog chews you buy nowadays at any supermarket. They last the puppies half an hour or so, but the adults go through them in a few minutes, so I try and make sure the puppy gets his on his own, or it soon gets taken off him.

If you intend to show your puppy he must have correct dentition, in other words forty two teeth, which include six insissors, top and bottom, two canines top and bottom again, and six pre-molars each side, three top and three bottom. The pre-molars are not used very much, and are not counted as a serious fault in England if one is missing. I do like full dentition and have it in all my dogs. It is of paramount importance on the Continent though and any dog there will not be place if even one pre-molar is missing, so its just as well to try to only breed from dogs with all their pre-molars if you intend to try to export puppies in the future.

Beardies do have a different way of teething, or rather, their jaws are inclined to grow differently to any other breed of dog I have ever known,

Pure Magic of Willowmead, 2 C.C.s, 3 Res. C.C.s

in as much that the top and bottom jaws can grow at different rates. I well remember bringing Barberry home from Mrs Willison and when I went over her, I discovered she was badly overshot. As I already had Poodles, and if their mouths were wrong they stayed that way, I rang Mrs Willison, only to be told it was quite alright, it would correct. It did, and by six months old she had a beautiful tight bite. I have regularly seen overshot puppies since and providing the bite was correct at six weeks of age, it usually does seem to be fine by six months, but these days there seems to be quite a few mouth problems not correcting, and I am now seeing, when I am judging, badly overshot bites and also wry mouths and undershots. These do seem to have increased rapidly over the last few years, so I feel it is a problem that needs careful attention, before we end up with more bad bites than good ones.

When you are looking at seven to eight week old puppies, check very carefully for the width of the bottom jaw and if it is very narrow and does not fit well inside the top jaw, I would be very suspicious of it going overshot. I have heard of dogs being very slow maturers with their teeth too. One puppy never did have any puppy teeth on his bottom jaw, but the adult teeth came through OK by six months and I recently had a puppy myself, who at six months, had one bottom insissor through, instead of six, and all four canines were very very slow coming to their full length, in fact, he was over two years before they had grown to the correct adult length. It does seem to be something that is developing in the breed, so it is a good thing to double check if you are interested in showing your puppy at a future date.

Providing you are buying your puppy as a family pet and loving companion, you will not need to think of show training, but training him to grow up to be a well behaved and obedient friend, and this can start as soon as he arrives home with you. House training is covered in another chapter, so we can forget that and go on to other simple lessons. Usually, the first thing you need your puppy to do, is to sit. Now with all training, pay great attention to what you are doing before you concentrate on the puppy and think of your commands. Always call the puppy's name to get his attention before you give a command, such as Fido sit, rather than, "there's a good boy, sit down nicely", which is not a good idea. Dogs are very intelligent and will probably sit after a long sentence command when they are a lot older, but a baby puppy is still learning your language and needs as few words as possible. Always, for any command, use his name first, then to make him sit, press his bottom firmly down as you say "sit". Give him lots of praise as soon as he has sat down and tell him he is good, and he will very soon know just what you mean, and do it at once. I usually like to give a titbit whilst I'm training and that gives added impetuous to the puppy to learn. A thing to watch out for is not to give a double command, such as Fido "sit down". That is two commands, sit being one thing and down is another, as down is used to get the dog to either get down if he is jumping up or lie down rather than sitting down.

The next thing to remember is that he must learn one thing at a time and have really understood the first thing before you go on to the second, so when he has really got his sit, go on to teach him go down, so then you say, "Fido down". Hold him down whilst you praise him for a few seconds, and he should soon have understood the movement and go down.

Care of your Old Beardie

One day, you will suddenly realise that the bouncing Beardie of yesterday has slowly become an older dog. He gets up a bit more slowly instead of leaping to his feet, his hearing might not be quite so acute, which can be quite an advantage in a thunderstorm, if he is one of the many Beardies who really hate thunder, and his sight might not be quite so keen, all signs of approaching age.

There are a few things that you can do to help your older Beardie. Providing you have maintained the cleaning and care of his teeth, they should still be in excellent condition, but it would not hurt to clean them twice a week now, instead of the previous once a week. Nails will probably be growing faster, as he is not able to race around quite as much as before, so when you groom, always check the nails. If they are starting to grow long, just keep the ends nipped off with a good pair of nail clippers. I prefer the guillotine type but it is purely a matter of preference. When you first start clipping the nails, look carefully for a white nail where you can see the pink quick growing down the nail, cut just below where you can see the quick, which with each cutting will slowly grow back so that you can get the nails progressively shorter. Cut the black nails where you cannot see the quick the same as the pink ones and you should be fairly safe. It would be a good idea, before you start to cut nails, to buy some of the preparations available, from a good chemist, to stop bleeding, so if you do inadvertently catch the end of the quick, you have something to hand to stop the bleeding straight away, otherwise you could have blood everywhere, which is a nuisance. Better not to cut the quick if possible, as its obviously painful, and you could run into a problem with the dog, next time you try to cut his claws.

As age increases you will find that your Beardies coat will change too. It can either get very sparse and lacking in undercoat, can loose its water proofing, so instead of the dog being nice and dry under his strong outer coat and warm thick undercoat, he is soaked through to his skin, and being older as well, could easily catch a chill, so its as well to towel dry, if he should have got too wet on his walks. He will also need more grooming which can become rather more difficult if he gets a little arthritic, as a lot of older Beardies do, and you will need lots of patience, as he finds it harder to stand and needs more help to get up on his table. If your bitch has been spayed, her coat could become extremely thick and soft and will tangle very easily, so again, lots more time for grooming.

With exercise, it really depends on the dog. Some older Beardies will still want to go long walks, but others might find the going a bit more than they can cope with, so don't push him if he starts to slow down, and next time try not to go quite so far. I find my oldies are quite content to follow just behind me on their walks, letting the youngsters rush around and play. More attention needs to be paid to their eyes too. The sleep which collects in the corners

Braelyn Broadholme Crofter, aged 14 years

seems to increase with age, so needs checking everyday carefully. Should they get a mucus discharge, go straight to the Vet, as the older the dog, the less chance they have of overcoming illness through their own good health, and something a young dog can throw off easily, an old dog can be very ill with.

Ears too need a very regular check, but providing you have kept the ears clean as mentioned previously, you should be able to spot trouble before it gets a hold. Remember to have a good sniff occasionally, as you can smell problems long before you can see anything wrong.

Slowly too, as age increases, sight and hearing get progressively less acute. The first sign of lack of sight, I have found with my Beardies, is night blindness. Usually, as they start to enter their teens, when I take them out for the last walk at around nine thirty, in the evening, I notice they start to stay fairly close behind me, rather than rushing off to race around the orchard, and if things have been moved, such as wheelbarrows and they are not aware of the new place, they can walk into them, rather than being able to use their night sight. As they get progressively older, they can get very little night sight, so I usually put them on the lead for the walks in the dark, when they trot around perfectly happily, knowing they are quite safe. I have never had a Beardie lose all its sight, all mine have been able to see perfectly during daylight hours, but due to the fact that I trim dogs, I have had plenty of contact with dogs of other breeds, that have lost all their sight, and know how clever some of these animals can become. One little Poodle was so clever, I had been trimming him for years so he knew the routine, and I was happily carrying on with the job, not paying anymore care than with any other dog as regards watching he didn't fall off the table or something similar. The dogs I trim all get so well behaved, I know I can completely trust them to be good, when his mistress told me he had been completely blind for six months, I was quite astounded as that dog had never even put a foot over the edge of the table, and he could not see the edge at all. Needless to say, I kept a very tight hold on him in the future, as I was very concerned that he might fall off, once I knew. He would trot all over the house and never once walked into any of the furniture, even when it was moved to fresh places, but he was rather exceptional, as most dogs, although they use their noses to compensate for the lack of eyes, do walk into objects if you move things about the house, so if you really want to consider your dog, its much kinder to leave things where he knows they will be, so can avoid walking into them and banging his poor nose.

The time I find rather more distressing with losing sight, is when the sight is getting pretty bad, but the dog can still see shadows and movement, but that is all. He has not adjusted to the loss of his sight and cannot tell how far off things are, he's walked into things and hurt himself, see's a shadow or movement and flinches like mad, really jumping back, getting very confused and upset. This is the time you need to be very patient and consoling to him. He is upset and confused enough and needs help, not impatience from his owners.

Young children must be taught too, not to upset or to mess about with the old dog. If he is getting somewhat arthritic, is fast asleep and some young tot races and falls over him, some old dogs will not take very kindly to being rudely awakened. Your old dog needs lots of sleep, infact they seem to sleep most of the day, and they go very sound asleep too. I remember with Barberry when she was approaching her sixteenth birthday, I used to have to look at her for several minutes to make sure she was still breathing, as she was so sound asleep, and several times I did wonder is she had slipped away in her sleep. This is something which we all pray will happen to our dogs, to be the perfect end to a long, happy, trouble free life and to go quietly in the night whilst fast asleep. Sadly, this does not usually happen, and I have always had to make the decision for all my dogs. They tell you when you must do the final thing for them you can see it in their eyes.

Some many years ago now, I had a Poodle that at fourteen and a half years old, needed to go to the Vet. She suddenly was taken ill, we knew she had a bit of kidney trouble, but had been fine with it, but now she was ill, so off to the Vet. He injected her and she seemed much better for two days, she then started to go downhill again, so back to the Vet and another injection, but this time she did not pick up, so I took her back again next day and said I thought he had given the wrong injection as we had not had the good response. My Vet then said no, there was nothing he could do, as both liver and kidneys had collapsed. I said should I take her home, to be told I could if I wanted to, but did I wish to watch her die slowly, she could only last two weeks, would get progressively weaker, was already concerned about the fact she could not hold her water and was rushing for the door, leaking all the way, which distressed her, was

Ch. Black Velvet of Willowmead, 10 years old

finding it difficult getting into her bed, only about three inches off the floor, was not at present in pain, but soon would be; did I really want to put her through that and live with myself knowing it was just to keep her for a few more days for my benefit, certainly not hers. There was only one answer, and its one lesson I have never forgotten. Please, always think of your dog, before your own loss, when the end comes and don't hang on to make him suffer. Vets are very reluctant to say you must give the dog the last injection, especially when they can see how upset you are, but please do not let the dog suffer, but let him slip quietly away, with one injection from the Vet, preferably with you holding him to comfort him in his last moments.

Care of Stud Dog & Matings

BEARDIES are lucky, in as much that as a breed they are not oversexed, thank goodness. I have seen dogs in other breeds that once they have been used at stud, are impossible to live with as household pets. They will mount anything and everything including chairs, cushions, people's arms and legs and particularly children, urinate everywhere, infact are a complete nuisance, and can end up having to be castrated or put to sleep, so its as well to really think hard, if your Beardie is your only pet and friend, has never paid more than a passing interest in other dogs and is happy and well adjusted, whether it is worth, just for probably the only time in his life, to try mating him with a friend's bitch. He hopefully would not develop some of the habits just mentioned, but easily might. What he has never had he will never miss, so when asked, I always say do not use pet dogs at stud. If you are showing your dog puppy though, and he has had a successful show career, and has a very good pedigree, you could be asked to use him at stud. I like to start my boys off at about twelve to thirteen months of age, but have used two dogs at eleven

Immature stud dog! Mating is the last thing on his mind,
Willowmead Man of the Moment, aged six months

Mature stud dog, brushed and waiting. Ch. Britannia Just Jeffrey

months old and both produced large litters. I have heard of some dogs being used even a bit younger and have been fertile and also some not being able to sire puppies till they are about thirteen to fourteen months old. I had one myself, who I mated at twelve months, but no puppies, yet at fourteen months a nice litter, and I heard from his sire's breeder that he also was a late maturer, so it never hurts to ask at what age the dogs' sire first produced puppies.

It is also a good thing to find out what sort of stud dog your puppy's sire was, as good keen sires produce good keen studs, and reluctant stud dogs can easily produce the same problem in their offspring. It is also a good idea to check the size of the dogs testicles. Beardies can have very small testicles, and there have been several dogs that have gone sterile at about three to four years of age. I would not be happy to use a dog with very small testicles as I think its going to be a problem we will have to watch in the breed in the future and can save ourselves a lot of trouble by being careful now. Also never use a monorchid (only one testicle decended into the scrotum) or cryptorchid (no testicles decended) as he would not produce any puppies, but monorchids certainly can. It is considered most likely to be hereditary, is a fault in the Standard and most judges will not place a dog with only one testicle, so there is no point in breeding it on.

To get back to our puppy, he is about fourteen months old and hopefully his first bitch will be a nice sensible matron, who knows all about being mated. She is the best help and encouragement you can have for a maiden dog. A good bitch will flirt with the dog, even getting up and mounting him to show him what to do and stand perfectly still when he does get his courage up and start to work. I always like to have two people at least to help, and never leave two animals to mate unattended, either or both can be seriously injured, if one or other go bonkers whilst tied. I had a bitch once, one of my own of course, who was a maiden and I was trying to do the mating on my own. The bitch seemed to behaving perfectly, stood beautifully and we got a tie first time the dog mounted. I had just turned the dog when the bitch erupted, threw herself on the floor screaming, caught me totally off balance and, of course, pulled the dog down with her. I managed to hang on to the tails and got them both back up, as the dog was fighting to stand up again, then we did finish the rest of the tie with two perfectly calm animals. I ended up with a badly pulled muscle in my back, and was not able to relax for several weeks with it, but thank heavens both dogs were fine, with no damage and the dog was not put off matings either, so do try and have help of at least one person to hold the bitches head.

I like the bitch to arrive with a strong tight collar, show slips or choke chains are no good at all to hold on to a bitch's head and steady her. I have my shed in the garden that I use for grooming and stud work. I have a carpet that I put down so both animals can get a good grip with their feet and its more comfortable to sit on whilst the dogs are working. First the bitch is taken into the shed and has five minutes to look round and see her surroundings, as the dog is groomed in there he already knows the area. I then check the bitch to see if she is ready for mating, always do this before you bring the dog in. I once had a bitch that had a really bad yellow discharge and if I had not looked, the dog would have, at the least, been upset unnecessarily through not being able to mate the bitch after being introduced, or at worst, caught her infection and had to be withdrawn from stud, possibly after mating other bitches and passing it on to them too. I also once had a bitch that was not anywhere near being in season, she belonged to another breeder of many years standing too, and I said I didn't think the bitch was in season, but her owner said she was sure she was. I brought in the stud dog, he took a quick sniff and looked at me as if I had gone silly, wandered off and ignored her. He was a very keen and efficient stud too, so I'm afraid that lady and her bitch had a wasted journey. The other reason for checking the bitch before the dog arrives is, should she need any hair trimmed off round the vulva, its much easier to do it then and the dog will certainly appreciate a clean and tidy girlfriend.

I then go and collect the appropriate stud dog. The treatment is exactly the same for maiden and experienced dogs, they are brought into the shed, the bitch keeps her lead on in case she gets difficult and both animals have a little time to get acquainted. Most bitches, unless they are like most of mine, the type I call brazen hussy's, take a few minutes to warm up to the dog and if you will only have a bit of patience, and you can get the bitch's co-operation, it makes life much easier and pleasant for all concerned. The bitch often hides behind her owner at first, but usually after a few minutes of nice talking to by the dog, she comes out and says 'hello' to him. They usually start to flirt a bit and when the dog has completely got her confidence he will attempt a gentle mount. This is when we start to get to work properly. The owner of the bitch is requested to hold the bitches head firmly by the collar and steady her, and I take the rear end. I prefer to train my dogs to let me guide them, as it makes for a much quicker and easier stud. I place my right hand under the bitch and guide her vulva between my first and index fingers, making sure her tail is out of the way, and make a small circle of my left hand. As the dog mounts and starts to come out, with the lightest of touch you guide the dog to the bitch and as soon as he enters the bitch he starts to tie. Without guiding the dog leaps aboard and bounces all over the place, too high, too low. Lots of young dogs work too low and hope to hit the right spot and tie. This bouncing and messing about can take three days and everybody ends up pretty exhausted. I must stress though, if you do try to guide, it must be with the very, very least amount of touching the dog, otherwise he will leap off, and even if he feels you there at all, will not try or work. It is a very difficult thing to learn and you could put a sensitive dog off stud work altogether, so do be careful.

Properly done, a dog that has total trust in you, even with difficult bitches, will mate very quickly. Guiding a stud dog is very much a knack and if you do not find you can do it easily, it is better left alone, as most dogs manage themselves perfectly adequately, otherwise there would certainly be far less dogs in the world than we have at present. It's a method that suits me and so I use it, but done incorrectly, its best not even tried. Also, some dogs will not accept it either, so don't be discouraged if it doesn't work for your dog, it might be that he is one who resents it anyway.

I would be very loathe indeed, to try to mate a maiden dog to a difficult bitch, you could easily put him off stud work for life. He really does not know what is expected of him on his first stud, and has not developed the keeness of an experienced dog. He's usually young, and fairly submissive because of age, and if a bitch is very nasty, and quite a few certainly are, some because its the wrong day, so they will fight really hard not to be mated, so if your young dog gets bitten, or even growled at, or as some bitches scream as he mounts, its enough to put any young man right off the idea. I have a friend who tried to mate her young dog to a nasty bitch for his first stud and it was two years before he eventually started mating bitches again, even though she tried him with several in that time and

Lady keeping an eye open for a handsome Romeo.
Ch. Willowmead Plain and Fancy

made him a champion, but then he had a good bitch and now is working really well. I am lucky in that I usually mate my stud dogs to my own bitches for their first studs, so rarely have the problem of difficult bitches to start with. You now have your dog and bitch introduced, the bitch has started standing and your dog mounts, as I have already said some dogs will bounce about trying to find the right spot and as soon as they do and commence the tie you will see a totally different strong thrusting movement. Do check that he is tying the bitch and is not just coming out without being in the right spot, as some dogs are just too keen and come out too soon. If he is doing this, push him down quickly, as if he stays up he will come right out and you will then have to wait several hours, or even the next day with some dogs before you can get another mating.

That is another advantage of guiding a dog, you can tell if he is entering the bitch when he starts his tie thrusting. When he has completed the tie, he will stop thrusting, and lie over the bitches back. I usually hold the dog up for a few minutes before I allow him to turn, as sometimes if he should turn too quickly, the tie can break and again you have to wait, before you can get another mating, so after a few minutes, only one or two, gently slide the dog down to the bitches side, then pass his rear leg over her back so they are standing back to back and you all relax.

The bitches owner still holds her head and I hold either both dogs tails or back legs, whilst the tie continues. A tie can last from a few minutes to around an hour, but is usually between ten and thirty minutes. You can then sometimes see the dog arch his back a slight bit and move away from the bitch. Usually the bitch drips steadily for a few seconds, which means the dog has passed plenty of semen and fluid so hopefully a good litter will result.

I once had an over enthusiastic owner pick his bitch up immediately, to carry her back to the car, and all the fluid poured out of the bitch down his trousers, so its as well to wait a few minutes before taking her back to the car. I usually ask bitch owners to carry them to the car, as it does save them leaving scent all over the place for my others dogs to get upset about and saves the bitch urinating immediately after mating. It's probably an old wives tale, and irrelevant, but it used to be considered not a good idea to let her urinate for an hour after mating.

Whilst the tie is taking place, the bitch usually stands reasonably still, some squeak, some yell and some can really struggle, but most, thank goodness, stand still and if really ready, enjoy it. Some dogs seem to have a need to wander all over the place, or prefer to stand with their heads hidden in a corner. Some also seem to keep walking with their hind legs. This, apparently is quite a good thing, and usually only very keen, fertile, dogs will do it, so if your stud dog looks as if he is trying to do a marathon whilst tied, don't get upset, just congratulate him and hope for a nice big litter. When the tie has broken and the bitch is returned to her kennel or car, if you have any other stud dogs, it is usually a good idea before you put the happy boy back in with his friends, to wash him down with some tepid water and soap solution, to get the stud smell off him. I have never had any trouble with all my stud dogs till one I have at present. I have always just popped the dog back into the kitchen with all the other dogs and bitches, and never had a moments trouble, but one of the three I have at the moment, if he has not had the stud himself, but one of the other two has, and I have not washed him down, will get a bit jealous and insist on mounting the dog that has just done the mating, so I decided to wash the dog who had done the stud, just under his tummy, and that worked, as it got rid of the smell and he was ignored when put back into the kitchen with the other dogs, so the problem was solved.

Occasionally though, some bitches just are not keen on being mated, sometimes it can be her wrong day even though she looks right and the dog is keen. More often, she is ready but just not feeling in the mood for love, as she has probably travelled hundreds of miles. I'm afraid its a case of holding her tight and carrying on. A great many maiden bitches can be pretty reluctant, usually due to the way their owners have treated them, always scaring off any dog that sniffs her and encouraging her to sit or snap at the interested male, so its no wonder that when the stud dog does just that she is only reacting as she has been taught. My dogs regularly check the girls, who obligingly roll over on their backs and hold a leg up, so when the day comes for them to be mated, its all fun together, and easy for everyone concerned, especially the animals.

If the visiting bitch just refuses to have the dog anywhere near her and continually snaps and growls at him, we have to end up with tying her mouth up, but I only use this as a last resort, and only then is it safe for the stud dog, the owners and my hands. I hate to do this as I find the bitches do not like it and can get pretty uptight, so never use it if there is the least chance you can win her over. Some bitches that have been flirting quite well beforehand, will completely go off the idea if taped, so its worth trying hard first, before you try taping her.

Some bitches hardly seem to swell at all when they come into season, and those can be pretty difficult for the dog to penetrate, or even find the right spot. There is a very good lubricating jelly obtainable from most chemists, that can be used to help the dog slip in. Petroleum jelly is not recommended, as there seems to be a question mark over it inhibiting the passage of sperm, and can mask the season smell of the bitch, so make the dog loose interest.

There is another situation that can arise in stud work and that is called an outside tie. The dog does not fully enter the bitch and if you let

Results of all those fun and games. Puppies from Willowmead Wish upon a Star and Willowmead True to Memory

him turn himself as soon as he wants without checking they are tied, he will just slip out and you have lost everything, one reason that I always hold dogs up on the bitch for a few seconds. Check that they are either tied or if its an outside tie, you need to keep the dog up on the bitch's back in the mounting position and slip your two first fingers behind the swollen balls, not the testicles, of the dog, and physically hold him inside the bitch, keeping both animals quite still, otherwise the dog just slips out. Providing he is fully out and pumping semen through, this is as good as any tie and can last as long as a normal tie, but I usually find I have had enough after about five to eight minutes, which has been quite sufficient to produce good litters. I had a Min. Poodle who never tied any bitch and always had to have an outside tie. He always produced big litters and I also know of a well-known Champion Beardie who also never did an ordinary tie. I used him myself and had a litter of eight puppies, two of which became Champions too. Sometimes the bitch will grip the dog sufficiently firmly that you can let the dog go, but this is rare, and never try and turn a dog with an outside tie, or it will definitely break, its safer to leave him up on her back and take the weight yourself for as long as you can, or until the tie breaks naturally.

If the bitch is on her right day and has had a good tie, I really don't think there is any need for a second mating, but if there is any problems or if the owners of the bitch are not sure of the day the bitch came into season, or there is a history of small litters, or missing altogether, it can be a good idea to have a second or even third mating. As mentioned elsewhere, I had a bitch that had to be mated very late, and it was only by trial and error we found her correct days. If she had only been mated once I might never have had any puppies from her, so if the bitch continues her season and carries on flirting, even with the family cat, as one bitch I had visited did, do bring her back for a second or third mating. The only time that might not be possible, would be if the dog had another bitch visiting at the same time. I have had it happen, but only once in all the years I have been breeding. Beardies are not quite as numerous as some breeds yet, thank goodness.

You can certainly get some funny things happen whilst you are busy helping at matings with your dogs. The following story was told to me by Althea Richardson, owner of the Caramac Bearded Collies about one of Mac's (Champion Swinford Sky Rocket at Macmont) last studs.

It's December 1989 and Mac is aged thirteen. His grandson, Caramac Cracker-Jack has a bitch booked for stud but unfortunately he is not particularly interested on her first visit. The owner of the bitch arranges to return the following day and asked if Mac could be used if Cracker-Jack remained uninterested. Althea agreed as he is still a very fit dog and saw no reason not to.

Anyway, after one hour they realised that it was going to be down to Mac, who of course was well aware that they had a bitch in season on the premises. Althea says that she should explain that she does her matings in a very long Utility room which has a cushion floor covering, so she always puts some rubber type underlay down at one end where the bitch usually stands.

Mac came into the room with a grin on his face - he just couldn't believe his luck. He went over to say hello to the bitch (she wasn't being over friendly, but certainly not resisting) and then he tried getting up. This is where his brain took over because he realised his back legs just were not what they used to be. He went up to the far end of the room and at this point Althea wondered if he just wasn't interested. No fear, he knew that he would have to take a run at her and he came galloping down before they were ready - threw himself on the bitch (who like them was totally unprepared) and they all ended up in a heap on the floor. At this stage they all realised what he was up to and got their act together, which was just as well because he went straight back to the end of the room and was already galloping their way again. It was the look on his face that sent everybody into hysterics but all they could do was to support the bitch and wait for him to land. On his third attempt he mated her and she seemed totally bemused by his antics - I'm sure he won her over this way but Althea says she was so impressed by the way he worked out this method, it was pure determination on his part.

Althea said that unfortunately no puppies were produced as a result of this mating but it was an experience never to be forgotten.

There are a few more amusing stories of the perils of doing stud work told me by Wendy Neal. Wendy says their telephone is guaranteed to ring at the most inconvenient times. You know the ones, the second you lift a hot heavy casserole from the oven, the moment you sit down to dinner, the instant you step into the bath.

So Wendy was quite pleased to have Alex, aged four, at hand when a bitch arrived to be mated to Penfold, Wendy's stud dog. He could usually be trusted to be polite to callers. His brother had a less refined telephone manner, tending to snatch up the phone and shout something along the lines of "Mummy's in the toilet" before smashing down the receiver on a doubtless speechless caller.

True to form, the phone shrilled out at that point just before the tie. Alex leapt dutifully into action. "I'm afraid Mummy can't speak to you at the moment" he said. "She's making babies with Penfold, Please can you call when they're finished?"

Wendy still doesn't know who that caller was. Had it been a friend they would surely have mentioned it. No one ever did, so she could only presume it was a little or unknown acquaintance.

Stud dog work introduces one to the parts of life other activities cannot reach.

The dogs are generally no problem. Most manage to do what comes naturally despite the efforts of their owners and since loosing his virginity at the ripe old age of thirteen months Penfold has never failed to mate a bitch, even if they've had to send the owner to watch the daffodils grow while the nuptials take place.

Mating dogs seem to bring out the untold hangups of the owners and the scenarios can be quite embarrassing. Wendy says she will never forget the day a pair of Golden Retrievers breeders arrived on her doorstep, desperate for help.

They had been trying for three days to mate a couple of dogs who seemed more interested in staring at the ceiling. She soon discovered why.

The poor stud dog, a maiden, hadn't moved an inch before his owner started yelling. "Go on Harvey, you can do it boy, you can do it son." Harvey couldn't, and Wendy couldn't blame him. She couldn't help wondering if the owner tried the same technique with her own husband, and if it had the same effect.

The cheerleading lady was dispatched to watch the TV in the room next door. Harvey breathed a sigh of relief and within five minutes the dogs had mated and tied.

Another couple arrived, the wife sensible and confident, the husband a quivering heap who looked likely to faint any moment. He was asked if he could wait in another room and they sent him away with a bottle of whisky. One hour and one mating later they found him sitting quietly grasping his glass in one hand and the much depleted whisky bottle in the other. His wife led him away.

Some stud work stories have become legendary.

One very prim lady arrived to have her bitch mated and firmly informed the stud dog owner her pet was well trained and would be no problem to mate. As soon as the dog walked into the room the lady snapped quickly, "Mate now, Trixie", and her bitch immediately rolled over on to her back. The owner beamed, "we're not having any of that kinky business", she said.

Sometimes, of course, things do not go to plan. Some of the best stud dogs seem to have the libido of inebriated garden slugs. Wendy knows of at least one determined owner who travelled more than a thousand miles in repeat journeys trying to get his bitch mated to a particular dog. The dog was unimpressed by the Herculean efforts of the owner and persistently looked at the bitch as if she was yesterday's breakfast. There was no mating.

Some dogs are very choosy about who they mate. You hear their distraught and frustrated owners explaining how they will only perform if a bitch is absolutely "spot on", or if it is brown, or if it isn't raining. They seem to take their dogs failures on a personal level and criticism cuts to the quick. If you think about it seriously, their pain is ridiculous, the fact is some dogs have a lower libido than others, and who can blame them? Why should they want to copulate with every Tessa, Dolcie and Harriet that appears on the doorstep?

Everyone knows that a tie is not an essential ingredient for a successful mating, but every one wants one and Wendy knows many owners (usually male) who seem to take personal pride in the length of tie achieved by their dog. The fact the length of tie can be dependent on the bitch is completely ignored.

One stud dog owner, however, was a little perturbed after her dog had mated a bitch and remained tied for well over an hour. She 'phoned her vet for advice. "Pin a medal to his chest", he said. The record tie, incidentally, is something over three hours.

The funniest story Wendy has ever heard was of a couple who took their Beardie to a particular stud dog and spent several long evenings trying to effect a mating without success.

The following afternoon the husband, I suspect in a fit of pique and frustration, took the bitch down to the village pub and had her mated to the local Don Juan, a Whippet.

Are you sure you wish to stand your dog at stud!!!

Breeding, Whelping and how to rear a litter

SO you think you would like to breed a litter. Lets imagine that you have a reasonable quality bitch, who in your eyes looks perfect, and you decide that you would like her to have a litter, several friends have said they would love to have a puppy, as she has such a delightful disposition. You acquire some dog books, and find the name of a breeder not too far away and ring him or her up.

The first thing you have to consider is her age. I usually like to mate my bitches for the first time at about two years of age, one, they are usually out of coat, and therefore not looking too good for the showring, and most important, are just nicely mature to cope with motherhood, and from the show point of view, a litter usually matures a bitch to go back into the ring later.

So assuming your bitch is around two to three years of age, the second question is, has she had her hips X-Rayed for Hip Dysplasia, and her eyes tested to find out if she has any eye problems. Both these conditions can be hereditary, so you do not want to pass them on to future generations.

Then what is her pedigree. I once had a lady ring me up with a bitch she had just acquired, she did not have the pedigree, saying it would be coming shortly from the previous owners. I pointed out to her, that unless I could see the pedigree, how could anybody possibly tell if it was not my stud dogs daughter, and there is no way I would do a father, daughter mating.

Providing the bitch has a good pedigree, then she needs to be seen. I know to every owner, their bitch is perfection, at least to all good owners she is, but the perfect dog is yet to be born, so she will definitely have some faults, and the stud dog owner will need to see what hers are, and decide which would be the most suitable dog, both in type, and pedigree-wise, to correct her faults and compliment her pedigree.

If the bitch is a really good specimen, with a very good temperament, calm, gentle, outgoing but not wild, no really outstandingly bad faults and a correct coat, then we must consider some other points before we go ahead.

Is there someone at home during the day, as puppies are very demanding little things and will take many many hours of attention, people out at work do not have the time to cope with the considerable demands that will shortly be put upon them.

Are you prepared for the risks involved? Ask any insurance company which is the biggest risk factor in their policies and the whelping bitch is the answer. You could easily discover the bitch has to have a caesarean section, with the possibility of loss of both bitch and puppies. She could abort, re-absorb, miss all together, be a non breeder, or a dozen other things, books are written just on this subject alone. Don't book a holiday, you might not have all the puppies leave at eight weeks, you could easily still have some around at three to four months of age, or even older.

There is one thing I always ask of people who bring their bitches to my stud dogs, are you capable of culling?. I do not believe that any maiden bitch belonging to an ordinary or pet owner, as opposed to an experienced breeder, and it being both bitch and owners first litter, that the bitch should be asked to rear more than six puppies. When the vet comes to check the litter after whelping, that any puppies more than six, should be put down. The bitch can usually rear six easily and successfully and both she and her owners can enjoy the experience, whereas, if she should whelp a large litter, such as nine or ten, that is very hard work indeed, even for an experienced breeder to cope with and its very hard work for the bitch, even with the best help, also six puppies are much easier to sell than ten. Most pet owners have the puppies in the kitchen or similar room and ten puppies would be very difficult indeed as they grow up a bit. The first thing I look for in a stud dog, when I choose a dog for one of my bitches is type. I have always tried to mate the same type of dog to the similar type of bitch, with any small faults she has, not to be carried by the dog, such as, if the bitch has an overlong foreface, and the dog also has an overlong foreface, most of the puppies will also have this fault, there are a great many different types in Beardies at the moment. Size seems to be a problem that is developing, so if your bitch is pretty large, try to find a smaller dog that you know produces correctly sized puppies, not all small puppies, as two wrongs do not produce a right, and should your bitch, alternately be on the small side, don't rush off to the biggest dog you can find, or you will probably end up with some extra large and some extra small puppies.

Don't be afraid to ask what the dog can produce, most stud dog owners are only too pleased to help with advice, as the last thing they want is poor quality puppies from their dog trotting around.

The stud dog should also have his eyes certified as clear of hereditary problems, and his hips X-Rayed for Hip Dysplasia with a good score.

Hips can be done a little later, as I like to start a dog at stud round twelve months of age and X-Ray between eighteen months and two years of age. Providing both parents have good scores, he should also be reasonably assumed to have a good score. Should he turn out to have a poor score I would withdraw any dog from stud. Since H-D X-raying started for Beardies in 1966, I have always X-rayed all my stock and tried never to use an outside dog whose hip status is unknown.

Next we must consider pedigree's, I like to line breed, and prefer to use my dogs on bitches that have similar lines and tie up to my own line, with regular outcrossing. I never inbreed, such as father/daughter, mother/

son, full brother/sister, and do not like grandparents to grandchildren either. One I find very successful is the following pedigree

Parents	Grandparents	Great Grandparents	Gt: Gt: Grandparents
Sire Ch. Willowmead Star Attraction	*Sire* Pure Magic of Willowmead 2 C.C.s, 3 Res. C.C.s	Ch. Brambledale Balthazar	Ch. Osmart Bonnie Blue Braid
			Brambledale Heathermead Moonlight
		Ch. Willowmead Super Honey	Ch. Wishanger Cairnbhan
			Ch. Broadholme Cindy Sue of Willowmead
	Dam Ch. Willowmead Juno of Tambora	Ch. Osmart Bonnie Blue Braid	Ch. Bravo of Bothkennar
			Ch. Blue Bonnie of Bothkennar
		Ch. Edelweiss of Tambora	Ch. Wishanger Cairnbhan
			Burdock of Tambora
Dam Ch. Willowmead Plain and Fancy	*Sire* Ch. Briaridge Lyrical Lord	Ch. Pepperland Lyric John at Potterdale	Wishanger Buttertubs Pass By Quinbury
			Pepperland Pandamonium
		Briaridge Erin Blue	Rossbourne Cynpegs Hobo
			Briaridge Black Annabelle
	Dam Willowmead Silver Lace 4 Res. C.C.s	Ch. Kimrand Simon	Ch. Edenborough Star Turn at Beagold
			Kimrand Summer Dawn 2 C.C.s
		Ch. Willowmead Super Honey	Ch. Wishanger Cairnbhan
			Ch. Broadholme Cindy Sue of Willowmead

Also the pedigree on the following page has been proved to produce a very successful line.

83

Parents	Grandparents	Great Grandparents	Gt: Gt: Grandparents
Sire American Ch. Willowmead Red Ruairidh	Sire Champion Benedict Morning Mist	Ch. Osmart Bonnie Blue Braid	Ch. Bravo of Bothkennar
			Ch. Blue Bonnie of Bothkennar
		Glendonald Gladsome	Jayemi Shin
			Bracco of Bothkennar
	Dam Champion Willowmead Perfect Lady	Ch. Edenborough Blue Bracken	Rowdina Grey Fella 1 C.C.
			Blue Maggie from Osmart
		Ch. Willowmead Super Honey	Ch. Wishanger Cairnbhan
			Ch. Broadholme Cindy Sue of Willowmead
Dam Willowmead Winter Memory 1 Res. C.C.	Sire Pure Magic of Willowmead 2 C.C.s, 3 Res. C.C.s	Ch. Brambledale Balthazer	Ch. Osmart Bonnie Blue Braid
			Brambledale Heathermead Moonlight
		Ch. Willowmead Super Honey	Ch. Wishanger Cairnbhan
			Ch. Broadholme Cindy Sue of Willowmead
	Dam Breckdale Pretty Maid 1 C.C., 4 Res. C.C.s	Braelyn Broadholme Crofter 1 C.C., 2 Res. C.C.s	Ruairidh of Willowmead, 1 C.C.
			Bobby's Girl of Bothkennar
		Breckdale Cala Sona River Danube	Alastair of Willowmead 1 C.C., 2 Res. C.C.s
			Westernisles Cala Sona Loch Aber

Both have the tie up of Super Honey, who was an outstanding producer and very strong indeed in fixing type, I have improved on one or two small points that I look for, but its basically the same construction as Honey's that I look for in both puppies and adults.

I always try to outcross regularly. There cannot be a complete outcross in Beardies, as all the dogs go back to the original few that Mrs Willison re-established the breed with, but with the many lines now developed, you can at least re-introduce some more or less fresh blood reasonably often.

If the breeder you first contact does not have a suitable dog, any good breeder will be only too happy to recommend another dog with the correct attributes and pedigree to be a good mate for your bitch. Do not be afraid of having to travel a fair distance to find the right dog. Don't forget, you will have five or six new lives to consider, dogs that will hopefully live fourteen or fifteen years, which is a long time for a mistake. All this should be attended to well before the bitch comes into season, one, you need to be ready, and two, she might come in early. Bitches can be very erratic with their timings.

When a bitch is due in season, I recommend that she is checked every day, so as not to miss the first day. As all my dogs live together with me in the house, my boys always let me know as soon as a bitch comes into season, but if you only have either, one or more bitches, the start can easily be missed by several days, then the correct date for mating can be somewhat confused.

Don't grab the poor girl and peer at her every few minutes, otherwise she, as well as you, will get somewhat neurotic about the whole thing. I find that if I gently run my hand down her back, from the head to the tail, when she is eating and very gently check her vulva, they are usually too busy with dinner to worry about anything I am doing, and will show colour easily. If you cannot touch your bitch whilst she is eating, and groom on a table, just pop her on the table for a few seconds brushing and check her then. Do not check her just after she has spent a penny, as even if she is in full season, she will not show colour then.

Usually the first day there is a copious discharge and the bitch will lick and clean herself regularly, a good sign to watch for, and another tip is, just before she comes in, she will usually urinate far more frequently than is her usual wont. Don't worry, if after the heavy start, she seems to almost go off and lose very little colour for three or four days, so long as she is still swollen, it is nothing to worry about. She will start to lose heavily again prior to mating. I usually find that most of my bitches start standing around the ninth day and are well and truely flirting by the twelfth to fourteenth day, which are the usual dates I mate. I find the thirteenth day about perfect for most of them, but there is the exception to every rule, and some bitches are dead right on the tenth day, or some make it later.

I have a bitch at the moment that is very late indeed. I mated her on her thirteenth day, she did not flirt at all being a maiden, that is a bitch that has never been mated, so as she looked ready on her thirteenth day, I took her down to London to the dog I wanted to use. She was duly mated without much difficulty, and as everything seemed OK, I did not bother with a second mating, end result, no puppies. So for her next season, I decided to use my own young dog, again, I tried on the thirteenth day. She was not really co-operating, but was not difficult, and they were still

85

tied in ten minutes, as it was a maiden dog, I was quite pleased. On her seventeenth day, she was really standing and flirting like mad, so I decided to try a second mating. She was very easy indeed and we had a very fast mating. She was still standing on her nineteenth day, so I did a third mating, again very easily. She was out of season on her twenty first day, and whelped one day early to the second (seventeenth) day mating. She has just had her second litter, and was mated again on the sixteenth and eighteenth days, and whelped one day early to the eighteenth day. Which just proves that its no good saying that you must mate on the tenth or fourteenth day, you have to go when the bitch is ready if you want to have a nice litter of puppies.

Usually, if a bitch has taken after being mated, she will go out of season fairly quickly, but again, do not worry if she goes for the full twenty one days, losing colour till the eighteenth day, I have had this with some of my girls and they have produced large litters.

One of the most important things to attend to after the bitch has been mated is not to let her get out or a roaming Romeo get in to her. A bitch will conceive to two, three or more dogs if she is mated to several different dogs. There are two things to be done, should it happen within twenty four hours, you can dash off to the Vet, and have her injected, this will start the season again, but the chance of her conceiving, if you mate her again later in the induced season is not very good at all, or if it should be longer than the twenty four hours, I'm afraid you will have to leave things to go their natural course and let her whelp.

There is now a method of testing called DNA which can prove which puppy belongs to which parent, so all is not completely lost. Where as before DNA, you could not possibly sell any puppy as a Beardie, as there would not be any method of telling, a puppy could look a totally correct Beardie and be the offspring of a mongrel dog.

The only disadvantage of DNA is its extremely expensive, being very new, but hopefully as time progress's, the cost should come down.

Hopefully no such disasters will take place and with care should not happen.

The bitch has been successfully and easily mated and returns home. Do keep an eye on her for any incorrect discharge, some bitches seem to develop infections from the air and if not attended to, could lose the litter. She should go out of season normally, and dry up as usual. The vulva, if she is pregnant, does not usually go down in size to quite as small as it would without being mated, so do not panic if she still looks swollen.

For the first three weeks there is no need to change anything, except to give her extra exercise in preparation for an easy whelping. At three weeks I like to worm the bitch, she should have also been wormed prior to mating. At coming up to four weeks in whelp she will usually go off her food, some bitches go off completely and will not eat much for several days, some bitches just slow down as they eat, and perhaps leave a few crumbs, instead of their usual completely clean plate. When she starts

86

eating up well again at about five weeks, you will need to start increasing her food. You will also find that she is starting to drink a lot more water, so make sure she always has access to fresh water at all times.

Do not do a sudden large increase in food, do it slowly, just an ounce or so on each meal. As mentioned previously, I always feed my dogs twice a day, but if you should feed only once a day, change to twice, or if she gets very large, three smaller meals are better than two large ones. You will find that by six weeks she will be eating considerably more. If she was eating eight ounces of meat per day in two feeds of four ounces each, she can double or even treble that, I have had bitches that normally have four ounces each meal go up to twelve ounces per meal, plus, of course, the equivalent increase in biscuit mixer meal. Do not change her diet, if she has been fed tinned meat as I feed mine, keep to the sort she is used to, if you feed a semi-moist or dry, stay with what she is used to. Do not feed milk, adult dogs cannot digest milk, so all it will do is give her diarrhoea and lose a lot of the goodness she needs from her food.

Also at about six weeks, she will have a vaginal discharge, providing this is a fairly clear sticky discharge without much smell, this is a sure guide that she is safely in whelp and I have not seen it in any bitch not in whelp, should she have a bad smelling discharge, that is wrong, and vetinary help should be sought without delay, or if she has a dark coloured or bloody discharge, again straight to the Vet.

You will find as the bitches girth increases in size, she will start to slow up a little. It is better to go several shorter walks rather than one really long one, and if she says she has had enough, do not insist on going further. There is always one who races about throughout the entire pregnancy, like a mad hat, even on the day of whelping, and still stays perfectly fit and healthy, I've had that sort too, but usually bitches take great care or themselves when pregnant.

A bitches recognised term is supposed to be sixty three days, most maiden bitches, (a maiden bitch is one that has not previously whelped a litter,) whelp two or three days early, but I have had one litter nine days early, and one five days over, the nine days early was rather worrying, as that is considered somewhat dangerous and the vet, said I would be lucky to have any survive, as the bitch was a very good mother indeed, she only lost two, one bitch had an infection through the cord, and a dog puppy was overlaid, we reared the other seven quite successfully. The puppies were very small at birth, and had very pink noses and paws with no coat on them, but it soon covered, and they all ended up as good sized adult dogs. The bitch that went over five days, had a much harder time whelping, as her puppies were so much bigger, but she was an experienced matron and very fit, so whelped without complications or vetinary help.

Prior to whelping, you should either have bought or made a whelping puppy box. As soon as you are sure she has taken and decided where she is going to live with the puppies for the first few weeks, the most common place seems to be the kitchen, as there is usually a floor covering that is

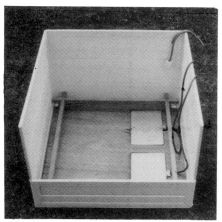

White whelping box. Low side up only, pig rail and heated pads in position

Above: White whelping box with high side up to keep puppies in when getting older

Right: Wooden whelping box with puppy pop open, can be closed when puppies are small

easy to clean, five or six little puppies can make an awful lot of puddles and poops, when they become active and carpet is certainly not suitable.

I always whelp and rear all my puppies on the polyester fur fabric, easily obtainable from shows and good pet shops, plus breeders. I always keep plenty in, as all puppies go to their new homes with a piece of blanket to help them settle in. The advantage of the blanket is, it is easily washed in the washing machine, drys quickly, the puppies are always warm and dry on it, as all liquids go through to the paper underneath, which can be changed whenever necessary and puppies can get their little toes into it to grip better when feeding, instead of something that they can slip on, such as paper. They also learn to walk much earlier due to the improved grip they have. I use heated pads under the blanket, and find the heat comes through beautifully, using the pads on the one side only of the box, the bitch can go and lie on the side with the pads when she feels chilly, or if too hot, can lie away on the cooler side.

I have found the bitch on the one side with several puppies feeding, and the rest of the litter, curled up fast asleep, quite content, on one of the heated pads. If you should wake them up, they toddle over to Mum for a quick feed, before they go back to sleep, usually on the pad again.

But before we get too much into puppies, there are several things to know about whelping. I find with all my bitches that they eat well until a few hours before whelping actually starts, so if she starts in the evening, breakfast will usually be refused and definitely dinner. Some will eat some breakfast, but leave the greater part, be fairly restless for the rest of the day, panting and fidgeting about. As soon as I see these signs I get the whelping box into the kitchen and even a maiden bitch hops straight in and lies there happily. I then put plenty of newspaper in, which she spends time chewing and scratching up into small pieces.

To try and get a good idea of the exact, more or less, time she will start you can take the bitch's

Box dismatled for easy storage

temperature. Sterilise the thermometer and grease with a little vaseline, get someone to hold her head to steady her and pop it into her anus. I have found that the temperature slowly drops from the usual 101.5 to 97 over a matter of 3 or 4 days, although it quite often drops to 99-100 and stays there for a couple of days before dropping rapidly to 97. I have never found it to go below this but could have missed it of course. The temperature only stays down at 97 for a short while, then rises quickly, usually when the temperature starts to rise you have 12 hours before the first puppy is born. I have once had a copybook whelping, Toomi's temperature started to rise at 10 am and the first puppy was born at exactly 10 pm, but it was sheer luck, I probably caught the exact time her temperature started to rise. I usually only take the temperature morning and evening, obviously there are many hours in between when things can start to happen.

When the bitch starts to whelp properly she will show signs of bearing down, (straining to pass the first puppy). The first contractions will be so slight you might not even notice them, but they will rapidly get stronger and she will often give a small "ooff" as she pushes hard. Most bitches will continually lick the vagina and will clean up any fluid that passes. When she has really started straining I change the paper and put thick folded papers in the box, mainly so that I can change them quickly as the puppies are born.

You will also need a sharp pair of scissors, sterilised in a bottle of surgical spirit, several clean dry towels, a bucket nearby to pop afterbirths in, and a comfortable chair to sit on as you could be in for a long session. I also have a paper and pen handy too as I like to note down times, colours and sexes of the puppies as they are born. I sometimes weigh them as well which can be very interesting later.

If you have any other dogs they need to be put right out of the room as the mother may well attack another dog coming near when she has her puppies. Also the other dog could kill the puppies as the bitch attends to the one being born at the time if you are not there to see to things, I have heard of this happening more than once.

Don't panic even if the bitch seems to be straining really hard providing she has not been at it for more than 2 hours. 2 hours seems to be the magical amount of time that is accepted as safe, both prior to the first puppy's arrival, and inbetween each individual puppy's birth. Longer is considered getting into the risky area. You will see her give some really strong pushes and on lifting her tail you should see a bag appearing. If it is a correct presentation, the puppy should appear head first, but Beardies seem to have as many as 50 per cent born rear ends first. This is not a breach birth as a proper breach is when the tail appears first and the back legs are tucked up under the rear end, which is a very difficult birth for the bitch, back legs popping out feet first is not too difficult at all.

We will hope its head first though, and after a few more hard pushes, out will pop the rest of the puppy. Do not panic if it seems to take ages for the rest of the puppy to follow the first half inch of the head, so long as the bag is intact, the puppy will be perfectly alright and if the bag is broken and the head is out, the puppy can breath, so again do not panic as you can upset the bitch. Always keep calm and reassuring with her all through the whelping, she has enough to cope with, without panicking people around her.

Usually as the puppy pops out, with a maiden bitch, she will give a yell, and sometimes will not look at the puppy, she does not yet realise its her baby, and that horrid thing hurt her, so its up to you to break the bag from the puppy, this is where you need your scissors and towels. Remove the bag from the puppy, breaking it with your fingers, hold the cord tight between finger and thumb on the puppy's side of the cord, and cut the cord on the afterbirth side, keep a tight hold of the cord for a few seconds to stop the flow of blood, leaving the cord approximately one inch long from the puppy, then let go and get the towel, the puppy will probably be sqealing and wriggling by now, so gently rub him up and dry him as best you can. As soon as he is a bit dry give him to the bitch to lick, if she will, sometimes she will not even look at the puppy, so gently put him into her tummy to start to suckle, if he will. Some puppies immediately start sucking, some need teaching how to drink, but I would not bother with the first couple to be born, the bitch needs to come to terms with her new family before you start pushing things along too fast.

You will, in the mean time, have popped the afterbirth into the bucket and pushed it away from the box.

Some bitches pop their puppies out every fifteen or so, minutes, some have them by two's, before she has time to sort out number one, number two is already arriving, which is again, a good time for you to be there to give any help needed, some will go the full two hours between each puppy's arrival. These are the bitches I do not like, as it makes it such a long time for everybody concerned. The ones I really prefer are the bitches that have a nice litter of between six and eight puppies, all whelped in a couple of hours. It does happen, but not often enough.

By the time the bitch has three or four puppies, she should really be helping to attend to things herself. If she only likes the puppies after you have done everything for them, push her head round as the puppy presents, and she will usually realise that she must start to break the bag and attend to the puppy herself. Do not worry if she eats the afterbirth, this is perfectly normal and actually gives her a feed to carry her over the first few hours of the puppies life. If she should be straining hard for more than two hours and nothing is showing, do not hesitate to call the Vet. There are so many complications that can arise, I have had one bitch that presented with what is called a traverse birth, the puppy did not come down the right canal for birth, but started going up the other horn of the uterus, so blocked everything, the Vet. had to turn the puppy and bring it down the right way. There are many other situations that can need vetinary help. You should have informed your Vet that your bitch is due to whelp on such and such a day, so he will not be unduly surprised if you need to call him out for help. Luckily though, Beardies are very easy whelpers so hopefully you will not have any trouble with her.

You will know when she has finished, instead of being still restless, panting and shivering, she will, after the birth of the last puppy, slowly become more and more relaxed, any very slight strainings will completely stop, and she will have a well needed sleep, completely happy with all her puppies, either feeding or sleeping contentedly.

I sometimes, if the bitch needs it, give a drink of water about halfway through a large whelping and always about three hours after the last birth, take her out to relieve herself. You can then change the paper in the box whilst she is outside. If its in the middle of the night, I then usually go to bed myself and leave her in peace. If its during the day, I take her out to the kennel, previously prepared for her and her family. I always have another box in the kennel, with her blanket, heated pads and an outside heater on, so the temperature is about 70° in the kennel for the first couple of days and nights. If its warm Summer weather, you will not need the heater on during the day, but its usually cold enough at night in England to need it for a few nights to start with, even in mid-Summer, and definitely at any other time of year. If you intend to keep her in the kitchen, I do not, as all my other dogs live in the house with me and we are mainly in the kitchen, but if yours is the only dog there is no problem. If you have another dog, I would suggest you put up some type of barricade to prevent the other dog getting into the puppies for the first couple of weeks. Afterwards, hopefully, they will all get on well together.

When the bitch has finished whelping, it is as well to contact the Vet to come out and check her over for retained afterbirths or puppies. They usually give a pituitary injection to contract the womb and it also helps to bring the milk down, sometimes an anti-biotic to prevent infection. You can also arrange with him to come out to do the dew claws in approximately three to six days time. I usually like the fourth day, as I find the puppies are fairly strong by then but not so big as to be very wriggly, which makes them difficult to hold. I have never seen a dew claw on the back legs of a Beardie, but have seen it on poodles, and have heard of it a couple of times on beardies, so it does exist.

Contented mum with new born whelps.
Willowmead True Delight

Assuming that your bitch whelped overnight, by morning she will need a good breakfast, don't forget that she did not eat much the day before, so will most likely be pretty hungry by now. Just give her normal food, but only maintenance rations, the puppies do not take too much from her for the first couple of days, so I find her usual amount of food is sufficient, then after two or three days, when the puppies demands grow, you will need to increase rapidly. I feed as much as she will eat, whilst still cleaning up her dish. I do not leave food down for her at any time, if she doesn't eat it all up, I feed a bit less next meal. She will need even more food whilst feeding the puppies, than she needed whilst in whelp, and she will drink water copiously, so make sure there is plenty of fresh water easily available at all times, day and night.

You will probably find that for the first few days, the bitch will be very reluctant to leave her babies and you will probably have to lift her out of her box to go outside. I usually cover the puppies up whilst

Contented day old puppies

Day old puppies

she is away with a large towel or blanket, they usually all cuddle up in the dark and go to sleep. I always take a lead out with me too, as sometimes she will be in such a hurry to get back to her babies, that she will not stop to do everything and if she is on the lead, you can take her a bit further.

I am lucky, in as much that I have a large orchard so do not need to leave my premises for exercise, but if you need to go out onto roads, I would suggest using a dilute wash of TCP or something similar, to wipe over her teats, round her mouth and paws, before going back to the puppies, for the first few weeks.

Another sad thing which sometimes happen is that the bitch, even though she tries to be very careful, can overlay a puppy. If it does not squeal very loudly and at once, it very soon is either squashed to death or suffocated. The first thing, either you or the bitch, will know about it, is when she gets up, she will find her dead baby. Some bitches are very careless indeed, and will just plonk down and not bother if a puppy squeaks a bit, as there are plenty more sqeaking all over the place. These are usually older mature matrons, younger bitches are usually much more careful as a rule. Another situation that can cause a bitch to overlay her puppies, is the fact that she is too hot. I know the books I have read all suggest the bitch and puppies should be kep^t at 80o for the first few days. I find 70o can be too hot. The bitch will continually sit up to try and get a bit cooler, as all the puppies are also snuggling up to her, she gets very tired indeed, can drop down asleep, not realising there is a puppy underneath her, and consequently, squash it. At a^{b}out 65o, the bitch happily allows all the puppies to cuddle up, they get her body heat, and all are comfortable.

Should the bitch overlay a puppy, you might find she could become distressed, if you try to remove it from the box, and leap out of the box to see where you are taking her baby. Get a towel or piece of blanket, and pick up two puppies, the dead one and a live one, slip the towel over the dead one and show her the live one, then replace that one into the bitch, she will happily lick the live one you have replaced and you can rapidly remove the dead one, underneath the towel so she cannot see it go.

There is one problem I have come across with a bitch getting too much milk, even before the final puppy is born, you can feel the milk getting hard around the teat, with a bitch that is lactating well, you can never feel milk, but if you squeeze a teat, a good flow soon appears, when she is getting engorged, you can feel hardness round most teats. The puppies usually suck and cry a little, as its such hard work to get even a small amount of milk down. I tried several different methods to sort the problem out, as the Vet could not help, he could start milk, or stop milk, but not regulate it. The best method I found was to almost starve the bitch of food for as long as necessary. I would only give her one ounce of meat and two or three grains of biscuit for her meals, for the first couple of days, water ad. lib. of course. I did not find it necessary to stop her water. Usually by the third day, the milk was starting to clear, and the stronger puppies were moving it from all the teats. I would make sure that any smaller puppy would get a good feed from the best teat as many times a day as I possibly could, making the strongest puppies feed from the hardest teats.

I found this worked better than all the other methods of trying to draw off milk etc. that I tried. The bitch was usually ravenous, but as soon as the problem was sorted out, you could rapidly increase her food, making sure the problem does not redevelop. It was usually in older bitches that this happened, but I did once have it start to show in a three year old in her second litter, so it can happen at any time.

When the puppies are about three days old, it is time to groom the bitch thoroughly, she will be somewhat reluctant to leave her puppies, but it is most important that her coat is completely brushed and combed through. Some bitches have very long coats, especially the bitches that are being shown, and they can easily start to knot with all the puppies wriggling through it and climbing all over Mum. If knots start to appear, you can find a puppy get tangled up in a knot, also if the bitch gets up quickly and jumps out of the box, the puppy can be hanging in the knot and be dropped on the floor outside the box. If nobody is there to pick the puppy up and put him back into the box, he will soon get very chilled and hypothermia set in, also he will yell as he is cold and lost, the bitch will start to get distressed, leave the rest of the litter, who then also start to yell, and you end up with a very upset and confused bitch and puppies.

Contentment - Lyndonbrae Lorelei

It's really much easier to groom her well every three days, until the puppies are four or five weeks or so, old.

Another couple of things that need close watching throughout the time the bitch is feeding her puppies are, one, the puppies nails need trimming regularly, they grow just like cats claws and are equally sharp, so if not cut will scratch the poor Mum dreadfully. I prefer the guillotine type of nail clipper, as you can see exactly how much nail you are cutting. Do be very careful not to cut the quick in the puppies claws, they are very tiny, but the quick is quite obvious growing down the nail. It is better to just trim the ends off and do them more often, rather than try to save time by only doing them occasionally and cutting too far up the nail.

The second thing to watch out for is long hairs twisting round the bitches nipples. This can happen very fast, and if not noticed almost at once, can be cutting right through the nipple, and will, if not removed, completely cut the end of the nipple off. It is very painful for the bitch, especially when the puppies try to suckle, and of course, you will loose the milk from that teat. The hair winds round and round and can be very difficult to remove. You will need a very sharp pair of scissors, and I find snipping very carefully with the points, the best way to cut through the hair. It is not possible to pull it off if its already become embedded and is too tight to get the scissors underneath to cut through. Do get someone to steady the bitch, if she is at all fractious, otherwise you could end up with bad cuts on her tummy, and even if she is a show bitch, when you will be trying to keep as much coat as possible, it's far safer to cut all the hair off that keeps on tieing round the nipples. Do check several times a day, if it has once started, as it seems to get tied up again in a matter of hours, and needs regular removal until the nipple heals up.

The puppies eyes usually start to open at around ten to fourteen days old, then they very rapidly start to grow up and by three weeks you need to start weaning them. I feed a milk powder that is as near to a bitches milk as is possible to get. Your bitches milk is very rich indeed with a high fat content, so giving the puppies cows milk is not really very good for them. I make about quarter pint of milk in a jug and with a small dish start to feed. I have a bit of trouble at the moment with my hands and have found the best method is to get each puppy out of the box and stand him on a small box covered with a towel, so his paws will not slip, hold him steady with one hand and hold the dish just under his nose with the other hand. They usually start to lap at once, but some can be too greedy and nearly choke themselves, so I hold the head to prevent them swallowing, or putting their noses under the milk and blowing bubbles. They soon learn to lap properly, and not get in too much of a mess. I also have a cloth handy to wipe their chins after feeding, otherwise as you put them back into the box, they get into rather sticky mess licking each other. The idea of feeding on the box is so that the other puppies cannot get at the milk dish whilst you are feeding each one individually. As you feed each puppy on his own, you can make sure, by feeling the weight of each puppy, that any one not as fat as the others, can get a little more, so catch up with his litter mates.

I always feed the smaller ones first, letting them eat as much as they like, before popping them back into the box, with the largest and fattest last, so if there is not so much milk left, he will not need it, being fat anyway. It also evens out the size of the puppies as they grow.

I feed a milk only feed, once a day for two days, when the puppies are three weeks old, with an average sized litter, providing the bitch has plenty of milk, is lactating properly and everything is going well.

Should she have any problems do not hesitate to start weaning earlier if neccessary. I had one litter recently of seven puppies, all went well for the first week, on the second week I noticed some of the puppies were not growing as fast as the others. This is not too unusual. I always make quite sure that any smaller puppy has a good teat for milk and stay with the bitch till she lets the milk down, so that I know all the puppies have had a good feed. You can tell when the bitch lets the milk down, as when the puppies first start to feed, they will be pummeling the bitch and seeming to work hard, when suddenly its all systems go, their little front legs go straight and they are really swallowing as fast as they can as the milk comes down fast. This only lasts a few

Puppies grow at a great speed.
3 week old puppies

7 week old puppies

10 week old puppies

moments, then its all change, with all puppies trying another teat to see if there is more milk there, instead of the one they have just emptied.

If you do not stay and watch the puppies, the smallest one will very rapidly get pushed out to the empty teats, so steadily fall back. Well, with my litter, two puppies were definitely going back and not growing at the same speed as the bigger ones. I made sure they had plenty of food from Mum, but each night they went back again, they were lively and obviously healthy, so at two weeks of age, I decided there was either something wrong with them or they were just not getting enough food. So I mixed up some milk and tried to see if they would feed, as I have never had puppies of two weeks lap before, they usually totally refuse any extra supplement. These two were just very hungry and lapped straight away. I had previously tried them with an eye dropper and milk, but they had completely refused it, so I thought they were getting enough milk. Now they soon started to catch up with their bigger litter mates. So if you do have any problems, consider the milk flow and does Mum have enough for her family.

This is very rare in Beardies, its the first time I have ever had it happen and have not heard of it either, but it obviously can occur and is something to look out for. I did start feeding all the puppies at 2 1/2 weeks old, and she dried up very much earlier than any other bitch I have ever bred from, as I have not had another litter from her, I cannot tell if she will do the same thing next time. She was fine with her first litter, but only had four puppies and this was her second litter with seven puppies.

To go back to weaning the puppies of a normal litter, when weaning commences at three weeks, I feed a milk drink, once a day, for two days, preferably when Mum has been out for a couple of hours, should you decide to feed the puppies when they have just had a good feed from Mum, they might not be so keen to eat and will take much longer to feed, whereas if Mum has been out, they are getting hungry, and soon polish the milk off.

On the third day, I give two milk feeds, one morning, one late afternoon, again when the puppies are hungry. On the fourth day, I introduce a bit of meat, mashed well into the milk. I use either a good tinned puppy food, or a complete dried food, sometimes a combination of both, about one ounce of meat the first day. The dried food I soak till it becomes very soft, then I mash it up with a fork, as I do with tinned food, so that it looks like a puree. The puppies usually love their first meat meal. I then do two more days of one milk only drink, and one milk and meat feed. I then give both meals with milk and meat, increasing daily both the milk and meat to appetite. You soon learn how much each puppy needs by feel and looking at his fat little tummy, do not over feed at this stage, but do make sure that each one has enough.

I usually feed each puppy individually for about five days, then try two together round a bowl, and when they are eating sensibly, put three round a bowl together, increasing the size of the bowl, as the size of the dinner and the puppy also increases.

By this time they are off the box and eating on the floor, so its easier to look after all of them together.

On approximately day seven, when the puppies are four weeks old, they have two milk and meat meals, and one milk drink mid day, with the other meals, morning and early evening, after another three days they go on to another feed, a drink of milk just before bed at approximately 9.30 at night.

All the time you need to steadily increase the food you are feeding the puppies, after another few days, I make the four feeds, breakfast, lunch, dinner and supper, all milk and meat feeds, and a drink of milk around mid-afternoon. At about five and a half to six weeks old, you need to start to include some biscuit mixer meal. I usually soak the meal for a few days to start with, and mash it up small, they can very rapidly go on to the small puppy meal unsoaked, but if you use a larger adult meal, soak it for a little longer. I do give my ppuppies a handful of dry biscuit meal from about five weeks old, to go to bed. For the first couple of days, I watch to make sure they can eat it safely, without getting it stuck in their throats, but have always found by five weeks, they can cope well, and enjoy chewing it up.

Steadily increase the amounts of food, till each individual puppy is having eight ounces of meat per day, divided into the four meals, and approximately two to three ounces of biscuit meal by eight weeks old.

This is the diet sheet I give out when the puppies leave me at eight weeks old.

Diet Sheet for an Eight Week Old Bearded Collie Puppy

Breakfast: 2 ozs. Chum Puppy Food, Mixed with $\frac{1}{2}$ oz. Chum Mixer biscuit. Twice a week add an egg - cover all with milk.

Lunch: 2 ozs. Chum Puppy food, mixed with $\frac{1}{2}$ oz. Chum Mixer biscuit - cover with milk.

Mid-Afternoon: Drink of Milk.

Dinner: 2 ozs. Chum Puppy food, $\frac{1}{2}$ oz. Chum Mixer biscuit, cover with milk.

Supper: 2 ozs. Chum Puppy food, $\frac{1}{2}$ oz. Chum Mixer biscuit, cover with milk.

* Do not feed food directly from the fridge. Allow to reach room temperature before feeding.

Increase the meat meals (Chum Puppy food) by 1 oz. per week (i.e. 8

weeks 8 ozs. - 9 weeks 9 ozs. per day and so on) until the puppy is having approximately 16 ozs. per day. Bitches may need slightly less than dog puppies and less Chum Mixer biscuit.
Also increase Mixer to approximately 10/12 ozs. per day.

At 4 months drop the milk drink.

At 5 months drop Supper.

At 6 months drop the Lunch so that the puppy is now having 2 meals day - you will need to, the same time as you drop each meal, increase the remaining meals to the appropriate amounts.

Give a hard dog biscuit to go to bed, with baby puppies, a small soft biscuit.

ONLY large marrow bones RAW.

If loose, a little arrowroot is very good mixed with each meal or given alone as a small feed - make with half milk - half water. Half a handful of bran just mixed into each meal soon firms up the motions too.

The puppy has been wormed twice but it is advisable to worm again at approximately 4 months - 6 months - 12 months and then once yearly with tablets from your Vet.

16 ozs. equals 1 lb.   2 lbs. equals approximately 1 kilo.
If you cannot obtain Chum Puppy food, any good quality tinned puppy food will do.

I usually find that the puppies start to get out of the box at about three to four weeks of age, they are now able to reach the top of the sides of the box and soon climb up, sometimes using a small brother or sister as a stepping stone to reach the top. Then of course they fall over to the other side. I find it a good idea, to make the landing side softer and safer, to put a thick piece of blanket round the box, so that it makes a soft landing, and is also somewhere warm to cuddle up, if they are outside the box for any time, rather than the cold floor. As soon as one has been out a couple of times, I take down the opening side of the box, and give the puppies the full kennel to play in, its safer than having one or two continually out. I always find that they go back to bed in the box on their heated pads, even the smallest one.

At four weeks I usually take the bitch out for all the night, the puppies are still feeding from her and taking quite a lot of milk, but are starting to pull her, and she is very glad to be away. They are quite capable of being all night without her at four weeks old.

Also at four weeks I usually start putting the puppies outside the

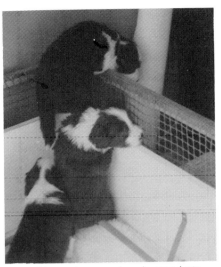

Up and away - Lyndonrae Late Arrival, Lively Lad and Leese

kennel into their run, which is half concrete and half grass, if the weather is reasonable, preferably sunny and mild, but not if its raining and cold, just for a few minutes to start with, gradually increasing the time as they become accustomed and acclimatized to the outside world. It doesn't take them long to discover the delights of being outside, and I find it fascinating to see which puppy is the first to go off to explore his new environment, or the one who sits and yells for his familiar surroundings. It is also so much easier to change the box and papers in the kennel when all the young inhabitants are outside, instead of trying to help you.

I usually find by this stage too, that the bitch only wants to stay in with the puppies to feed them and is soon glad to get out and go back to a pleasant life in the house.

At around five weeks, I start to stand the puppies on a table, to start to assess their show potential, or what faults they might be developing. It is easy with incorrect markings, as these puppies, even if really beautifully constructed, will not be accepted in the showring. The ones with correct markings can start to be checked for how they are progressing, and I usually trim them under the tail to keep them clean and healthy too, as the coat is starting to really get some length already, and if not tidied up, and if missed for a few days, the puppy can become totally tied up behind and not be able to pass his motions, when he could very rapidly get into difficulties, which could result in, at the least, a trip to the Vet at worst, can die, which would be a terrible thing, just at the beginning of his life.

You will probably find, at about this age, you will need to check the puppy's eyes each morning for bits of sleep in the corners, clean them if necessary, with a bit of damp cotton wool, also check ears for any dirt, and if any signs, have them cleared up with medication from the Vet. All this can be done on the table, when you have them up for show standing, another thing to be done on the table is a quick brush, really more of a gentle rub over with the brush, just to get him used to it, for a few seconds. He will soon enjoy being attended to, but do have two people there, if at all possible, as baby puppies can be terrible wrigglers and it would be dreadful if he slipped off and fell on the floor, he could easily break a leg,

101

or his neck, something not to be recommended.

Also as the puppies grow, do be extra careful when you hold them, sometimes as you go to put them down, they will start to wriggle, as they realise they are nearing the floor. My mother was putting down a poodle puppy once, who was seven weeks old, and she wriggled out of her, not quite tight enough grasp, fell awkwardly on to the floor, and broke her front leg. It was, thank heavens, only a greenstick break, but it still necessitated being in plaster for three weeks, and as she was being collected two days later, her new owner was somewhat disappointed at having to wait so much longer for her eagerly awaited puppy. I had another breeder drop a puppy too once. This was again a very wriggly puppy, and she was dropped from waist height, luckily she did not break anything, but she was very shocked indeed, and for about the next twelve months she would go rigid whenever she was picked up. I kept her, and was able to regain her confidence, but was furious with the girl who had dropped her. It was the last time she was invited to see any of my puppies.

It is a good idea to attend to each puppy every day, on the table, so that when the new owner puts him onto the table for grooming, he is quite happy there, and stands still. You can also feel the weight of each puppy in turn, and so realise if one should start to drop back, and either make sure that one gets a little extra dinner, or if one might be starting some illness, you can catch it quickly before it gets a good hold. Watch the puppies eat all their food, as sometimes they can all start eating well, but if you should go away to change their beds or similar, you will not notice if one starts to leave the food too early, or if the bossy one of the litter starts to push out a smaller sibling, so the little one does not get enough. It is not unusual for the bossy puppy to start to growl at his brothers and sisters whilst they are eating. I usually find this can start happening, from about seven weeks old. One of the best ways to prevent this, is to feed the bossy puppy from a dish on his own, it does entail sitting there holding him, while he eats his dinner and the other puppies finish off their own too, but it is worth it.

I usually like to bring the puppies into the house for a bit of a play, and to get used to the different smell, sounds and noises of a household before they go to their new homes.

They usually take everything happily in their stride and think its great fun to rush around looking at all the new experiences, a quite different type of situation to the grass and quiet of the run outside. If you have reared the litter in the house, of course this would not apply, but you will need to take the puppies outside, one, to learn to be clean in the house, and two, to harden them to the outside world. When the weather is nice, it is a good idea to get a small puppy pen put up in a shady spot. I would like a bed, or small basket or box also put in the pen, so the puppies have somewhere to sleep, especially if the ground is at all damp. If you give them the run of the whole garden, it is amazing how quickly the garden flowers will disappear and if there is the smallest hole, they will soon discover it and go visiting the neighbours, so it is safer all round in a secure puppy pen.

To start with only leave them out half an hour or so, gradually increasing the time they stay out, until they can be left outside all day in nice warm sunny weather in the Summertime.

A brief summary of things to remember.

Things to check throughout pregnancy and whilst rearing the litter. Plenty of exercise for the first five weeks, decreasing according to the bitches needs and her increasing waistline. Check no bad coloured discharge throughout pregnancy and weaning of the litter. She will have a clear sticky discharge, from approximately six weeks in whelp, increasing in volume until whelping, after whelping, she will have a slight blood coloured discharge, which can continue until the puppies are three months old, so long as its slight and the bitch is obviously healthy, this is quite normal.

The bitch will go off her food at about three and a half to four and a half weeks in whelp, do not tempt or insist she eats, if she doesn't finish up her food, just remove and offer food again at her next meal. She will soon eat it up again after a few days.

Start increasing her food at about five weeks in whelp, and slowly increase to between three and four times her normal maintenance rations.

Get everything ready for the whelping in plenty of time, as she can whelp up to nine days early, or five days late. Do not leave her over five days, otherwise you can loose both bitch and puppies.

Worm pre-mating and between three and four weeks in whelp. Inform your Vet of the due date of the litter, so he knows she is in whelp. If you want the Vet to check she is in whelp, the best time is around four weeks. These days there is ultra sound scanning, which is completely safe, and can tell you whether to expect a large or small litter.

Get box, bedding and heating sorted out in plenty of time. Accustom the bitch to the box and area you want to keep her and the puppies for the first few weeks, or the whole time you have the puppies with you.

Trim all the hair off the bitches tummy, and clear the nipples, so that the puppies can feed easily, well before the due date.

Get in milk powder in case you need to supplement any puppy, also puppy feeding bottle, or if not easily obtainable, an eye dropper is quite suitable.

Do not leave the bitch much longer than two hours between puppies as they are being born, and get the Vet out when she has finished whelping to check her over.

Remove dew claws between three and six days of age.

Start to wean puppies at three weeks.

Remove bitch at night from four to four and a half weeks of age of puppies, she should be completely weaned off by seven weeks, but if there is still milk there let the puppies strip her out once more, then keep her well away until they have all gone, or until she has quite dried up and will not let them feed again, then she can start to play with her family once more.

Worm puppies at five and six and a half weeks and if necessary, at seven and a half weeks.

Should the puppies or the bitch, get loose motions, give a handful, or more if necessary, of bran, mixed up with each meal. This should tighten her up within hours, if it doesn't work, it is probably some infection and veterinary advice should be sought.

Showing

Training your Puppy for the Show Ring

A DOG has to be six months old before he can be shown in a Kennel Club registered show, but there is a lot of work and preparation to be done before that day arrives.

Any puppy that is intended for the show ring needs to start his show training at eight weeks old. No, don't panic, all you need to do at this stage is every time he is groomed, when you have finished brushing him on the table, just set him up as you would in the show ring, as an adult. Gently place his front legs straight under him, making sure he is standing completely straight, then run your hand down his back and with your left hand steadying his head, with your right hand, place his rear legs into position and hold still for a couple of seconds, then praise him, give a pat and release, putting him down off the table to play. You cannot give enough praise at this stage, in fact, all through show training, praise cannot be overdone, as you want him to really enjoy his showing.

When you have set him up for a few times and he is starting to stand still for a few seconds, you can then start to go over him. First, feel his head and look at his eyes and teeth. It sometimes helps to say 'teeth' when you do this, then the dog knows you are going to open his mouth. When he is quite happy with you checking his bite, go on to check for pre-molars so he is used to the sides of his mouth being looked at, as well as the front. Carry on to feel the reach of neck, shoulders and length of back, running your hands all over his body. Pick up a front leg, so that he learns to balance on three, run your hands down his legs and press on his back and quarters so that when a judge does just that it does not come as a shock and make the dog move because it was something new.

5 week old puppy being stood.
Ch. Willowmead A Star is Born

He must also be groomed twice a week, so that his coat is properly looked after and he will get used to being handled whilst you are doing

3 month old puppy stood correctly on his table. Side view, front view and rear view of Willowmead Man of the Moment

that too. He must also go out regularly in the car, as there will be plenty of travelling to shows and if he is happy and relaxed in the car he will arrive at a show in a happier frame of mind. I always carry all my puppies round towns from eight weeks old, so that they are fully accustomed to all traffic noises and the hustle and bustle of busy shopping centres, as they will meet plenty of noise and people in show situations. I usually lead train in town too. The puppy will be approximately fifteen weeks old and has been carried round town for some weeks, so is completely happy with the surroundings. I just put him down in one of the shopping precincts, usually they are off straight away, just to say 'hello' to all those lovely people, but there can be a short time sometimes when a puppy just stands there somewhat confused, as it all looks rather different from ground level. If this happens, then I just stand quietly by and praise and pet him till he gets his confidence, so when he starts to walk I just follow, and usually in a few minutes he is trotting along. You may have to go back and forth a bit till he gets the idea of going along with you, but its never been more than a few minutes and we always walk back to the car park and lead training is accomplished.

As soon as he is confident on his lead, he can go to ringcraft classes. Ringcraft is for show training, not obedience, so mind you don't get the two mixed up, as obedience is directly the opposite to show training. Ringcraft classes are excellent for getting the puppy used to the show atmosphere and a good variety of different breeds, and to be in close

4 month old puppy set up on the ground. Willowmead Touch of Class

5 month old puppy set up on the table. Ch. Willowmead Plain and Fancy

proximity to other dogs without getting either too excited or frightened. I usually prefer to do a bit of show training at home before I take my puppy to ringcraft lessons so that he already knows what is expected of him on the lead, and is fairly confident on that score, so can enjoy his classes.

To get him used to showing on the lead, I go out onto the lawn just with the puppy on a show slip and start off with standing him for a few seconds, which he has already learnt on the table. Then walk round the lawn in a circle, with the dog on my left side, lead in the left hand, fairly short, so you have direct contact with him. It is no use having a long lead at this stage, otherwise instead of learning to walk by your side, he will wander along sniffing at the ground, or pulling to one side or the other, to play. We go round the lawn once, usually with several checks, a quick pull and command for 'head up' everytime his head goes down to sniff. Next, a quick stand then walk into the middle and he is set up for the judge with the command 'stand'. As I live on my own, I usually have to be judge as well as handler so go over the puppy as he has learnt on the table, very gently for the first few times, getting progressively firmer as his confidence grows. After he has been gone over, I then do the triangle and the straight up and down for the judge, we finish with another couple of circles, varying the speed with commands of gently for a slow walk and quickly for a fast run. Do not let the dog break his trot, so only go as fast as he can go comfortably.

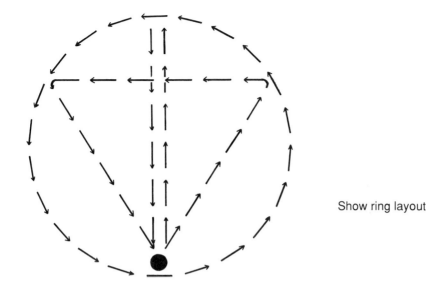

Show ring layout

Some dogs can go a lot quicker than others, so adjust your speed to suit his ability. If you have done your training successfully at home your puppy will slot into his usual routine at his ringcraft classes with ease and confidence and his first show will be a happy event for both of you.

Whilst you are doing the training at home, you will also need to keep an eye open for shows. Most ringcraft clubs have schedules at the classes, so you can pick them up there. The weekly dog papers, Our Dogs and Dog World also advertise every week the shows for the whole country, from the small exemption show to Championship events. I usually look for local open shows with Beardie classes, for a puppy's first outing, so that he doesn't have a long journey for his debut. Most open shows usually have between four and six classes, sometimes with a puppy class, so a nice introduction to the show world is made. The schedule has the classes available, date, venue and judges names, with the form for you to fill in with your dogs details, which is all on your pedigree. Dogs registered name, date of birth, breeders name, and names of sire and dam are all written on the form, with the numbers of the classes you wish to enter in, so you have entered your puppy in his first show. You have attended his classes, and its now the day before his first show and the time has come to prepare his coat for his first big day. Groom well, then he has to have his whites bathed. I usually do this last thing in the evening. He goes for a good walk, then I have a baby bath which I put in the kitchen, and a bucket, small plastic jug and shampoo ready with towels and chalk. I use Bob Martins Cleansfur, and have always found this excellent. I put warm water in the baby bath and have a full bucket by the side, then put

Getting down to handle. Willowmead Touch of Class

Showing on a loose lead. Willowmead Man of the Moment

the front legs of my puppy in the bath, washing his face first, then his collar, chest and front legs, rinsing well with the fresh water from the bucket. I squeeze the water out and turn him round and put his back legs in the water and wash his rear feet and tail tip. If you do not have access to a baby bath, you can always use your own big bath, but do not wash the dog all over, as it softens the coat too much and makes it all 'fly away'. When you have finished rinsing him, dry him thoroughly on the towels and then puff a little chalk powder into the whites and rub well in. He is still damp at this time, so the chalk really whitens the coat and stays there. Pop him out on a lead to do last jobs and keep in a warm kitchen to dry off properly overnight. Hopefully, the weather will not be raining next morning, but after his walk, which cannot be a long one and only in a clean area, not through muddy fields please, re-dry his paws and re-chalk, before putting him in the car to leave for the show.

I never feed my dogs before we leave for a show, it will only give them an uncomfortable journey to the show, and you could make a puppy start to be travel sick by feeding just before a long journey. The day before, you should also have packed the car with your show paraphernalia, which can consist of a trolley table, which is a table that has collapsible legs and wheels, so that you can, with the aid of a pulling handle, put all your bags and chairs etcetera on it.

How not to set up your show dog. Willowmead Golden Memories

Another picture of Willowmead Golden Memories. This time presented correctly

The things I usually pack into my show bag are, brushes and combs for grooming, also, if the show is benched, a bench blanket for your dogs comfort, benching chain to make him secure on his bench, lead and collar, and food and water for the dog. I usually take my own water, as although there is always water obtainable at the show, my dogs prefer water brought from home. Towels are a must in case its raining and you need to dry him off, dry shampoo for the feet should they get a bit dirty walking in, and I also have both mac and boots for the dogs, really invaluable, as there are very few days when the ground is completely dry for the dogs to walk in without getting either wet or muddy.

For myself, I always have a light mac and a good rain hat packed, and usually take coffee and food to Championship shows, but prefer to buy at Open shows, to help support club funds, as its usually all home made catering, so very good too.

Two other things I always pack, for even if you do not need them yourself, there is always someone who will, one is plasters for cut fingers or similar, the other is some type of headache pills. A nail file can also be useful, as I seem to break a nail fairly regularly at shows and trying to groom a dog with rough nails can be awkward, as its continually snagging in the coat as you brush. Nail clippers for the dogs claws in case your dog should break a nail, either en-route in the car or actually at the show. A pen for marking up your catalogue and last, but not least, some money, as there is always something you find you need to buy from the many stands that are at every show these days, selling everything conceivable concerning the care and welfare of dogs, plus often many things not at all connected with dogs, but sometimes very useful for birthday or Christmas gifts for family and friends. All Championship shows are benched, but very few of the others are these days, so I also have a crate for putting the dogs in when necessary. I have found when I have two or more dogs at a show, my crate is invaluable, as there is not always someone to hold the other dogs when you are in the ring, or even grooming, prior to showing. The dogs love them and feel secure, and do not get trodden on by the mass of people usually rushing around. The crate also can go on the trolley table to be taken to the ringside at Open shows, so you can watch the judging and enjoy it too, whilst you groom.

It is usually a good idea to accustom your puppy to his crate at home, by just leaving it up in the kitchen for a few hours, several times, with the door left open. They will normally go in of their own accord, but if not, a few biscuits put in will soon get him trotting in happily.

I always like to arrive early at a show, especially with a new puppy, so that he has plenty of time to get used to the new surroundings and meet the other dogs that he will soon be in the show ring with. Give him a good walk round, so that he feels comfortable, then get him well groomed ready for his debut. It does not hurt to go into the ring for the

Perfectly prepared show dog ready for the ring.
Ch. Desborough Dulcinea of Snowmead

113

first few shows, before the judge arrives and go through your show procedure, and let him see the ring and meet some of the other dogs, then he knows that he is there to work, not to play this time.

Championship shows are a help to get to know the other people in the breed, as you always are benched in alphabetical order so usually have the same people next to you at each show, so will soon get to know them. The dogs also get very friendly with each other, and readily make good friends. After his walk round you need to brush and comb him very thoroughly so that he looks his very best for the ring, making quite sure all the chalk is out of his coat. So long as you only put a small bit in the coat, it should all have vanished long ago, as Kennel Club rules are against chalk in coats these days. Watch the ring closely, if you are not in the first class, as it is up to you not to miss your class, and be ready to go in as soon as your class is called, with hopefully, your happy, well prepared puppy.

There can be some very amusing things happen when you are busy showing dogs. Ian Copus of the Rallentando Bearded Collies told me one story that really made me laugh even if, as Ian says, it wasn't quite so funny at the time. Ian with his wife Hattie and another lady doggy exhibitor were travelling together to a show in Scotland. The girls were sitting in the front of the car, chatting away, and Ian was on the back seat with a seven month old puppy who had crept onto his lap, curled up and gone to sleep. Ian decided to follow suit and dozed off. He woke up a bit later and thought "that puppy is pretty warm on my lap", then he suddenly realised he wasn't just warm, he was also damp. Obviously the puppy had leaked whilst asleep and Ian was somewhat soaked.

He told the girls and they decided to stop rapidly at the next service station as they were travelling up the motorway. Ian, of course, did not have a change of clothes, but the friend said she had a track suit in her show bag, intended to be worn whilst she was handling her dog in the ring, but Ian was welcome to the trousers until they could sort something out later. The track suit was a beautiful shade of bright pink.

As it was very early in the morning and very little traffic around, they soon arrived at the service station and Ian, complete with pink track suit trousers nipped into the Gents. Whilst the girls exercised all the dogs, including the puppy, to prevent her having another accident. Ian breathed a sigh of relief to find the Gents quite empty, popped into the "loo" and changed his trousers and pants. As he came out, adorned now in the beautiful pink track suit, still no one around, he started to rinse out his pants in the wash basin, when of course, the inevitable happened, in walked two huge lorry drivers, who stopped dead and just stared in horror. Poor Ian just wrung out his nether garments with great speed and fled, one look at their faces just told it all.

Judging

JUDGING can be fascinating, if very hard work, so lets go right back to the beginning, as that is where you really start, long before you even dream that you might become a judge.

The Standard of the breed is your bible and even before you start showing at all, you must learn to interpret the Standard. One person recently said to me, I am looking forward to my first judging engagement. It's quite easy really, you just place the dogs that have been doing a lot of winning, then you cannot go wrong. This is *not* judging, any fool can place previous winners. To become a good judge will take years of studying the dogs in the show ring and outside at home, slowly learning construction and movement, learning to appreciate the good and bad faults, working out for yourself the degree of fault and how much each fault will cause loss of working ability to the dog. Always remember, Beardies are working dogs, not lap or toy dogs and must retain the attributes that have made him what he is, a very intelligent working animal that has the ability to go all day without tiring. We must never loose the wonderful animal that has come to us from hundreds of years and generations of careful breeding to obtain the best dog for his job, so sit at the ringside at shows and watch. Look at each dog individually, and try and see how he fits the Standard.

There are several different types of Beardie so you must decide which is the type, that for you, best represents how you have interpreted the Standard. Never, never fault judge, you will only end up in a mess. I have seen several different judges fault judging, and it is appalling. Everyone sits and watches and cannot understand what on earth the judge is trying to do, as they always end up with a complete mixed bag of every different type of dog. You can see type in the ring and until you can differentiate between the types, you are not ready to even think of judging. Decide which is the type you consider correct and mentally, after watching the dogs move, place them in order. Don't forget, it is the dogs you are judging, not the handlers, so you must learn to shut the person out of your mind completely, a very hard thing to do when you are a novice and you know its Mrs X from the top winning kennels, handling her pride and joy. You must never just place that dog first if he doesn't deserve it, but at the same time, you must never put him down to third or fourth because he belongs to Mrs X and she always seems to win, so you will be clever and find better dogs owned by another exhibitor. Mrs X has probably been in the breed thirty years, has learnt how to breed and select puppies, handles to get the best out of her dog and presents him to perfection so will certainly not waste time with second rate stock.

Novice exhibitors too can also breed real flyers and learn to handle and present equally well, so remember, block out all the handlers and concentrate on judging the dogs.

One thing that can be very deceptive indeed in Beardies, is size, and a strongly made small dog can look bigger than he is, whereas a slightly boned tall dog can look smaller than he is, so try and train your eye to the correct size, and if it should worry you, take a measuring stick into the ring. I am very concerned that Beardies are getting considerably bigger than the Standard of twenty one/twenty two inches dogs and twenty/twenty one inches bitches, and have measured at several shows lately. I have found it very useful indeed, as several dogs that I would have sworn were about twenty three inches, easily went under the stick at twenty two inches, and I have always considered I had a fairly good eye for size.

Everybody has preferences for certain points of the dog, considering one point such as a dark eye in a slate dog to be more important than a slight ballerina front in another, but that is what makes judging interesting. Learn to read the construction of the dog through your hands as well as your eyes, as with Beardies, a cleverly groomed coat can hide a multitude of sins, and clever handlers never stand the dog to show his

Learn to train your eye to the correct height of the dog

faults, so you must find them for yourself.

I like to go into the ring, walk up to the stacked dogs and get a first impression. I then send the dogs round once or twice, as it settles the dogs into the showing conditions and they know they are there to work, also you can see how your first impressions stand up to movement.

Stand back and get an over all impression of the dog, look at front, side and rear view, then walk to the front of the dog and go straight to his head, don't dither about, patting and chatting to him, just take his head gently into your hands and commence to evaluate it. Dogs can sense at once if you are nervous and wonder why, "is it something to be afraid of"? and can sometimes back away from a person exuding nerves all over the place.

Whilst you are going over the dog, I always ask the age of the exhibit. This, I feel is very important, as with Beardies they can develop at greatly different rates, some puppies at six months can look very raw, others over mature and more like eleven months of age. Again in the older dogs, anything from ten months to two years can be in very different stages of development, but if you have a four year old, who has light bone and looks two, that is a bad fault, where-as an eighteen month old still has plenty of time to develop the correct proportions and must not be faulted to the degree you would the four year old, who certainly will not improve much more by that age.

Do not creep up to the dog and grab his head, whilst standing by his shoulder, as I have seen a judge do recently, or even worse, grab him from behind, and start to work up his body from the middle of his back, another most undesirable trick perpetuated on one of my poor dogs by a novice judge. The dogs do not like either of these approaches in the least, and it can really upset young puppies just starting out on their show careers, and will certainly upset the exhibitors if their dogs are made distressed.

Please remember baby puppies are just that, and I always feel that a young puppy should enjoy his first few shows, so do not condemn him if he says "hello" to the other puppies whilst the rest of the class is being judged and shows some high spirits on the move, providing he is under control, certainly not yapping, that upsets the rest of your class, always remember he has plenty of time to mature and learn correct ring behaviour. I would not appreciate an older dog misbehaving though, as by then his owner should have taught him the right way to go about things.

I then go over each dog individually, feeling head, checking ear set, strength of skull, looking at eye colour, shape and set, looking at teeth, bite and pre-molars and feeling and looking at foreface for length and strength. I then check neck length, arch and set into shoulders, then feel for shoulder angle and check for loaded shoulders. I also check at the same time as I feel for loaded shoulders the width at the withers, if it is too wide or too narrow, as ideally, you should just about have a finger width between the blades. Feel for breadth of chest between front legs, bone and straightness of legs and reset the front legs to see if the dog is actually straight or if he was just placed straight by his handler, sometimes lifting and gently dropping a front foot, as if he is either pintoed or ballerina fronted it will show when the foot drops on its own. I then check for depth of chest and if he has the correct unusual shape of rib that a Beardie should have, or is barrel ribbed. Going down the ribcage I feel for length of loin, leaving the body, I feel tail set and length which should be at least down to the hock. If a dog, check for testicles, he should have both apparent in the scrotum. I then reset the rear to see if he is cowhocked or has other faults. It is usually a good idea to press firmly but gently on the quarters, as this can also show if a dog is cow-hocked or not. His hindlegs from the hock down should remain dead straight and bending down again, I feel the bend of stifle, as it can be misleading with a very heavy coat and I want it so that the point of the hocks are just behind the point of his buttocks.

Some dogs are stacked so overstretched that the topline goes from the level desired or can be made roach backed by being stood with the legs too far forward. I also look at the topline and see that it is nice and level. All this can be done in a few minutes and you should have a good mental picture from your eye and your hands. I have seen judges waving hands all over the dog and you know they have hardly felt a thing of importance. The thing I hate more than anything, is rough judges. You certainly do not find out anymore about construction by poking or pinching any dog, in fact I really don't think you can feel anything with rough handling and I have had young puppies really upset by such judges. One poor youngster nearly had his head pulled off by a very rough judge, who repeatedly looked at his teeth. Needless to say, these are judges I don't bother to show under twice.

As soon as I have completed my examination of the dog, I request the exhibitor to move the dog in a triangle first, then straight up and down, to assess movement, near side and front as they go away sideways on and return to me with the straight up and down to confirm any faults. When the last dog has been gone over and moved, the whole ring stands their dogs. If it is only a small class, say up to fifteen, I can usually select the ones I like straight away. Up to about twenty five, I like to just do a quick check on heads and look at the general dog before pulling in my final selection. With classes of around thirty five to forty dogs I usually split them on examination into two, the ones I like and the ones I have found too many faults in for re-consideration. When I have my final few left in the ring, I usually check heads, then a quick construction check and send them round the ring again, usually in the order of placing.

Should I spot something on the move I do not quite like as much as before, I can then change my placements before the final awards.

So let us go back to learning how to judge. The first thing really, is to start to go over your own dogs and find the good things and the faults. Go to shows and ask the more experienced people to point out to you the construction, good and bad of your dogs, and chat to other exhibitors, asking why such and such a dog was placed first or last, and slowly your eye will start to recognise the different constructions and good and bad points of each dog. Most Beardie people are only to happy to help novice exhibitors to learn.

When you have shown for some time and have started winning with your dogs, you have obviously learnt how to handle and present correctly. The next thing is to go and look at several litters of puppies. Usually when you look at a litter that belongs to a fellow showing breeder, rather than a litter from a pet bitch in a pet home, the puppies will have been trained already to stand on a table and be gone over as a show dog, for the breeder to assess the show potential of the whole litter, and which puppy will go as a show prospect or which will go as a pet quality puppy. Usually, people are quite happy if you are a novice to set the puppies up and point out the correct construction and all the faults of the various puppies. We are very lucky with Beardies as an eight week old puppy has all the construction there, that it will have as an adult. They change greatly between ten weeks or so and six months, but its all there at eight weeks, which really makes choosing a pick of litter somewhat easier.

When your own bitch that has hopefully done quite well in the showring, is old enough, you might decide to let her have her first litter. This is the best way of any to learn the different construction of the dogs, as you can spend hours playing with the puppies and really look, don't just see pretty fluffy bundles, study each and everyone of them and really look at movement too. That can be the most difficult thing, as young puppies seem to have two speeds, flat out gallop and stop dead. They do sometimes trot and then you need to be in the right spot to be able to assess the correct movement, but you have at least eight weeks or so to be able to look and learn.

There are also lots of books that you can read on showing and judging, and believe me, the more you read and learn the more you discover there is to learn. I feel that you really need to be showing and breeding for a least five years before you have enough knowledge to start thinking of taking a judging engagement, but in the meantime there are judging seminars that you can attend. These are most instructive and you spend the day having a mock show where a few students go over a class of around six dogs then have to place them in order of preference explaining why they did it and have tutors explain where they have gone wrong or congratulate when placements are correct. Movement is fully explained and construction is covered to explain why such a dog who is made in a certain way will move as he does because of his bone conformation.

The next step could be to be asked to judge at a fun-day, where a small show or match is being held. My local ringcraft has a match once a month and usually a member is asked to judge and this can be their first judging experience. In the Midlands, our Garden Party day is one where we hold a match and inexperienced or aspiring judges are usually asked to officiate to give them experience without pressure, as it is all for fun and not too serious.

All this time, you have been making friends and getting known in the world of dogs and as the other dog people are the people who run the smaller shows they know you are interested in judging and will ask you to judge at a small show, usually one or two classes of Beardies at a Limited or small Open Show. The feeling when you step into the middle of the ring for the first time is one you will never forget, but remember you are doing this for pleasure, so give the dogs your full consideration, never pre-judge, and enjoy yourself. Always be very gentle with all the dogs, patient with puppies and novice owners, courteous with the exhibitors and give everybody an equal chance. Never forget the exhibitors have paid quite a lot of money for the privilege of your opinion and give you the honour of going over their dogs, so rudeness, roughness and bad manners have no place in a dog show judge.

If you have made a good job of your first judging engagement, you will find that you will be asked to officiate at other small shows and you will be given more classes. The next step is the bigger open shows where you can have as many as six to eight classes and the sexes start being split. When you have been judging for a bit, you need to go on to the various breed club judging lists. With most of our Clubs you have to be proposed for the lists and seconded. Thereafter, once a year, the membership vote on each individual person and hopefully you have made a good job of your judging engagements that you gain sufficient votes to be included on the Clubs judging list. You will start at the bottom on the Open Show list, but once on the list, these lists are sent to all show secretaries, so you could be asked to judge at shows all over the country.

The criteria for the lists for the Bearded Collie Club are as follows:

Open Show List

Nominees must fulfil qualification (1) and at least 1 other qualification.
1) Have judged a minimum of 30 Bearded Collies in total in Breed Classes in at least two licenced shows.
2) Have owned or handled Bearded Collies for at least 5 years.
3) Have bred or qualified 2 or more Bearded Collies for the Kennel Club Stud Book.
4) Be on the Open Show judging list of at least one other Breed Club.

Championship Show List

Nominees must fulfil qualification (1) and at least 2 other qualifications.
1) Have been on the Bearded Collie Club or Southern Counties Bearded Collie Club Open Show List for at least three years or already be approved by the Kennel Club to award Challenge Certificates in the Breed.

2) Have judged at least 15 classes of Bearded Collies in at least 2 separate Open Shows with a minimum of 120 dogs in the classes.
3) Have owned Bearded Collies for at least 10 years.
4) Have bred or qualified either one Bearded Collie Champion *OR* two Bearded Collie individual CC winners, *OR* five Bearded Collies for Kennel Club Stud Book entry.
5) Have awarded Challenge Certificates in at least one other breed.

I will just explain here the Kennel Club Stud Book qualification. To get your dog in the KC Stud Book, he has to win a number which is allocated by winning first, second or third in either Limit or Open classes at a Championship Show where CC's are on offer. You do not have to apply for the number, it is sent to you direct from the KC and thereafter you do not use your registration number anymore. If the dog is used at stud or has puppies, if a bitch, you always use the KC Stud Book number for registration. In fact, wherever you need your registration number, you now use the Stud Book number which is much easier, as it is always much shorter than the registration number.

You will eventually be asked to judge a club open show. Two of the committee's of the British clubs choose the judges for their shows, and the rest vote on judges which means forms are sent out to the membership of the club and people are nominated for each show, open and championship, then the membership vote and the person winning the vote is asked to judge at one of the club shows.

Once you have judged a club show you are well on the way to gaining championship status. Again, as you can see by the nomination forms for the different lists, when you have obtained sufficient knowledge and experience judging smaller shows, plus breeding, showing and hopefully winning with your own dogs, you can be put forward for the championship show list.

As before, you have to be nominated, voted on, and win sufficient votes to be included on the 'B' list. Then you have to wait till you are asked by some show secretary if you would be willing to judge and award CC's, as this will be your first time, the secretary will send you a Kennel Club form for you to fill in and return, which will then be sent off to the Kennel Club. Some of the things the form asks are how many shows have you judged, how many dogs in total, dates and classes of the shows, what dogs you have qualifed for the Stud book etcetera. You then have to sit back and wait, hoping that you will be sufficiently qualified to be passed by the KC committee. Providing you have had sufficient experience, the reply will come through, passing you to award CC's. Be prepared for a very different days judging to the usual small shows. In Britain our usual entries at championship shows are round the two hundred dogs mark and that is a lot of dogs to go over. Classes can have around forty dogs in them, many of which are of top quality, presented to perfection and behaving beautifully, so judging can be a really hard days work. I well

Ch. Desborough Destiny of Sammara - A beautiful Champion bitch

remember at a show, a few years ago, it was the judges first championship show engagement, she had started the day off looking bright and full of beans but by Post Graduate bitch she was looking really tired and acknowledged to me that she had not realised what hard work and what a long day a championship show days judging was before.

Once you are awarding CC's, the next step is being asked to judge abroad, usually a club show rather than a general championship show. This can be very pleasant and it is very interesting indeed to see the quality of the dogs in the different countries. I was the first English person to be asked to judge outside the UK at the first club to be formed in a foreign country, this being the Dutch Bearded Collie Club in Holland. The show was held in the Hague, and if I remember correctly I went over by plane to Amsterdam. I travelled over to the show for the next few years by ferry and usually went with a few friends. We always had a marvellous weekend with fantastic hospitality from the Dutch people we stayed with.

All the European countries are quite happy for you to judge providing you are passed to award CC's in UK, but with America they send you a form to fill in from the AKC asking what your experience of judging is also what if any dogs you have exported to the US and how many are champions. They also send you various forms and leaflets on their judging procedure, which is very helpful. At the show, in America, before you start judging for the first time, the AKC representative, who is at every championship all breed show has a chat with you and gives you the disqualifications again, which you must observe, something I have not found in any other country. Several countries leave it until you actually get into the ring to tell you the rules of their country and as each has different rules, unless you have good stewards, it can get somewhat confusing. In all the continental countries you have to critique each dog as you go over it, all this is written down by your secretary at a table in the ring. All mine, so far, have been written in English and translated if the exhibitor needs it, when they are handed out to each exhibitor in the ring, as they leave at the end of the class. You also have to grade each dog, as either excellent, very good or just good.

In Great Britain, it is considered that you should critique the first two dogs in each class at a championship show and the first in each class at an open show, but usually first, second and third at club championship shows. All the judges that have been officiating for a long time write critiques but sadly, a great many of the newer judges do not seem able to write critiques. It is a shame, as I know many people really look forward to reading about their own dogs. In America and Canada you do not write critiques at all breed championship shows, only at the club events, and usually the first four placings, which are then published in the breed club magazine.

There is one thing that I feel I must mention about the markings on Beardies. Quite often, in the white area's, if the dog is born black and has very strong pigment, i.e., eye rims, nose, lips, you will see small spots of black hair growing. This is more obvious in young puppies, and usually blends in and is harder to see in an adult, as the long white hair seems to mask it. Please do not condemn the dog for this. Shepherds look for this as one of the signs of a good working dog, along with as much pigment on the roof of the mouth, and, if you can find it, three strong hairs from the small pimple under the chin. All dogs have these pimples, for want of a better word, two on each cheek and one underneath. Working ability is only shown by the hairs under the chin, not the cheek hairs, and it must be three, not more or less.

I once met a novice exhibitor at a show who was almost on the point of retiring his puppy from the showring because the black hair spots had developed in her puppy coat. I managed to dissuade him from his plan, and she consequently won really well, as his dog grew up, but some judges who are far from knowledgable had condemned the poor dog for something that is most desirable, providing you believe, as I do, that the breed was bred for work and we should do all in our power to retain his working ability, as well as having first and foremost, a super pet and loyal companion, and a dog we can have fun with, either showing, doing obedience or agility, amongst his many other traits.

Beardies at Work, Obedience and Agility

BEARDED Collies have long been working sheep and cattle dogs, and thank goodness, quite a lot of them still do work solely for their living.

When I first started breeding Beardies, the British Kennel Club allowed unregistered dogs with little or no pedigree, to be passed by an authorised judge for registration. Mrs Willison was very keen to see what a dog would produce in its progeny before she liked to pass it for registration. I did not know this, and had two puppies Romany and Sweetheart, offspring of Moonmaiden of Willowmead mated to a working Beardie in Scotland, and I thought the easiest way was to enter them for a show in London, where I knew Mrs Willison would be so she could see them at the show and hopefully think them good enough to pass as Beardies. They both won all their classes, and so Mrs Willison, somewhat reluctantly, I must say, duly signed the Kennel Club form for registration. I am so glad she did, as all my line goes back to Sweetheart of Willowmead. It also gave me a really good working strain in my line, which I have strived to retain, hopefully with success, as I still sell some puppies solely for sheep or cattle work.

Beardies have also proved that they are extremely versatile in as much that they also have acted as qualified Mountain Search and Rescue dogs in Scotland and as fully trained Guide Dogs for the Blind.

I was approached by a childrens television programme called 'Blue Peter' in the late 1960's about training a Beardie as a Guide Dog. Blue Peter has done a lot for guide dogs, but mainly with Labradors, and they thought it would be interesting to try with sponsoring a Beardie. I was most enthusiastic and immediately offered a puppy. Sadly the training school at Leamington Spa was concerned about the coat, feeling that a blind person might not be able to cope with the grooming required, so the project was abandoned. Then I discovered that in the late 70's Mrs Foster of the Bredon Beardies had two puppies from a litter to my own Crofter, a dog and a bitch, accepted for training at Leamington. Both these puppies did not complete the courses. The dog was sent home as being too good to be castrated, as all guide dogs have to be, and the bitch was not quite the right temperament for a guide dog, but two more puppies from a subsequent litter to Crofter, both passed with flying colours and were fully fledged guide dogs, the first ever for the breed, I believe. The blind owners found no problems with grooming the coats and since, there have been several other Beardies happily and successfully accompaning their blind owners and doing their very worthwhile jobs in life.

Beardies also make excellent obedience dogs as they so love to please and learn very quickly. I well remember one story told me by a new owner. He had taken his six month old puppy to his first obedience lesson and as it was all completely new to both dog and owner, they decided to sit out the first lesson and just watch to see how things went on. It was held in the usual small village hall, and both watched carefully for a couple of hours. On going home, the wife asked what they had learnt and husband decided to try and show his wife rather than explain, as he wasn't sure of the terminology. He called his dog and to his amazement, the puppy executed all the basic lessons that they had both just sat and watched, to perfection, so don't underestimate your puppy's intelligence.

Agility is the latest craze in Great Britain and Beardies are particularly suited for this, being super jumpers, with perfect balance for the see-saw and bending poles, and love racing round the arena.

You do not have to be a totally dedicated obedience trainer though, to be able to compete in the Bearded Collie Working Tests. These are made up so that totally novice dog and owner can compete in the Primary Test, going through the Primary, Junior, Intermediate and finally the Senior Test. The tests are not competitive, so you are marked on your own dogs performance.

Bearded Collie Working Tests

The Primary Test

1. Examination by a stranger. The dog, sitting by the Handler's side, on a loose lead, shall allow itself to be handled by a stranger without showing nervousness or aggression. A change of position by the dog shall not be penalised but over-boisterousness or backing away through fear will be. Any attempt to bite will disqualify.

    20 points (16 to qualify).

2. The dog to walk on a loose lead beside the handler, waiting whenever the handler halts. This shall be done with changes of direction and paces. Distractions will be provided such as a stranger stopping the handler and talking, another dog on a lead approaching, of clapping by half a dozen people, which should not upset the dog unduly. If the dog barks, the handler should be able to quieten the dog immediately. This exercise is designed to show whether the dog will accommodate itself to the handler's pace and direction without pulling on the lead.

    20 points (16 to qualify).

3. Recall. The dog shall be held by its collar while the handler walks some distance away. When called, the dog should come right up to the

handler without any hesitation and have its lead put on. Movement of the handler towards the dog will be penalised.

20 points (16 to qualify)

4. The dog to be walked on a loose lead within reach of food placed on the ground, The dog should ignore the food when told to do so.

20 points (16 to qualify)

5. Tied stay of one minute. EXTRA COMMANDS ALLOWED. The dog shall be tied to a stake or any other convenient object and the handler shall walk at least twelve paces away. The dog should not panic, struggle or bark continuously.

20 points (16 to qualify)

The Junior Test
1. Stand for examination, on a loose lead. The handler can steady the dog as is done in the show ring but the dog should remain standing throughout the examination by the judge.

15 points (12 to qualify)

2. Heelwork on a loose lead, which should incorporate changes of both pace and direction. The dog is expected to sit when the handler stops. The same distractions may be provided as in exercise 2 in the Primary Test.

15 points (12 to qualify)

3. Recall to handler. The dog may be held by a steward or left in a stay position. When called, the dog should come direct to the handler and sit in front. No other finish is required.

15 points (12 to qualify)

4. Stay for one minute. EXTRA COMMANDS ALLOWED. Handlers will remain in sight and the position that the dog is left in will be at the handlers discretion. A change of position by the dog will only be penalised slightly but movement away from the spot where it has been left will disqualify.

15 points (12 to qualify)

5. Retrieve any handler's article. The dog may be held whilst the article is thrown but should go straight out to pick up the article and deliver it to hand without dropping it. The handler may give such encouragement as he sees fit.

25 points (20 to qualify)

6. One foot jump off lead. The handler may jump with the dog if he wishes. No slip collars to be worn during jumping. Should the dog fail to jump further attempts are allowed for a loss of two marks for each attempt.

15 points (12 to qualify)

Open Dog Class, Joyce Collis judging - Dogs from left to right: Ch. Sunbree
Sorcerer, Ch. Grizlinda Morning Monarch, Ch. Swinford Sky Rocket at Macmont,
Pure Magic of Willowmead 2 C.C.s - showing different methods of handling

Below: Ch. Osmart Bonnie Blue Braid
in his Scottish outfit

Above: Ch. Willowmead Summer Wine

...exhibit to the St... Willoweround Star of Magic... owner Sandra Franz, in Canada...

Herding Beardies - Ch. Britannia Ticket To Ride, H.C.

Agility - The double jump

Left: The Triple jump

Right: A Frame

The High jump

The Long jump

The Triple jump

A Catwalk

Another High jump

Sit and Stay

Going through the Tyre

3 ft. high with 3 ft. spread - Triple jump

The Intermediate Test

1. Heelwork. A very short stretch of heelwork on the lead is to be immediately followed by a much longer stretch of heel free. The position of the dog to the handler must be consistent, fairly close, but not impeding the handler's progress. Changes of pace and direction will be included and the dog should sit when the handler halts. The same distraction may be provided as in Exercise 2 of the Primary Test. 15 points (12 to qualify)

2. Stay for three minutes - NO EXTRA COMMANDS ALLOWED. Handlers will remain in sight and the position that the dog is left in will be at the handlers discretion. A change of position by the dog will only be penalised slightly but movement away from the spot where it has been left will disqualify. 15 points (12 to qualify)

3. Recall from the sit or down position to the handler's side as the handler is walking away. 15 points (12 to qualify)

4. Stop on recall. The handler will leave the dog in a stay position, recall the animal and stop it on command when it has come part of the way. The handler will then return to the side of the dog. As this exercise can be a life saver, it is essential that the dog stops immediately on the first command. 10 points (8 to qualify)

5. The dog will jump a two foot hurdle. No slip collars to be worn during the jumping. Handlers may run up to the jump to encourage the dog but may not pass the obstacle before the dog does. Reasonable control should be demonstrated when the dog has cleared the jump. Should the dog refuse or run out further attempts at the jump are allowed for a loss of two marks for each attempt. 10 points (8 to qualify)

6. The dog will retrieve to hand (a dumbell) provided by the handler. The dog is required to go straight out and bring the article straight back without dropping it, and to sit and present the dumbell to the handler, who will take it on the Steward's instruction. Any movement by the handler towards the dog will be penalised. 10 points (8 to qualify)

7. Stand for examination. The dog will be on a loose lead and is required to stand steadily while handled by the judge. The handler should stand at least one pace away from the dog. 10 points (8 to qualify)

8. **Handlers choice of:**
   Elementary seek back: for handler's visible article (other than a dumbell) dropped by the handler surreptitiously. The dog must be sent back at least fifteen paces and should deliver the article to hand. 15 points (12 to qualify)

OR:

Elementary Search:
Pieces of three inch wooden dowelling or garden hose pipe will be provided by the **Organiser** of the tests. The handler of the dog will have **four** articles to scent up which will be placed by a Steward in a marked area roughly 12 yds by 12 yds square, unseen by handler or dog. The dog is required to find and deliver to hand **one** of the four articles. The handler may move round the perimeter of the search area but must remain outside it. A separate area must be used for each dog. The time limit is two minutes. The articles must not be given to the dog before the test or reused afterwards.

15 points (12 to qualify)

The Senior Test
1. Heel free at fast, slow and normal paces. At one point the dog will be left at either the stand, down or sit at the handler's command. The handler will continue as directed by the steward until reaching the dog when both will continue forward together. The dog will be required to remain at heel while its handler walks through a crowd of people and dogs who are clapping and cheering. Excessive commands by the handler or barking by the dog, will be penalised. Further distractions may be included at the discretion of the judge. These may include unusual objects and food left on the ground.

15 points (12 to qualify)

2. Stay in the down position with the handler out of sight for five minutes - NO EXTRA COMMANDS ALLOWED. A change in position by the dog will only be penalised slightly, but a dog which moves away from the spot on which it was left will be disqualified.

10 points (8 to qualify)

3. **Handler choice of:**
    See back. With the dog walking at heel, the handler will surreptitiously drop an article provided by the judge when told to do so. The dog and handler must proceed at least thirty paces before the dog is sent back to find the article and deliver it to hand. There is a time limit of three minutes from the time the dog is sent to find the article.

15 points (12 to qualify)

OR:

A Search. The search shall be a marked area roughly twelve yds square to find and retrieve an article provided by the judge with handlers scent placed by a steward unseen by handler or dog. The handler may move round the perimeter of the search area but must remain outside it. A separate area must be used for each dog. The time limit is three minutes.

15 points (12 to qualify)

128

In both a) and b) the article provided by the judge should not be smaller than a matchbox, be fairly inconspicuous in colour, and not made of any material likely to cause injury to the dog's mouth.

4. Stand for examination off lead. NO EXTRA COMMANDS ALLOWED. The handler must be at least three feet away.

20 points (16 to qualify)

5. The dog to jump a five foot long hump.

10 points (8 to qualify)

6. The dog to jump a two foot six inch hurdle.

10 points (8 to qualify)

In both 5 and 6 the handler may run up to the obstacle in order to encourage the dog but must not pass the jump before the dog does. The handler should demonstrate control over the dog following the jumps. Should the dog fail to jump a further attempt may be made for the loss of two marks. No slip collars to be worn during jumping.

7. The dog to be sent away (a minimum of twenty five yards) to a spot marked by its handler's belongings and dropped beside them. The handler will return to the spot, pick up the marker, walk away and finally call the dog to heel. 20 points (16 to qualify)

Agility

Something that Beardies really love is agility and providing you are reasonably fit too, it can be great fun for both of you. Even if you don't go in for competitive agility, you can still train your dog up for a bit of fun together.

Long Jump

You will definitely need to do a bit of basic obedience training, such as sit, down and the recall, but it does not require the perfection that competition obedience needs, in fact, it would be a hindrance to get to the perfection stage.

The other thing to remember is do not start your puppy to jump too early, although you can certainly do very gentle work as your puppy grows up, serious training for agility should not be started until the dog is about twelve months old, and anything over a few inches high with his jumps should definitely not be attempted until he is about one year old too, which all gives you plenty of time to teach the puppy to be extremely obedient with his sits and stays etc well before you get into serious agility training.

A Frame

Although any normal Beardie can jump two feet from a standstill with no problems, you must start agility with low jumps and slow paces to get

See saw

130

A nice jump

the dog under complete control at all times, as you must be able to call a dog off a jump at any time, for if, when he is doing competitive work he should go over a jump in the wrong sequence, he will be disqualified, so implicit obedience is a must. NEVER use a choke chain collar when training, his normal leather collar with a buckle is most suitable.

You will need to find someone, or a school, to teach your dog the 'A' frame, dog walk and see-saw, as you need expert tuition for these items, but jumps and tunnels can be taught at home. So start with some jumps and see how both you and your dog progress, and if you are both suited to agility work. Some dogs just don't have the inclination, so its no good trying to force him, it will only end in an upset owner, and a very confused and distressed dog. Luckily though, most Beardies really love agility, so progress to teaching him his jumps. Jumps should have an easily dislodged crossbar and to start, do not set the jump at more than one foot high. Sit the dog in front of the jump on a loose lead. Give the wait command

Beardie hair flying everywhere

Making it look easy

and walk round the jump, keeping the lead loose; stand facing the jump on the other side and ask the dog to jump over, using the command 'over' and lots of encouragement. When the dog is jumping on command, try walking at the side of the jump whilst the dog is jumping over. Remember, the dog must jump on **your** command, so do not command either too early or too late. Do not let the dog get too excited and don't pull on the lead at any time.

Progression can be made from here, by asking the dog to jump two jumps in a straight line, still on the lead at walking pace. Progress can be furthered from two jumps off the lead at your own pace, but always remember to make haste **slowly** and keep the jumps low.

Tunnels

Teach the dog to tackle the ridged tunnel first, by keeping the tunnel as small as possible, and getting a helper to hold the dog by the collar; you to go to the other end of the tunnel and call the dog through. The tunnel can slowly be lengthened, but kept straight. When the dog is more confident, you may try walking at the side of the tunnel encouraging the dog through, the command 'through' can now be used.

The flat tunnel can now be taught in the same way, but the canvas must be held up to start with, and only dropped onto the dog very carefully, otherwise you could very easily lose all the dogs confidence that you have slowly built up with the ridged tunnel.

If both you and your Beardie have successfully and happily learnt both jumping and tunnels, ask at either your Vets or obedience classes, for the local Agility Club, and go along and learn the more complicated obstacles, and hopefully end up competing with the best.

Schedule of Tests, Courses, Obstacles and Marking
(with kind permission of the Kennel Club).

1. Courses
a. The following Regulations apply to the construction of courses:
    (1) Test Area shall have a suitable surface and measure a minimum of **35 yards x 35 yards for outdoor venues.** Indoor venues may be smaller but must be appropriate to the size of the Test.
    (2) Design: The course should require a dog to traverse at least 10 obstacles but not more than 20 and all jump obstacles should be the same height in any test up to the permitted maximum except that no variation is permitted in the height of the Hoop (Tyre). Obstacles which the dog is required to clear should have a minimum of **4 yards** between centres except that this may be reduced to **3 yards** when the following obstacle is placed at 90 degrees or more to the preceding one. **The distance between the finishing pole should be wide enough to allow a dog to pass through without impediment.**
    (3) Safety: Obstacles and equipment in the test area must not include unnecessary protusions and where "wings" or side supports are part of an obstacle they must be appreciably higher than the part to be cleared by the dog.
    (4) Under NO circumstances may any obstacle involve the use of FIRE.
b. The Judge is responsible for the design of the course and must at all times give total consideration to the safety of the dog.
c. No practice is allowed on the course save that competitors will be allowed to walk the course without their dog(s) before the test begins.

2. Obstacles
The following obstacles meet with the approval of the Committee of the Kennel Club. However, organisers may submit other obstacles for approval, if desired.
a. **Hurdle** - Height: 2ft 6ins maximum. Width: 4ft minimum. The top bar or plank must be easily displaced by the dog. A wall should have displacable units on the top.
b. **Spread or Parallel Jump** - Two single Jumps as in item a - (Hurdle) placed together to form a double spread. When both

hurdles are set at identical heights the spread must not exceed 2ft. If the top bar on the first hurdle is at least 6ins lower than the second hurdle the maximum spread may be 2ft 6ins. The feet of the side supports (wings) should not be interlocking and the uprights should be in line.

c. **Brush Fence** - Dimensions and details as for item a - (Hurdle). This obstacle must have an easily displaceable top unit.

d. **Hoop - (Tyre)** - Aperture diameter 1ft 6ins minimum. Aperture centre from the ground 3ft. The height of the hoop should not be lowered. The frame and fixtures must be substantial or secured in such a way that dogs cannot knock the obstacle over from either direction.

e. **Table** - 3ft square minimum. Height 2ft 6ins minimum and 3ft maximum. To be of stable construction with a non-slip surface.

f. **Long Jump** - Three to five separate units comprise a long jump. The maximum overall length 5ft. Height should not exceed 1ft 3ins maximum. Marker Poles with a minimum height of approximately 4ft should be placed at all four corners.

g. **Water Jump** - The overall spread shall not exceed 5ft with a minimum width of 3ft. A low hurdle or brush, with a maximum height of 2ft may be placed in front of the water. Marker Poles with a minimum height of approximately 4ft should be placed at all four corners.

h. **Wishing Well or Lych Gate** - This obstacle will have a roof of which the bottom will not be less than 5ft from the ground. It will have a displaceable top bar the height of which will be 2 ft 6ins maximum. **The minimum width should be 2ft 8ins.**

i. **Collapsible tunnel** - Diameter: 2ft minimum. 2ft 6ins maximum. Length 10ft minimum. Circular of non-rigid material construction. It must have an entrance of rigid construction with a depth of at least 1ft 6ins that can be fixed or weighted to the ground. **Minimum entrance height 1ft 7ins clear** (with suitable padding), if entrance has a floor this must have a non slip surface.

j. **Pipe Tunnel** - This obstacle should have a diameter of a minimum of 2ft and should be a minimum of 10ft in length.

k. **Weaving Poles** - The minimum number of poles should be five and the maximum number 12. They should be a minimum of 1ft 6ins and a maximum of 2ft apart, between the poles. The poles must be of rigid construction and with a minimum height of 2ft 6ins **and a diameter between ¾ and 1½ ins.**

l. **Pause box** - Defined area 4ft x 4ft.

m. **"A" Ramp** - Two ramps 9ft long by 3ft wide hinged at the apex 6ft 3ins from the ground. The last 3ft 6ins from the bottom of each ramp should be a different colour to indicate the area with which the dog should make contact. Each ramp to have anti-slip slats at intervals but not within 6ins of the start of a contact area.

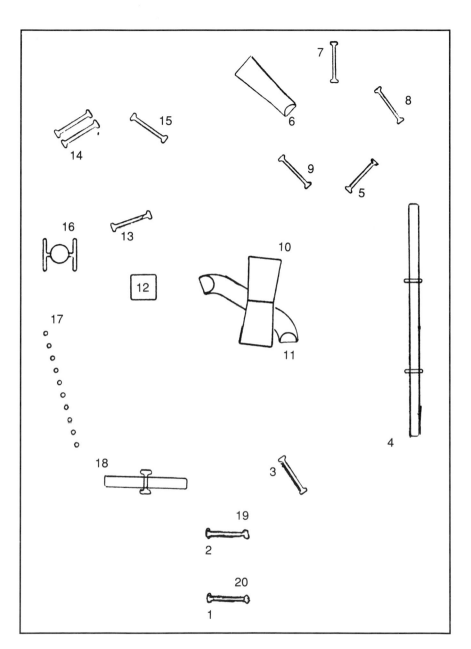

A good Agility Course

n. **See-Saw** - This obstacle will consist of a plank firmly mounted on a central bracket. The length of the plank should be a minimum of 12ft and a maximum of 14ft. The width should be 9ins minimum and 12ins maximum with the height of the bracket being a maximum of 2ft 3ins from the ground. The last 3ft from each end should be a different colour to indicate the area with which the dog should make contact. The plank should be non-slip or have anti-slip slats at intervals but not within 6ins of the start of the contact area.

o. **Dog Walk** - A walk plank of approximately 4ft 6ins high with firmly fixed ramps at either end. The planks should be a minimum 12ft and a maximum 14ft in length and a minimum of 9ins and a maximum of 12ins in width. The last 3ft from the bottom of each ramp should be a different colour to indicate the area with which the dog should make contact. The ramp should have anti-slip slats at intervals but not within 6ins of the start of a contact area.

p. **Cross Over** - Four Planks approximately 12ft long. Widths 9ins minimum 12ins maximum securely fixed to a metal table frame 4ft high with a top 2ft 8ins square. The obstacle may be used with two or more planks but must be of stable construction. The last 3ft from the bottom of each ramp should be a different colour to indicate the area with which the dog should make contact. Each ramp to have anti-slip slats at intervals but not within 6in of the start of a contact area.

3. Marking
a. Standard marking
All course faults in units of five. For time faults see paragraph b below.

(1) **Table-Pause** - faulted at judges discretion.
(2) **See-Saw - Must be touching the ground before the dog alights from the obstacle.**
(3) **Wishing Well - a dog should be faulted if it touches the base or dislodges the pole.**
(4) **Long Jump and Water Jump - a dog should be faulted if it touches any part of the obstacle.**
(5) **Hurdle/Wall - a dog should not be faulted if any part of the obstacle is touched and does not fall.**
(6) **Weaving poles** - (Maximum 2 faults) **incorrect entry** - one fault (not to be classed as a refusal) - **further error one fault** - failure to complete correctly before continuing to the next obstacle elimination.
(7) **All other obstacles** - fault for failure to negotiate correctly.
(8) **Refusal/ Runout** - fault for each refusal/runout.
(9) **Three refusals/runouts** - elimination.

(10) **Out of control** - elimination.
(11) **Out of control** - elimination.
(12) **Contract area - fault for each failure to make contact.**
(13) **Course time -** at the judges discretion.

b. Cumulative Marking/Time Faults.

Faults incurred for failure to negotiate obstacles will be added to the faults incurred for failure to complete course in set time. A single fault will be added for each second, or part thereof over the set time.

c. Other Marking.

Any variation in the form of marking must be clearly defined to all competitors prior to competition.

Ailments & Diseases

ONCE upon a time we all thought Beardies were one of the lucky breeds that seemed to be clear of almost every hereditary problem. Sadly we have discovered this is far from being true.

One condition that can be greatly helped is hip Dysplasia, when this condition was being first brought to light in the sixties, it was thought there were eleven breeds that did not have hip Dysplasia, one of which was Beardies. Then a six month old puppy was diagnosed as having serious H.D. The breeder immediately contacted the Bearded Collie Club and all members were informed and we promptly started to X-ray stock. I was one of the first breeders to have all my stock X-rayed with Cindy Sue, Crofter and Will O'Wisp. They were also the first H.D. X-rays my Vet had ever done, so you can see how little was known about the complaint in those days.

The scheme was arranged by the Kennel Club in conjunction with the British Veterinary Association, and you had to send to the Kennel Club for forms. The vet, as now, took the X-ray, and returned the forms to the B.V.A. In those days you would only have three results, clear, breeders letter and fail. The clear means the dogs hips were excellent, breeders letter meant there were slight imperfections in the hip, but so slight the B.V.A. considered the dogs hips were certainly good enough not to cause any trouble to the dog in the rest of his life, so he was suitable to be bred from. The fail was anything else from slightly malformed hips to really bad ones and you had no idea of what degree the condition was.

The German Shepherd people, with the help of Dr. Willis, a geneticist, formulated a scheme, where instead of just having three reports, the hips would be scored, the score to read from zero (good) to 53 on each hip, making a total of 106 for both hips.

Some enlightened Beardie people contacted Dr. Willis and managed to join his scheme, which was called the B.V.A. and Bearded Collie hip Dysplasia scheme. This happened in 1982. Southern Counties Bearded Collie Club, in trying to get all the dogs scored, that had previously been X-rayed under the old scheme, assisted with half the payment for the scoring. I took full advantage of this, as I was up to thirteen dogs having been X-rayed by then, so was extremely grateful for their help, as the original X-raying was pretty expensive. I have always X-rayed all my stock since the original dogs in 1969, and have found the system of scoring fascinating. Sadly there are far too few Beardies being X-rayed and the consequence is there are considerably more dogs being discovered to have really serious H.D. Several six months old puppies have had to be put to sleep to prevent further suffering. A dog that lives near me has had to have major surgery at only six years of age. The average score at the moment in Beardies is nine, with the worst score being sixty nine. The average score is slowly creeping up for the breed, as so many dogs that have not been X-rayed are still being bred from, such a short sighted policy can only do the breed harm ultimately.

Several European countries will not let anyone breed from either dog or bitch, until they have been X-rayed and passed as good enough hips to be breed from, a situation that some clubs in other breeds are already asking for in England now, so it could well happen with Beardies too.

Eyes are another thing that can easily be checked before any consideration is given to producing puppies. On the whole we do seem to be in a very good state with eyes, but if care is not taken, we could easily have a problem develop here.

Eyes need to be checked by a Specialist, and again the B.V.A. and the Kennel Club have a scheme and issue certificates for each dog passed as clear. It is much easier to have the dogs eyes checked as all that has to be done is for some drops to be put in the dogs eye to dilate the pupil, then the vet looks in it with his light and checks for hereditary cateract, collie eye anomaly and progressive retinal atrophy, the three most common hereditary dogs eye problems. Although I previously said we are lucky in Beardies with these eye conditions, all of which are very serious and can cause blindness at a very early age, I have heard of Beardies in the UK with hereditary cataract and P.R.A. and also both of these in Europe and America, so it is in the breed, and it behoves everybody to be very careful indeed not to breed it into the Beardies, as it could so easily race through the breed if a popular stud dog carried one of the conditions, we could end up as some other breeds and be in the dire straits of a breed with eighty per cent affected.

Another condition that seems to be causing worry in the breed that has just come to light in the last couple of years, is Addisons disease and Von Willbrans, and there seems to be a link between the two. Addisons is loss of the function of the adrenal glands. The dog has very low stress tolerance and can easily die. I have heard of several that have died as young as between 10 and 20 months of age. If Addisons is detected early enough, the dog can quite easily be put on medication and live a reasonable life, providing the adrenal glands are not to seriously damaged. But as Addisons is an extremely rare condition, it is not a thing most vets would think of first, so it could be as well to mention that it has been found in the breed in higher numbers than is usual.

Von Willbrans is a bleeding disease which affects the platelets in the blood, and if the dog has to undergo surgery it will not stop bleeding in the normal manner, or if it should cut itself, the bleeding is very difficult to stop. Von Willbrans is again, a very rare disease and not one a veterinary surgeon will think of immediately, so if you need to take your dog to your vet and he is baffled, it is as well to know both conditions are to be found in Beardies, and if you bring it to his attention, he could check for the condition before the dog becomes too ill to treat.

All dogs become ill at some time or another. Quite a few of the more simple things can be dealt with at home.

A fairly regular Summer problem is bee and wasp stings. Puppies seem to think that bees and wasps are lovely buzzing play things, and can easily be stung. If it should be on the paw or somewhere similar, some anti-histamine cream rubbed into the area of the sting should soon reduce the swelling, check the sting is not still in the dog, if it is, remove with tweezers, being careful not to squeeze more of the poison into the dog if possible. If the sting is in the dogs mouth, try and get straight to the vet as the swelling could be serious, or if the sting is on the dogs nose leather, again to the vet, as it could cause trouble with breathing. Another type of sting is a snake bite, we are very lucky in England by only having one dangerous type of snake, the adder, the other types of snake being harmless, but the adder bite is very serious, and should your dog be unlucky enough to be bitten by an adder, do get immediate veterinary attention. I have heard of several dogs that have been bitten by adders, and so long as you manage to get to the vet pretty soon, the dog can be saved, but if you should delay, thinking tomorrow will do, the dog will almost definitely die.

Beardies are very active dogs and are continually racing around, with the consequence they regularly knock up a toe, and the first thing you know is a cry of pain and a limping dog coming back to you. To find out if it is merely a toe, pick up the foot that is being carried, or that the dog is lame on and start to check each toe separately. First press gently but firmly on each toe nail, if there is no response from the dog and no blood from a torn nail then press each pad from underneath each toe. If it is a wrenched toe the dog will cry out when you press the damaged toe. If the whole foot does not give any pain, it could be ligaments or tendons pulled, although both are fairly unusual, or just a wrenched shoulder or hock. Shoulders seem a fairly common problem but I have never had a damaged hock in any dog I have ever owned. If I do have an injury, I usually put the dog on the lead at once and keep him on the lead everytime he goes outside, and only walk slowly with him whilst out. If there is not immediate, within hours improvement, go to the vet as it could be something more serious, but just a slight strain I find cures with a few days of rest, rather than the usual steroid treatment the vet gives, but I must stress that the dog **must** be kept on the lead for several days. If you let him run free, even once, all the rest of the previous few days will be undone, and he will have to stay on the lead for even longer. One of my dogs had a bad strain and I let him off the lead a little too soon and he ended up having to stay on the lead for two months before he was completely cured, so care at the beginning really does pay off.

One thing you must go to the vet with as soon as possible and everytime, is should anything happen to the dogs eyes. Any scratches, bites, blows or in fact anything to do with eyes must have professional treatment as soon as possible. I had a client once who decided he would ask my advice when I trimmed his dog two weeks after an accident had happened to the dog. He had to pay the vet and I didn't charge. I was furious when I saw the dog and sent him straight off to the vet. Sadly, too late, and that dog lost the sight of the damaged eye.

Teeth seem to be another thing that dogs are always breaking or pulling out, especially if you want to show your dog and it needs a full set of correctly placed teeth. Luckily, most judges know that dogs are dogs and very few will condemn a dog that has a broken tooth, especially if the bite is obviously correct, but it is possible if the dog is in pain to have fairly sophisticated dental treatment done these days. I have recently been to a lecture on animal dentistry which was very enlightening. The Lecturer was a human dentist four days a week and an animal dentist three days, including zoo animals, as well as a great many dogs. He did stress that he would not do corrective dentistry to falsify an incorrect mouth for the show ring, so don't all rush off with that hopeful show puppy whose mouth has gone wrong. Dogs can have crowns just the same as humans do.

Another thing I find my dogs do is swallow things. I once had a poodle and he was busy passing a motion and went on for ages. I discovered he had eaten a long piece of linen. Luckily, it went right through, and the first we knew of it was the result coming out the other end. Lace, one of my Beardies was not so lucky, she managed to get at some biscuits that I had thought were out of reach. The biscuits were in a strong plastic bag and to get at the biscuits she ate a small hole in the bottom of the bag. I caught and spanked her, and as I could see she had eaten some plastic, thought I had better try and get it back, so consequently made her sick to try and bring it up. The easiest way to make a dog sick is to always keep ordinary washing soda in your cupboard. Take the packet and remove the largest pieces; I usually get about six out and place in easy reach. Take the dog outside and pop them down her throat, they do not like the flavour at all, so watch your fingers on their back teeth. I have never got all six pieces down any dogs throat yet, usually one piece four or five the dog starts to heave and rapidly brings up all the soda and all the previous meal. If it has just been fed fairly recently, it is much easier to bring up all the previous meal, if a long time has elapsed it's harder to get the lot. Lace was very sick, but we did not manage to get the bit of plastic. I had hoped we had, but in about an hours time she started to be sick

141

involuntarily and had started to blow up. She was beginning to look like a heavily in whelp bitch, so was rushed off to the vet, where she had a saline drip injection in case she had to be operated on to open her up to remove the plastic which had obviously blocked her passage from the stomach. Then the vet gave her a relaxing injection in the hope of floating the plastic through. I just about made home before the injection started to work. All her muscles completely relaxed and was I glad it was a nice sunny warm day in summer, as she gently oozed urine and faeces, but it worked, and although I did not see the plastic, it obviously moved and Lace was saved from some fairly major surgery, so in other words, make sure that anything that is dangerous to a dog is well out of reach, as even the best behaved dog will steal at times. Lace was not a thief, never stole before and up to now, since, but she could have so easily died if I had been out that day instead of being at home. Always keep a box of washing soda in the cupboard too. I have had to use it several times to make dogs regurgitate things they should not have eaten.

One ate rat poison once and returned home from an excursion into the next door farmers barn with a blue set of whiskers instead of her usual white, washing soda soon brought that lot up. Another ate a whole packet of Ovarid pills, including the silver paper, so no matter how careful you try to be, there can always be the naughty one who does his best not to survive.

An abscess is not an uncommon occurrence, there are quite common anal abscesses and quite a few Beardies have suffered from these. The first time you see one it can look very alarming. I had a poodle that had the first one I saw. She started by looking very uncomfortable and continually checked under her tail. She had been perfectly happy earlier in the day, but as she went outside I suddenly saw this huge pink swelling just under her anus, then she gave a sharp yell and the abscess burst. It had only taken a couple of hours to come up from nothing to a large pink lump and burst. Simply masses of gunge came away and as I had no idea what it was rushed her off to the vet.

She was given an antibiotic jab and I was told to bathe it with warm water to clear the mucus away each day and let her clean it herself if she would. It healed quickly and dried up nicely. The second one she had I just bathed it and she licked it clean herself. When the vet saw it, I had another dog to take in for something else and just had her checked in case all was not well, but the vet said he had never seen an anal abscess heal so well and quickly, so if you can see that everything is going along well, and if the dog will help by attending to it himself, I would not bother going to the vet. If the discharge is not clearing up or starts to smell bad, then it would need veterinary attention. I have never had a Beardie with an anal abscess, but have found some of my older Beardies do need their anal glands clearing out occasionally. This can be done quite easily by their owners. I prefer either paper towel or kitchen roll rather than cotton wool, as you have more sensitivity in your fingers with paper, as cotton wool rather masks what you are looking for. Get the kitchen roll readily to hand, put the dog up on his table, get someone to steady his head and then lift his tail and feel gently just below the anus with finger and thumb on either side. If the glands are empty it should feel hollow and you can press gently. With plenty of abscess fluid or gunge, it feels hard as if there is a blockage there. The glands are full. Get your paper and cover the anus well, press gently but firmly either side, but just below, the anus. The dog does not usually mind at all. If the glands are really full, the liquid can shoot out at quite a speed and the smell is horrid, so be prepared with plenty of spare paper. If the liquid is just that, liquid, that is quite alright, if it is thick and porridge like, that is the first stage of it starting to turn to an abscess, so remove as much as possible without causing distress to the dog, but do it again in about a week when hopefully it will now be liquid, if not, repeat again in another week.

I well remember once I was doing the glands of a Poodle in his owners house I could tell from the feel that he had a great deal in his glands and pressed gently. The liquid really shot out, straight across the room and hit the television screen slap in the middle. I had the owner hurry off and get some strong disinfectant to wash the TV and kill the very unpleasant smell, so be prepared to either move fast or get plenty of paper to collect up the fluid. Sometimes, I think, it is better for you if the stuff is a bit thicker, even if it's not for the dog, at least you can catch it easier. The easiest sign to observe that the gland needs cleaning is from the dogs behaviour, he will often spin round and lick under his tail or scoot his bottom on the ground, as there is discomfort in the area and he is trying to press the fluid out himself. Should you see him doing either of these things pop him on the table and check and evacuate his glands at once.

Should he still be troubled and continue licking, I would suggest a trip to the vet, as it could be something more serious developing in his back passage and catching something early can save a great deal of money later on. If there is a fair amount in the glands, dogs can evacuate them if they have a fright. I put a bitch onto the vets table once, I cannot remember what she had gone in for, probably her yearly booster, but she promptly evacuated her glands everywhere. It did not make her very popular with the vet I'm afraid, so I used to take her to the vet with the kitchen roll and talc to kill the smell, at the ready. It is a good idea to smother the area under the tail with some sweet scented talc as soon as you have done the glands, it does get rid of the smell a bit, as the smell from anal glands is very distinctive and is extremely unpleasant.

Beardies have long ears and lots of coat covering them, so it's as well to keep a very close eye on their ears for problems. Every time you groom your dog, don't just brush and comb his feathers, but look closely at the ear canal. You can often spot trouble starting at a very early stage by having a good sniff. The ear should smell quite clean and sweet. If there is the slightest sign of an unpleasant smell, he is probably starting some sort of ear trouble which could be mites or excessive wax. Another sign to watch for is slight discolouration on the leathers inside. The canal looks quite clean, but it is almost like a bit of grease on the leather inside that comes off on your finger if you rub gently on it. Other signs of ear problems developing are scratching his ears, shaking the head and when it gets very painful, holding the head on one side to let air into the canal. Should you see brown wax, some people have thought the dogs ears have been bleeding as it almost looks like dried blood, but it is almost invariably wax, usually because he has a massive amount of ear mites down in the canal. It is much better to go to the vet quickly for ear trouble, as the earlier it's caught the quicker and easier it is cleared up, rather than leaving it until it's really bad and consequently sometimes incurable. I have even seen dogs that have had to be put to sleep because the suffering has been so severe from badly infected and neglected ears. If you also have a cat do make sure the cat is clear from ear mites too, as that is how the dog usually gets them to start with, so they can re-infect each other continually for years.

All Beardies have hair growing down in the ear canal, some far more than others, so it is a good idea to remove most of this hair. I never start to remove it until the dog is about twelve months old, providing the ears have stayed healthy of course. Should you get infections earlier, it will have to be removed before, but if the ears are quite healthy, whilst you have him up on the table busy grooming him, put some talc into the ear and very gently tap or shake it down, leave the ear and continue grooming. It is important to do this otherwise he will associate having things put into his ear, with pain, and if you need to put in medication at a later date, you could have a battle on your hands. After you have brushed another leg or whatever, turn his ear back and with forefinger and thumb very gently ease out just one or two hairs, once or twice. The talc seems to deaden the ear and gives you grip on the hair. Talk to the dog and soothe and calm him whilst you are removing the hair and praise him well as soon as you have pulled out the very few hairs.

Do not do it everytime you groom him or he will start to anticipate it and might resent it, also the grooming, which he associates with having his ears done.

I have several youngsters that are appalling babies when their ears are done, but only removing very little hair, it's done very quickly and a very nice titbit afterwards makes them look forward to it rather than fear and hate it. I am a great believer in having the dogs co-operation rather than having great fights for everything.

Once you have more or less cleared the ears, removing a few hairs every month should keep them pretty free of hair, and hopefully, of all ear troubles too. Whatever you do, only use your finger and thumb to clear the hair and never use instruments, you could cause damage to the ear canal if you start poking down the ear, and if you have an instrument in your hand and the dog suddenly shakes his head, it could damage the flap or canal. Do not poke down the canal to try and clean it, that is a job for a vet and best left to him. If you should start to pull the hair out with tweezers or similar, you could pull the hair the wrong way and cause pain and resentment from the dog who will resist strongly next time you try to remove some hairs, and it's always easier to do anything to the dog with his co-operation.

Another sort of abscess that can occur quite easily is one on the feet. Again, this will happen very fast indeed. Lace had one recently, although it is not as common in Beardies as it is in some breeds of dog. I have never had one in a Beardie before. The whole foot swelled up very fast and the one toe where the abscess was situated looked really sore, as well as swollen. This is a time to go straight to the vet, who opened the abscess up and cleared out a load of gunge. We thought it could have been a grass seed causing the trouble, but there was no sign of one, and it has remained a mystery ever since.

Grass seeds from wild barley are the worst cause for interdigital cysts and foot abscesses. If you spot any wild barley in the garden do get it all up at once and either burn or get rid of it completely as it can cause such a lot of trouble. The seeds are barbed and can be very difficult to get out once they have started to migrate into the skin. One Beardie came for grooming once, and the mistress had carefully checked the underneath of the dogs paws everyday on coming back from the woods, where they walked, as she knew there was wild barley there, but she forgot to check inside each toe and I found about five seeds well and truely embedded, a couple deep in a mass of puss. The poor dog must have been in a fair amount of pain, but had never gone lame or even licked her paws, so if your walk goes near to wild barley, do check all the dogs feet, underneath and inbetween all toes, as with all the hair a Beardie has on his feet, it is very easy to miss a small seed snugly hiding away.

All puppies need inoculating for the really serious illnesses that are always with us. These are distemper, leptospirosis canicola and icterohaemorrhagiae, hepatitis and the latest, parvo-virus. All these can be lethal, both leptospirosis and hepatitis can be transmitted to human beings and vice-versa of course, and although no inoculation can be always one hundred per cent, it is very rare indeed for the dog not to obtain very good protection. There is a common fallacy that once the dog has had his initial inoculation, that he will be immune for life. Unfortunately, this is not so, and he will need yearly boosters to maintain the correct protection.

Distemper can take several different forms, another name for it being hard pad, not heard so much these days but the nose and paws would go hard and cracked with this form. Another type would cause fits and damage the dogs brain, so even if he survived the illness it would end up with euthanasia.

Leptospirosis canicola attacks the kidneys and can kill in forty eight hours if not treated, although sometimes no treatment can save the dog if the attack is very severe. Rats are the main carriers of leptospirosis and a dog eating food that has been contaminated by rats could easily succumb, also sniffing where rats have urinated can be equally hazardous. Even if the dog catches the type that just makes him slightly off colour for a few days, the damage to his kidneys can be so severe that it knocks off several years of his life.

Hepatitis attacks the liver and can again be very rapid indeed in progression, veterinary advice must be sought immediately otherwise death could result. Symptoms for both distemper and hepatitis are very similar, and may include diarrhoea, vomiting, lack of appetite, rise in temperature, sometimes lethargy plus in some cases a nasal discharge.

Parvo-virus has only been with us for a relatively short time, and is widely considered to be a mutant gene from cat influenza. When it first appeared in the dog world a great many dogs died and until a vaccine was invented, everyone lived in dread of catching it. The main symptoms are sickness and diarrhoea, both of which are different from ordinary enteritis by the passing of blood in both and everybody who has had a dog with parvo says the smell is different from anything they have ever smelt, a really dreadful smell and one you never forget. Parvo is extremely contagious and the virus will live for many months in the ground, being very difficult to eradicate once you have it on the premises. There are vuricides these days that you can spray all the area with, including the house and garden, but it is much easier to have a quick inoculation.

Kennel Cough is actually now far more common than all the previously mentioned illnesses, and at last there is now an inoculation to prevent it. At least, the inoculation covers the most common ones as there are about twelve different types. The dog can still go down with one of the rarer varieties, even though he has been inoculated, but at least, you have done the best you can for him. At present, the inoculation only lasts for six months, so don't forget to have the second one inbetween his annual boosters. Kennel Cough can be just a few coughs and the dog is not at all ill, eats well and you will hardly notice it at all, or it can be really serious. I know of one Beardie who started with Kennel Cough and it caused pleurisy, he died, and several that it has damaged the heart so badly they have also died, so it certainly is not a problem to be dismissed lightly. It is also very contagious and is air borne, so your dog does not even have to get near to another dog to contact it.

One type my dogs went down with, they started sneezing violently for a couple of days before they started coughing, that one was a very virulent type, as nearly all of the dogs went down with it and it took three different types of antibiotics before we hit on the right one to cure it. Honey, who was about eleven years old at the time and was very ill indeed, never did completely get rid of the cough for the rest of her life.

Another type, the dogs just give a few coughs for a day, then really start seriously, they seem to have a fit of coughing ending with a gagging sound usually bringing up some yellow or white bile at the end of the paroxysm. One case we had, the dog also brought up a bit of his dinner with each coughing fit, so it was no good giving antibiotics in pill form as they also came back, so he had to be injected until he managed to stop being sick. Kennel Cough can also be very serious indeed, for very young puppies, so if your dog shows any sign of coughing, it is just as well to leave him strictly at home in case he should pass it on to a pregnant or lactating bitch that he meets or goes near, and definitely do not go to a show or classes until he is well and truly over his bout.

Enteritis is another very contagious infection although not usually as serious as the previously mentioned diseases. Enteritis can still, in its worst state, kill, especially the very young or very old dogs. It usually starts with sickness and within hours the dog usually starts severe diarrhoea.

There is no inoculation for enteritis and the best cure is to starve the dog for twenty four hours. Do not restrict his water intake as he will be dehydrated with the diarrhoea, unless he is being sick all the time, then only give a few sips until he stops being sick. When you start feeding again, give only light food and small meals for a couple of days, and I find a handful of bran on each meal helps a great deal with the diarrhoea. Do not make the bran too wet, just a teaspoonful of water on it to make it moist. Also, if your dog has antibiotics at any time, live yoghurt on each meal, when the course is finished, helps to put the good bugs back into the system that the antibiotics have removed with the bad bugs, and the dogs really love the yoghurt. It must be live yoghurt which is obtainable at health food shops, as supermarkets do not usually keep the right type.

All the diseases I have mentioned, need veterinary attention as soon as possible. It really is better and safer to go to the vet at once, and so much easier to treat the dog when he is in the first stages of illness, still having the strength to get better, rather than leaving him in the hope that he will get better himself, just getting weaker and weaker and having very little strength left to recover.

Worms can be quite a problem in very young puppies. The two types that we have in Great Britain, are round worms and tape worms. Round worms are like white pieces of string, all baby puppies have round worms, some more than others, and it is very important that puppies are regularly wormed with tablets from the vet. These are easily given to the dog. I crush the tablet up and feed on a light breakfast. The flavour is not noticable in the food and the worms usually start appearing by late afternoon, after dinner, usually going on passing the worms until the next day, but that is usually all you will see until the next worming in between seven to ten days time. The round worm migrates from the dam into the foetus whilst she is pregnant and, of course, when the bitch cleans the puppies as she is rearing them, she ingests worms and eggs, so will need worming regularly too, keeping her as clear as possible whilst she rears her litter. I have found that some of my bitches produce fairly wormy puppies every litter and other bitches have puppies with scarcely any worms even though I follow the same routine with all of them.

Don't forget to worm the dogs as well as the bitches, usually once or twice a year. The other type often seen is tapeworms. These are first seen by the owner usually as small approximate half inch segments, whitish pink and flat, adhering to the anus or on the faeces when it is first passed. The tapeworm itself can be about two feet long and the bits seen are only the ripe ends going out to continue the life cycle. Tapeworms have to go through a host such as a rabbit or sheep who eat the segments on the grass, pass it out, where it again gets eaten by the dog, who develops the tapeworm in the intestine. Again, tablets from your vet as soon as you see any signs. Some tablets clear the worm out from the dog whole, but mostly these days the latest tablets dissolve the worms internally and you don't see a thing, much the better way I feel having used both.

There are also hookworms and whipworms. I have heard of some in Cornwall brought in by imported dogs, even though they have been through quarantine, but it is very rare. Whipworms can be between two to five inches in length and have a thicker top end, tapering to a fine tail, consequently the name, whipworms. Hook or thread worms are about threequarters of an inch in length and resemble a thread of cotton. These can get into the soil and be very difficult to clear up, if your garden gets infected.

Heartworm is fairly prevalent in America and can be very serious indeed, also causing death if not treated. The larva is transmitted to the dog through a mosquito bite. The only way to tell your dog has heartworm is by having the blood examined, so its as well to go on to the anti heartworm tablets if you live in a heartworm mosquito areas. Hopefully it will never arrive in England.

A dog that sits and puts its nose up in the air and yawns a lot with the head up, can indicate a liver complaint. The dog is usually a bit lethargic, but still eating. The yawning can go on for quite a bit before the vomiting starts, usually only bile, not bringing back food, and the bile can be yellowish or green. Veterinary attention should be sought as soon as possible.

Famous Dogs of the Breed

THERE are so many famous dogs in any breed and Beardies have their fair share. In 1968 we had our first points trophy, offered by Mrs Jackie Tidmarsh, it is called the Tambora Points Trophy, and every dog that won it had to be of exceptional quality. Slightly later, in 1971, the Bearded Collie Club, the only club for Beardies in Great Britain at that time, held its first championship show. Again, the dog that took best in show was an outstanding specimen, we now have entries of over 500 at the championship show each year, and it takes a lot of Beardies to make that sort of entry.

The following chapter is about those dogs that have either won best in show or the points trophy, thereby being top dogs of the year. Some of the dogs have won both, so their name only, appears in one of the write ups to avoid repetition.

Then there are several dogs, either pre-championship show or points trophy, or never did win either, but at the same time, have made a great impact on the breed through their offspring, sometimes producing a definite type even through several generations and these dogs really must be included, as they are a great part of the breeds strength.

Championship Show Best in Show Winners.

1972 Champion Willowmead Juno of Tambora.
1973 Champion Edenborough Blue Bracken.
1974 Champion Black Magic of Willowmead.
1975 Champion Penhallows Pink Panther.
1976 No Show.
1977 Champion Pepperlands Lyric John at Potterdale.
1978 Champion Blumberg Hadriana at Potterdale.
1979 Champion Dearbolt Lady Ancorrie.
1980 Champion Pepperlands Lyric John at Potterdale.
1981 Champion Potterdale Patch of Blue.
1982 Champion Moonhills Gold Digger
1983 Champion Pipadene Camio.
1984 Champion Briaridge Lyrical Lord.
1985 Champion Willowmead Red Admiral.
1986 Champion Potterdale Ptolomy.
1987 Champion Binbusy Ballade.
1988 Champion Potterdale Priviledge.
1989 Champion Potterdale Premier.

Tambora Points Trophy Winners

1968 Champion Bracken Boy of Bothkennar.
1969 Champion Edelweiss of Tambora.
1970 Champion Wishanger Waterfall.
1971 Champion Willowmead Juno of Tambora.
1972 Champion Edenborough Blue Bracken.
1973 Champion Edenborough Blue Bracken.
1974 Champion Edenborough Blue Bracken.
1975 Champion Mignonette of Willowmead at Orora.
1976 Champion Mignonette of Willowmead at Orora.
1977 Champion Pepperlands Lyric John at Potterdale.
1978 Champion Pepperlands Lyric John at Potterdale.
1979 Champion Pepperlands Lyric John at Potterdale.
1980 Champion Osmart Black Thorn at Moonhills.
1981 Champion Willowmead Star Attraction.
1982 Champion Tamevalley Easter Song of Potterdale.
1983 Champion Ororas Frank.
1984 Champion Ororas Frank.
1985 Champion Potterdale Philosopher.
1986 Champion Potterdale Classic at Moonhills.
1987 Champion Sammara Standing Ovation.
1988 Champion Potterdale Classic at Moonhills.
1989 Champion Potterdale Priviledge.

Famous Dogs in the Breed

The first dog that one must really think about is Jeannie of Bothkennar, Mrs Willisons first Beardie and the foundation bitch of the post-war revival of the breed.

Jeannie's sire was a dog called Baffler and her dam was Mist, both working dogs, and her colour was a beautiful rich sandy brown. She only produced black and brown puppies.

Jeannie arrived at Bothkennar Grange in 1944, instead of a Sheltie puppy, originally ordered by Mrs Willison. With her Beardie appeal, she

Mr. R. Willison and Jeannie

Britt of Bothkennar

rapidly won the hearts of all the family, so stayed, instead of being returned to her breeder. She had two main claims to fame, she was the first post-war registered Beardie, and the foundation bitch of the Bothkennar Kennels.

Her second big event was to make her debut as a film star. Jeannie's film was called "Day of Grace". Jeannie was a fairly old dog when the film was made, but thoroughly enjoyed all the star treatment and her behaviour was exemplary, her previous obedience training proving how worthwhile it had been. Sadly, just as they finished the filming, the cameraman discovered most of the film was not usable, so it all had to be re-shot.

On the last day of the original shooting, Jeannie had slipped and hurt her back, so although she gamely carried on with all the re-shooting, the sparkle that had been shown in the early shots, was not to be seen in the finished film.

I believe there is still a few copies of the film around but have no idea where they are to be found.

After Jeannie, the dogs bred by Mrs Willison that really made the most impression on the breed in my opinion, were Britt of Bothkennar, 2 C.C.s, champions Bravo, Blue Bonnie and Beauty Queen. Mrs Willison sold Beauty Queen as a puppy, not realising her potential. Due to family troubles, Beauty Queen was returned to Mrs Willison, who was delighted with how she had grown up and decided she would stay at Bothkennar, it was certainly a good thing for Mrs Willison, as she subsequently made Beauty Queen up to become the breeds first Champion. We were awarded C.C.s for the first tme in 1959. Beauty Queen won her first at Crufts, and at the next two shows, her second and third. We only had four sets of C.C.s that year, so Beauty Queen really excelled herself.

Blue Bonnie won a total of seven C.C.s, two in 1960 and her third in 1961, whilst she was still with Mrs Willison, and four after she moved to Osmart and Ken and Jenny Osborne. Bravo of Bothkennar won all his three C.Cs in 1961 to become a

Ch. Bravo of Bothkennar

Champion and a further four, making a total of seven all told. He also went with Blue Bonnie to live at Osmart when Mrs Willison disbanded her kennels due to ill health. Britt only won 2 C.C.s, as he never carried very much coat, and although he was an ultra sound dog, he did look a bit out of place with the longer coats on the other dogs. Britt was born in 1955, Beauty Queen in 1957, Bravo in 1959 and Blue Bonnie in 1960.

Ch. Blue Bonnie of Bothkennar

Jenny Osborne tells me both Blue Bonnie and Bravo were certainly characters. Bonnie always liked to go at a good pace when she moved in the show ring. The time Jenny particularly remembers was once when Stanley Dangerfield, one of our top all-rounder judges was officiating, Bonnie did her triangle at her usual fast pace, but when she started the up and down she started to increase her speed and on going back to Mr Dangerfield, she just got faster and faster, shot past the judge, with Jenny panting behind, straight out of the ring and onto her bench. Mr Dangerfield, who was very amused by the whole incident, asked if they would both like to return to the ring now. Poor Jenny said she had to laugh, even though she felt somewhat embarrassed.

Bravo also managed to disgrace himself once at a show. He usually was very well behaved on his bench sitting quietly and sensibly, but this one day he just would not stay up and kept getting off the bench and disappearing underneath, Jenny just could not understand him. Bravo was benched next door to Mary Partridge of the Wishanger Bearded Collies, who as usual travelled with her brother Richard to help with the dogs.

Lunch time came and Mary and Richard returned to their bench to have lunch, when Mary suddenly gave a furious shout "Richard, you have eaten all our sandwiches, you greedy thing" Jenny very rapidly fished out from underneath the bench, a very self satisfied Bravo, licking his chops after thoroughly enjoying all Mary and Richard's lunch.

Mrs Joyce Collis of the Beagold prefix had two dogs, Champion Davealex Royle Baron, pet name Baron, and Champion Edenborough Star Turn at Beagold, pet name Noddy. Baron's sire was Marilanz Amber Gleam, dam Champion Cala Sona Loch Aber. Baron produced a very recognisable sort of dog as he was very dominant in type.

Joyce says if she had been asked to give her opinion on the Beardie that answered every one of the standard requirements she would have immediately named Baron. Baron was born at the Davealex Kennels. Joyce thinks he was sold at eight weeks, but either he was too lively, or something happened and he was returned to Jean and Derek Stopforth. He broke out of his kennel and mated an Old English Sheepdog at a very early age. Then he showed his keen stud ambitions by mating an Osmart bitch owned by Jean before he was a year old. That produced Davealex I Own Him. During his time at their kennels he was forever escaping and damaged himself badly. When Joyce visited Jean and Derek they offered Baron to her. Joyce learnt of Barons wild ways and decided to think it over for a bit, but there was something about that naughty dog which fascinated her and she soon made up her mind to have him. He was brought to a show and travelled home with Joyce.

Their life together then started, he was very easy to train, and groom, so before long he was taken to several open shows, he won some Best of Breeds, so they progressed to Champion shows, and eventually he gained three C.C.s and was made up to Champion. Joyce said she remembered shedding a few tears when he gained his title, but she always knew he had the potential to win well, he was such a handsome dog.

The three judges who thought him worthy of a title were Mr Ben Johnson, at Windsor 1973, Mrs Trudi Wheeler, Darlington, 1973, and

Ch. Davealex Royle Baron

Miss Lynn Evans at Leeds, 1975. He also won several Res. C.C.s in between those dates.

Baron was well known for coping with difficult bitches when he mated. Anyone with a difficult bitch would travel far to use Baron. Joyce remembers receiving a telephone call from Mrs Barbara Iremonger hoping that she could come to Baron as the dog she had tried to use would not mate her bitch. She arrived and left within the hour, with the bitch thoroughly mated and 63 days later she had a litter. Then she called again some months later, she was having more trouble mating her bitch, the dog would not co-operate. This was Christmas Day, and Joyce was getting ready for relations to arrive for a party. Anyway, she arrived and in no time the bitch was mated and on her way home.

Baron only tried to escape once while he was with Joyce. She doesn't know how he jumped a ten foot fence, but it was obvious he had scaled it, and gone down the village. Joyce was giving a lecture to the Young Wives Club, later, she mentioned that he had gone down the road looking for bitches. One young lady who obviously did not like her neighbours said "He should have come down our road there are lots of bitches living down there".

Baron was born black and white, but as he matured he had a lovely silver grey coat. He had a nice dark eye, and his expression was enough to melt any cold heart. Joyce says she has so many wonderful memories of that handsome dog, that even to this day he is sadly missed.

Joyce's other dog, Champion Edenborough Star Turn at Beagold, was sired by Champion Edenborough Blue Bracken out of Davealex Dawn Reign. Although Noddy also had a wonderful character, and Joyce loved him very much, there was just that extra bit of feeling that she had for Baron. Noddy was very ill throughout his young life, Joyce was constantly at the vets with him, in the end she decided to forget the vets treatment and start at the beginning and wean him on baby food, five meals a day, as he was skin and bone.

After several weeks he began to respond to her treatment, and so they went to a Championship show, and at ten months of age he won his first C.C. under judge George Leatt, at Manchester show in March 1975. His second was won at the East of England show under judge Mr Ben Johnson, also in 1975. His third and title at the same show in 1976 judge Mrs Jean Lanning. He then went on to win 13 more C.C.s. His final tally being 16 C.C.s with 11 Res. C.C.s.

Edenborough Star Turn at Beagold

Joyce remembers one time when Noddy had two C.C.s, and she was so keen to win his title, she knew that his handsome sire, Blue Bracken, would be in the same class again, and that the judge was a real fan of his, so that it was a foregone conclusion that when he arrived that he would beat Noddy. The class was called in, and Shirley Holmes and Blue Bracken had not arrived, Joyce felt very nervous as she hoped she might win if Blue Bracken was not there. The class was judged and still he had not arrived. The prize cards were handed out and Noddy won First. Still no Blue Bracken, all unbeaten dogs were called in, and although she should have known that it was too late for him to be included in the line up, she could not believe that luck would be on her side that day. Noddy did everything that was asked of him, and Joyce was handed the C.C. The applause started so Joyce knew her luck had held. She then saw Shirley Holmes and Blue Bracken come running to the ring, she had been held up in a car accident. But being the good sport that she always was, she congratulated Joyce on gaining Noddy's title.

Noddy would always behave well until there was appaluse, then he would jump and run round in circles, so each time they were on their way to a win, Joyce would always hope there would not be applause in the other rings. If there was she found it impossible to curb his exuberance to show off, so she just let him get it out of his system, especially as she knew he would calm down as soon as the applause ceased. Noddy's most famous son was Champion Beagold David Blue, who was made up to Champion by Felix Cosme, now in partnership with Joyce in the Beagold Kennels, David Blue was later exported to Norway, where he became an International Champion, and top dog, all breeds in Scandinavia for several years. Noddy died when he was $13^{1}/_{2}$ years old, he was born black and white and had a most profuse coat of excellent texture, he was a keen stud dog, but never so ambitious as Baron. Joyce bought him because she had plans to mate his offpsring to Barons offspring as the pedigree's tied up so well. Whenever she managed to carry out her plans it always worked very well.

One of the most dominant for producing a really recognisable type was Champion Osmart Bonnie Blue Braid. He was a great dog and made a great impact on the breed. Braid was bred by Mr and Mrs Ken Osborne, who gave him to their daughter Catherine, under whose name he was always shown. His sire was Champion Bravo of Bothkennar, his dam being Champion Blue Bonnie of Bothkennar and he was born on 1.12.1965 and died 15.4.1980. Braid, as his name suggests, was a lovely blue, with a gorgeous blue/brown eye, none of the horrid white type of eye that is seen sometimes these days for Braid or any of his offspring. He also produced all four colours in his puppies.

Braid's record is pretty impressive. He won eleven Challenge Certificates and five Reserve Challenge Certificates in fairly restricted showing, considering the amount of Challenge Certificates we have on

Ch. Osmart Bonnie Blue Braid

offer in these days. He made his debut in 1966 when he attended three shows. That year there were eight sets of Challenge Certificates on offer, and retired in 1972 when he attended two shows and there were fifteen sets on offer. He only once went under the same judge twice and that was at Crufts in 1972.

Braid sired thirteen English Champions namely Champions Brambledale Balthazar born in 1969, Nigella Black Tango also born in 1969, Willowmead Juno of Tambora born in 1970, Benedict Morning Mist also born in 1970, Dutch Bonnet of Willowmead born in 1974, Banacek Moonlight Blue also born in 1974, Charncroft Cavalcade born in 1975, Lochbarra Benjamin Blue born in 1975, Robdave Wild Affair born in 1975, Sheldawyn Black Jet born in 1975 Sheldawyn Blue Opal born in 1975, Orora's Frank born in 1977 and Osmart Black Thorn at Moonhill born in 1975. He also produced another twelve dogs that won either one or two Challenge Certificates, Mountain Dew of Tambora, Osmart Bracken Brown, Osmart Smoky's Silver Sabre, Rossbourne Cynpegs Hobo, Cynpegs Hollyberry, Marilanz Black Penny, Nigella

158

Nutbrown Maid, Orora's Honesty, Osmart Golden Raine, Osmart Queen of Clubs, Osmart Silver Cass and Scapafield Carbon Copy.

Jenny tells me the win that gave her the most satisfaction in all the years of showing him was the day at Windsor Championship Show in 1972 when he won the Any Variety Stud Dog with Progeny Class, with all four colours represented. I well remember the day too, as I had my own Juno there, and have a photo, a great prize, of all of us standing behind Braid. It was a great thrill when the judge walked across and handed Jenny the first prize card. It wasn't an easy win either, as the competition was very hot and included the well known Dobermann Champion Iceberg of Tavey and the Standard Poodle, Triple Champion (American, Canadian and English) Tall Dark and Handsome.

Jenny's proudest moment was the day Braid retired, it was the first Bearded Collie Club Championship Show, a day I remember extremely well as I had Juno there, Braid's daughter, and when I saw Braid I felt there was no way I could beat him with his record, as Juno was only two years old, but Juno went Best in Show and Braid was Reserve Best in Show. Best Puppy was Moonlight Mile, a daughter of my Crofter and a granddaughter on her dams side of Braid and best Opposite Sex Puppy was Marilanz Brigadoon, Braid's grandson. So his stock really wiped the board.

Braid wasn't just a show dog, he also really enjoyed all the rallies and fun days devoted to Beardies. He regularly competed in the races and fancy dress competitions, winning one dressed as a Scot. Sometimes he had almost human tendencies, one of his favourites was when driving with Jenny, if the visibility became poor and her speed (to him) became excessive, a paw would come over and tap her arm, whilst Braid 'peered' at the speedometer. He also had his favourite seat in the house, and visitors who sat on his corner of the settee usually asked why he was staring at them. On being told that 'Sirs' seat, many said 'sorry' and moved up, whereupon 'Sir' climbed up, looked over his shoulder, sighed deeply and settled down.

Miss Mary Partridge's Champion Wishanger Cairnbhan is a dog that has made a lasting impression on the breed. Cairnbhan was a really dark brown dog. His sire was Mary's first Beardie, Champion Wishanger Barley of Bothkennar, the breeds first Champion dog, mated to Champion Willowmead My Honey, a brown bitch Mary bought from me. Honey was a daughter of Will O'Wisp and Merry Maker, and Cairnbhan was very much like his dam in make and shape. He had a lovely outgoing friendly temperament which he always passed on to his children.

I used him at stud several times. The first time to Breckdale Merry Maid who was exported to Canada in whelp to Audrey Benbow. The second time to Champion Broadholme Cindy Sue of Willowmead, who had nine puppies and I retained Champion Willowmead Super Honey. The third time, again to Cindy Sue, she again had nine puppies, the most famous one being Champion Mignonette of Willowmead at Orora, who belonged to Bryony Harcourt-Brown. Cairnbhan produced many Champion offspring and even through many generations, there can still be seen the strong Cairnbhan influence.

Amongst the famous dogs of the breed there has only been one obedience Champion, namely Jenni Wiggins Obedience Champion Scapa.

Scapa at 11 years - The only Beardie to scale the dizzy heights
to Ob. Championship status

Scapa, not content with her obedience Championship, was also the foundation bitch for Jenni's Scapafield Beardies. Scapa's sire was Champion Bosky Glen of Bothkennar, her dam being Swalehall Martha Scrope and she was born on 17.4.1964. Scapa had three litters one to a blue dog, one to a brown dog and one to a slate dog, she had one blue puppy in each litter and all the rest were always slate, she had seventeen puppies all told in her three litters. One puppy, Scapafield Carbon Copy won 2 C.C.s, and she also had a dual Reserve C.C. winning offspring.

Scapa won the first of her Challenge Certificates at Ruislip and Northwood Canine Training Society on the 24th, June 1967, with a total of $296^{1}/_{2}$ marks out of 300. Her second Challenge Certificate was won at Bath Canine Society on the 6th, September 1968, with a total of $297^{1}/_{2}$ marks out of 300, and her third Challenge Certificate at City of Birmingham Canine Ass.on the 6th September 1969, with the magnificent

300 out of 300 marks, as near perfect as any one can ever get. The first trophy she ever won for the breed was at Ruislip and Northwood Canine Training Society and it is ironical that it was the Bothkennar trophy donated by Mrs Willison.

Jenni tells me Scapa was something of a character. Jenni always used to buy Scapa a rabbit for a special birthday treat, but on her fifth birthday, had decided not to bother this time. Jenni took Scapa for her usual walk in the local park, but when she arrived back at the car, discovered that sometime during the walk she had lost the car keys. What to do? well there she was with an obedience champion, trained to retrieve, so Jenni sent Scapa back into the park to find the keys. Very rapidly Scapa found the keys and proudly brought them back to her pleased Mistress. Poor Jenni didn't stay pleased for long though, because, as she bent down to take the keys from Scapa's mouth, Scapa swallowed them. So poor Jenni had to dash off to the vet to have a quick operation on her very naughty dog to retrieve the car keys, she tells me the vets visit was considerably more expensive than any rabbit would have been, so after that Scapa always had her birthday rabbit treat.

Ch. Brambledale Balthazar

Miss Lynne Evans Champion Brambledale Balthazar is another dog that I really feel has left a very definite mark on the breed, with the really delightful temperament that is still going through in, by now, the fourth and fifth generations down.

I used him on my Champion Willowmead Super Honey and kept Pure Magic of Willowmead, who won two Challenge Certificates and three Reserve Challenge Certificates, and you could not wish for a gentler or more obedient dog, a perfect dog to live with.

Balthazar, whose pet name was Angel, which aptly described him, was sired by Champion Osmart Bonnie Blue Braid, his dam being Brambledale Heathermead Moonlight. He was born on 8.11.69 and was a dark slate with full white collar.

He won a total of six Challenge Certificates, the first in 1973 and the last in 1975 including Best of Breed at Crufts in 1975. Amongst his champion offspring, was Lynne's Champion Brambledale Bathsheba, Champion Swinford Sky Rocket at Macmont, International Champion Brambledale Billet Doux, American Champion Brambledale Blackfriar and American and Canadian Champion Brambledale Blue Bonnet, amongst many others, too numerous for Lynne to recall them.

In his many litters, he would produce all four colours. When I asked Lynne for a story of Angel, she said she could think of so many amusing stories about all her other Beardies, but not Angel. He was always the perfect gentlemen, always gentle and impeccably behaved, she couldn't think of a single naughty or silly thing he ever did.

Although I have tried not to include my own dogs in this section, as I feel they have been covered in the chapter about the Willowmeads, I think there is one dog that I feel I must mention. She is Miss Maureen Reader of the Tamevalley Beardies 'Champion Dutch Bonnet of Willowmead', pet name "Mieke". Mieke was born on the 28th July 1974 and was a daughter of Champion Osmart Bonnie Blue Braid, her dam being my bitch, Breckdale Pretty Maid. Mieke was a really dark slate with white markings and won five Challenge Certificates and four reserve C.C.s. She was Maureens first Champion.

Mieke was a super brood bitch as well, producing six champion offspring, including in her first litter, the top Challenge Certificate winning bitch of several years standing, Champion Tamevalley Easter Song of Potterdale, her other Champion offspring were Champion Tamevalley Folk Lyric of Labooshar, International Champions Tamevalley Easter Hymn and Tamevalley Highland Melody, American Champion Tamevalley Highland Ballad and Australian Champion Tamevalley Highland Thistle. Mieke only produced slate, slate/tricolour and blue puppies.

Maureen tells me that Mieke had an uncanny knack of reading her mind. Maureen well remembers one day when prospective puppy buyers called to look at one of her litters. They met the visitors at the door and

Ch. Dutch Bonnet of Willowmead

after looking at the puppies and older dogs and answering certain questions that Maureen says she always asks people, she found that they were not suitable Beardie owners. But how to tell them without causing offence. Mieke took care of that.

The lady asked if she could "go over" Mieke and Maureen agreed, although Maureen had already realised that the lady had no idea of what she should be looking for in a show dog. Maureen put Mieke into a show stance and as the lady approached her she rolled on her back and waved her paws in the air. The lady stood back and let Maureen set her up again. The same thing happened twice more, the lady was getting very exasperated and said: "I thought this was a show dog" whereupon Mieke retired to the furthest corner of the room, put her head on her paws and flatly refused to budge again.

They said they would reconsider about having a Beardie and left. Mieke immediately came running to Maureen asking for a cuddle, with what seemed like a smile on her face and an expression saying "didn't I do well".

Ch. Charncroft Cavalcade

Champion Charncroft Cavalcade was really the foundation of Miss Pat Jones Wellknowe Beardies. He is a very typical son of his sire, Champion Osmart Bonnie Blue Braid, his dam being Champion Charncroft Cassandra. Cavalcade, pet name Kerry, was born on 24.11.1975 and is slate and white. Kerry won five Challenge Certificates and four Reserve Challenge Certificates and also numerous Best in Shows at Open Show level.

He produced two English Champions, Pat's own Champion Wellknowe Hill Scout and Jenny Wiggins Champion Scapafield Night Raine, up to the present date, as he has several offspring as yet very young, there could possibly be more in the future. He also has numerous Champion offspring abroad.

Kerry was interesting in the colours he produces, he has brown, slate and blue puppies with tri-colour only in his bitch puppies.

I had never been over Kerry in the show ring until he came under me at a Championship Show in Scotland in the Veteran class. He looked a picture both standing and moving and easily won the class. He came out again and won Veteran in 1989 when he still looked super at the age of fourteen years, Kerry also worked both sheep and cattle on Pat's farm, something very few Champions manage to do these days. In fact, it is to do with this, that Pat told me about his naughty habits. She said she never seemed to have to feed Kerry, he chose to open doors, jump fences, remove lids, overturn bins in fact do anything to steal cow cake, sheep pencils, or any other type of feed, taboo to him. I know just how she feels about it, as my own Ruairidh, who loved going with me to feed my horses, would scoff pony nuts as if there was no tomorrow. I didn't really mind, until the day I was running out of food and just had enough to feed Caprice, my brothers thoroughbred, for her breakfast. I was expecting a delivery later that day. Whilst I filled the hay nets, I heard a sound and discovered Ruairidh with his head deep in Caprice's bucket having eaten about half her breakfast. I soon shot him off, and poor Caprice had short rations until dinner time. Ruairidh wasn't at all sorry about his misdemeanour, and as usual helped me to finish feeding all the horses.

Ch. Sunbree Sorcerer

Champion Sunbree Sorcerer is another dog that has certainly left his type on the breed. Mrs Barbara Iremonger bred Martin from Charlie and Elsie Corderoy's Ch. Black Magic of Willowmead, from a mating to Southernisle Perilla. Martin was born on 31st October, 1976 and is a very dark slate, rather smaller type of dog. He produced all four colours in his litters and one of his claims to fame is the fact that he was the sire of the artist David Shepherds 'Muffins Pups' litter, so all the many pictures David Shepherd has painted of the pups are Martins children. Martin won seven challenge certificates in all, with several reserve challenge certificates too.

Barbara tells me that one of our top all-round judges once said to her, if you want to win well with a dog, he must be the type that will appeal to everyone. When Martin was born, she thought he looked as if he might fulfill this ideal. How right she was proved, when he first came out into the show ring he was never beaten from September to the following June, including being campaigned everywhere, at club open and championship shows and taking Crufts in his stride. Martin was a very easy dog to show, always being happy to do whatever Barbara asked of him. He had a very sensible temperament, which he passed on to his puppies, along with his beautiful dark expressive eyes and lovely sound flowing movement. The other thing he passed on was his really excellent pigment, which is carrying on through several generations as I have proved to my own delight onto the third and fourth generation now. With my Man of the Moment and Touch of Class.

Pat and Fred Randall's Champion Kimrand Simon, born on 4.5.1976 is a lovely light slate grey. I first saw him at ten months of age, when he won the puppy class at the show he was attending, and admired his lovely reachy movement.

His sire was Champion Edenborough Star Turn at Beagold and his dam was Fred and Pat's lovely brown bitch, Kimrand Summer Dawn, who herself won two Challenge Certificates. Simon won eleven Challenge Certificates and also a Championship Show working Group at the East of England Show.

In his litters, he produced black, slate brown, fawn and tri-colours, so

Ch. Kimrand Simon

a real mixed bag could be expected. Amongst his many champion offspring were Champions Kimrand Stargazer, Kimrand Saul, Lordryn Lady Palestrina and Taupbelle Sandyman, with International Champion Kimrand Tartan Tiger and Norweigan Champion Kimrand Sparkling Judy. Simon was also sire of my own Willowmead Silver Lace who won four Reserve Challenge Certificates and was one of his slate tri-colour children.

Simon was a most considerate fellow to his other Beardie friends, one that was a special friend called Jasper, for whom he would steal fruit and nuts from the bowl on the dresser (for himself as well, of course). As Jasper grew older and his teeth were not so good, Simon would crack the nutshells for Jasper and present him with the nicely shelled nut, so proved what a gentleman he could be.

Mrs Althea Richardsons, Champion Swinford Sky Rocket of Macmont is a dog that has really passed on his excellent properties to his children and they are going through now to both grand and great-grandchildren.

Althea acquired Mac in somewhat sad circumstances. He was bred by Mrs Eileen Collins, of Swinford Bearded Collies and sold as a baby puppy to Mrs Noreen Nicholls, of Macmont Beardies. Whilst he was with Mrs Nicholls, he won well and consistently in the show ring, obtaining firsts and seconds at Crufts. That was sadly the day before Mrs Nicholls died from cancer. The kennels were disbanded and Althea, who had already a pet dog from Mrs Nicholls took Mac, as she had already decided she would rather like to show dogs too. Althea soon learnt how to handle and present, and Mac continued his winning ways in Althea's hands.

He was sired by Ch. Brambledale Balthazar out of Ch. Charncroft Country Maid and was born 6.10.76. Mac won a total of three Challenge Certificates with the dubious honour of being the oldest Beardie ever to win a Challenge Certificate. He also won two Reserve Challenge Certificates.

Mac is a very plain dog in markings and is a dark slate grey. He has sired one English Champion, Moonhills Country Gentleman and has several Champion offspring overseas, including my own Finnish Champion Willowmead Spring Fantasy, Australian Champion Willowmead Spring Festival and several others as I liked Mac so much, I used him at stud several times. He proved especially well suited to my Champion Willowmead Super Honey.

Mac has sired approximately fifteen litters, as Althea does not have full details of his stud work while with Mrs Nicholls, and unless the bitch was dominant black, all litters contained brown and slate puppies. He is also credited with producing excellent dark brown and strong slates with superb pigment.

Althea tells me Mac was two when he came to live with her. He settled in immediately and has never given them any reason to regret having him. Quite the reverse, he is a pleasure to own and they know how privileged they are to have shared his life this past eleven years.

Bearded Collie Club Championship Show Best in Show Winners

Ch. Willowmead Juno of Tambora

Ch. Show B.I.S. 1972

The first Bearded Collie Club Championship show was held in 1972. Previously it had been only open shows, but by 1972 the Club had grown sufficiently for a Championship show to be held. The Kennel Club had granted us Challenge Certificates, commonly called C.C.s, so the event went ahead.

The dog to win best in show was my own Ch. Willowmead Juno of Tambora. Juno had previously been top Beardie during 1971, and this was her 4th C.C. In all she won five C.C.s. I usually like to win four or five, then they are retired. I feel to keep on chasing C.C.s is a particularly pointless achievement. Once you have made the bitch a Champion, she cannot be more, to go up to four or five just makes sure you really have a Champion and that one C.C. was not a fluke.

The only time I have broken this rule was with Ch. Willowmead Perfect Lady, when she won her three C.C.s at three consequtive Crufts in 1978/9/80, and I did want to win that hat trick as it has never been done before or since in Beardies.

To go back to Juno, she was bred by Jackie Tidmarsh and her sire was Ch. Osmart Bonnie Blue Braid, her dam being Ch. Edelweiss of Tambora. Juno was born black, turned a beautiful light silver in her juvenile coat change then went back to dark slate. She had a lovely straight coat and a three quarter white collar. She never produced any other colour puppy than black or blue, even though she was mated for her last two litters to Pure Magic of Willowmead, who regularly produced brown puppies, and several of her puppies proved dominant black or dominant black/blue, which is interesting for students of colour breeding as Braid was blue and Edelweiss was brown.

Juno loved the show ring. She went down to her first show held by the Collie Club of Wales in Cardiff, approximately a two hour drive. She was a travel sick puppy, never dribbled, was just sick, and as she had been sick about four times on the journey, I was pretty fed up by the time we arrived and went into the show offering her to anybody who would like her, all in jest. I'm not sure what excuse I would have had to think up if any one had taken me seriously. Well you can imagine my delight when she went Best of Breed, as she was only six and a half months old. At about her third show, she had just won her usual first and the steward was handing me the red card, when she suddenly started to heave to be sick. I rushed her outside the hall, where she only brought up a bit of bile. I was very concerned that she was going to be ill, maybe contracted some dreadful disease, but as she seemed perfectly happy and her tail was vigorously wagging, she obviously was not ill.

At her very next show she won her class again, and at exactly the same moment, just as the card was being handed to me, Juno again started to heave. We only made it to the ring side this time, and I was beginning to get embarrassed. At the next show, again Juno won her class, but this time I was ready for her, and as the steward gave me her, as usual, red card, and Juno started to heave, I grabbed her mouth and held it tightly shut, smiling through gritted teeth, accepted my card, holding a heaving dogs mouth tightly shut, whilst her tail wagged furiously at the other end.

I had cured her of her travel sickness by holding her mouth tightly shut, it worked extremely well, as she soon learned, after about three tries, actually that it was much nicer not to be sick, much to everybody's relief. After just two goes whilst she was winning her class, she gave up that game too, so I was able to accept her cards with just her tail wagging. She never tried it at any time except when she won first, which might prove something perhaps.

Juno produced several Champion children, English Champion Willowmead Summer Wine, sire my own Braelyn Broadholme Crofter, and English Champion Willowmead Star Attraction, who managed top puppy, top junior and top dog, his sire was Pure Magic of Willowmead. Abroad, her Champion offspring were, International Champion Mystique of Willowmead, Grey Lady of Willowmead, a club best in show winner.

American Champion Spring Magic of Willowmead, all children of Crofter. Juno actually only reared 23 puppies in her three litters to Crofter and two to Magic, so not a bad amount of Champions on the whole.

Ch. Show B.I.S. 1973

Ch. Edenborough Blue Bracken (see Tambora Points Trophy winners, 72,73,74).

Ch. Black Magic of Willowmead

Ch. Show B.I.S. 1974

1974 show saw Charlie and Elsie Corderoy's Black Magic of Willowmead gaining his third C.C. title and Best in Show, Smokey had won his other two C.C.s at Paignton and Birmingham City shows, all in 1974, gaining his Junior Warrent at Cardiff, making 1974 really a year to remember.

Smokey was born on May 19th, 1973 and died in November 1986. His sire was Edenborough Soaring High, 2 C.C.s, and dam, my own Breckdale Pretty Maid, 1 C.C. 4 Reserve C.C.s He was a lovely mid dark slate with full white markings. As well as the three C.C.s, the first at only thirteen months old, and his Championship at eighteen months, he won three more, making a total of six C.C.s in all.

He won best of Breed twice at Crufts, in 1978 and 1980, with the Best opposite sex and bitch C.C. my own Ch. Willowmead Perfect Lady.

He had a super day at the first Southern Counties Bearded Collie Club Show with his offspring from five different litters winning first, second and third in minor puppy dog class, first and second in minor puppy bitch class, first in puppy bitch class and first in junior bitch class and best puppy in Show. To show his versatility, from a sixth litter, his daughter won first pre-beginners and beginners obedience at her first show, voted by the judge as the one showing most promise, so every puppy took home a card. Smokey finished off a super career in the veteran classes by winning a Veteran Stakes and qualifying for the finals. Smokey also sired a Champion son, Champion Sunbrec Sorcerer, and produced all four colours in his many litters.

He wasn't always well behaved though, one September in 1981, when Charlie and Elsie took their caravan to Leicester Champion show, their two Beardies, Smokey and Summer, along with Satchmo, their Newfoundland dog, looked spick and span after extensive grooming, they bedded down, in the awning their usually well behaved dogs, unleashed, and looked forward to the next days competion. Morning arrived and to their horror, the three had turned overnight into slimy green monsters. Evidently they had sneaked out for a moonlight dip, and had returned carrying most of the ponds surface muck with them, especially Smokey, he did not have any white at all, every bit completely green.

As Beardies were first in the ring, a race against time to clean off the dried slime and pond delights had to be faced. Poor Charlie, with Elsie's help, worked desperately, and it say's something about Smokey's disposition, who, after all the hassle, he was as always, ever eager to please, went on to win the reserve C.C. and Charlie's cherished ambition, won the Veteran Stakes.

Charlie and Elsie were able to laugh about the incident afterwards, but there is also a message in this tale, if you are showing Beardies, steer clear of slimy green water - especially with Newfoundlands around.

Sadly Smokey never made the Veteran Stakes grand final, much to Charlie and Elsie's great disappointment, as they were snowed in that weekend, that bit they did not find quite so amusing.

Ch. Show B.I.S. 1975

Don Maskills Champion Penhallows Pink Panther was the girl for 1975 she was bred by Mrs Joanne Pickford of Penhallows Bearded Collies. Her sire was Champion Osmart Black Barnacle from Penhallows and her dam Osmart Copper Necklace and she lived for thirteen and a half years. Her colour was a dark sandy, a really beautiful colour and her eyes were exceptionally dark, almost as dark as my own Perfect Lady's, who had the darkest eyes I have ever seen on a brown.

Panther won five Challenge Certificates, four with Best of Breed and eleven Reserve Challenge Certificates. She also had one Champion son, Becktara's Mr Bosley.

Panther had three litters, her first produced five puppies two blacks and three browns. Her second litter was two blacks and four browns and her third litter, three blacks and two brown puppies, so she really gave Don a very even selection.

The time I really remember Panther, was the year I judged Crufts. She came under me in Open bitch and I really fell for her. She could not have shown better, did everything Don asked of her and really sparkled as she went round the ring, so I just could not resist her charms and gave her Best of Breed.

Sadly, there was not a Club Show in 1976, due to the Kennel Club refusing the Bearded Collie Club their set of Challenge Certificates, I understand the Secretary applied for the Show Licence late and so we lost the show for that year.

Ch. Penhallows Pink Panther

Ch. Show B.I.S. 1977 and 1980

The only dog to ever win a Club Championship Show Best in Show twice is Mike and Janet Lewis's Champion Pepperland Lyric John at Potterdale, and although Mike and Janet had had several other Beardies before Lyric John, he was the dog that really took off for them in the show world, winning right from the word go.

I believe I was the first judge who gave him a best of breed, at about fourteen months old. I was very impressed with him, feeling he really had everything I look for in a Beardie, apart from, at that age, a fairly light eye, but that certainly darkened considerably as he matured. It never became the colour I really look for, a dark amber, but was certainly quite acceptable.

Winston, as Mike and Janet called him, was sired by Wishanger Buttertubs Pass by Quinbury and his dam was Pepperland Pandamonium. He was born in 1975 and his colour is really outstanding, being a beautiful rich red brown. He was shown extensively, and won thirty Challenge Certificates all told, including Best in show at both Leicester and Windsor championship shows as well as his two Club Show wins.

172

His list of champion offspring is really outstanding and includes English Champions Potterdale Ptolemy, Pipadene Cameo, Dearbolt Lord Snooty, Multan Magikana, Potterdale Privilege, Tamevalley Folk Lyric of Labooshar, Ansasra Arden Prince, Potterdale Just William, Binbusy Cadence, Binbusy Ballade, Tamevalley Easter Song of Potterdale, Diotima Dream Baby, Grizlinda Morning Monarch, Shilstone Minuet, Briaridge Lyrical Lord and Moonhills Midnight Treasure.

Winston only ever produced black and brown puppies, not being factored for the dilutes. Janet tells me Winston was a very kind dog and if ever they had visitors with small children, he would get down with his head on his front paws so he was at their level. He also loved puppies and would lie on the floor and let them climb all over him, a very unusual trait in an adult male, as most make off at speed if puppies want to play all over them. He is also a great extrovert dog, and was well known for his unpredictability in the show ring. Mike, who almost always handled him, never used to know whether he would behave or not whilst he was being shown.

Ch. Show B.I.S. 1978

1978 was the second year running for Mike and Janet Lewis to win Best in Show, this time with Champion Blumberg Hadriana at Potterdale.

Ch. Blumberg Hadriana at Potterdale

173

Her sire was Blumberg De-Roos Erasmus, bred by Tine Leonard of Blumberg Beardies and the dam was Chloe of Blumberg.

Hadriana was born in 1977 and is slate and white. She won five Challenge Certificates and proved to be a very successful dam, producing six champion offspring, Champions Potterdale Philiosopher, Potterdale Patch of Blue, Potterdale Ptolemy, Potterdale Conclusion, Potterdale Phoenix and Potterdale Byron. In her puppies, she only produced black and brown.

I remember when I judged her as a youngster, I was very impressed with her lovely movement, good quality coat and beautiful dark expressive eyes. Mike tells me she has always been a very strong character and is something of a matriarch at home.

Ch. Dearbolt Lady Ancorrie

Ch. Show B.I.S. 1979

1979 show saw Dearbolt Lady Ancorrie as Best in Show. Annie was bred by Beverley Cuddy, who still owns her, on the 25th May 1977. Her sire was Champion Charncroft Corinth and dam, Beverley's Champion Edenborough Sweet Lady, her colour is a lovely silver slate. Annie won three C.C.s and four reserve C.C.s. Her first litter to Champion Edenborough Star Turn at Beagold produced ten puppies, slates, one brown and a slate tri-colour. Her second litter was to Champion Orora's

Ch. Potterdale Classic at Moonhills with the Crufts Best in Show Cup and her puppies

Ch. Osmart Bonnie Blue Braid at Crufts

Ch. Edelweiss of Tambora

Ch. Willowmead A Star is Born

Ch. Willowmead Black Magic at Crufts when he won Best of Breed
with Charlie Corderoy

Ch. Swinford Sky Rocket at Macmont

Ch. Edenborough Blue Bracken

Brenda White with Ch. Moonhill Gold Digger
and Ch. Osmart Black Thorn at Moonhills

Ch. Willowmead Star Attraction aged eleven years

Ch. Pepperland Lyric John at Potterdale aged 13 years

Ch. Potterdale Ptolemy

Ch. Binbusy Ballade

Ch. Binbusy Ballade relaxing with her daughter Carama Charisma

Frank, when she had seven puppies, this time both slates and browns. Beverley tells me that Annie is a very sensible dog who is a joy to own. However she hasn't led a totally blameless life!! She blotted her copybook when the family were entertaining an American Beardie person - Jan Masters.

It was a lovely summers day and they had decided to give Jan some traditional strawberry and cream tarts with afternoon tea. They had puppies at the time and Jan wanted to have a quick play with them before their treat. As only sensible Annie was in the room, they felt sure the cakes would be safe when they placed them high, out of all but the most acrobatic dogs reach. Suffice to say the temptation of strawberries and cream proved too great and Jan had to make do with a chocolate biscuit.

Annie has only strayed into crime on one other occasion - this time to eat two pounds of wrapped sweets (Quality Street). To do this she had to knock a glass bowl off the top of the TV set, and carefully pick her way through the sweets being sure not to cut herself on the broken glass.

Annie is a very well respected member of Beverley's and her parents dog family. She is now the oldest, but for many years she has seen it as her duty to teach the youngsters about Christmas. Every year they place presents under the Christmas tree for dogs and people alike. The dogs presents consist of chews, choc drops, biscuits and even the odd Mars bar - all smelling very tempting to Beardie noses. the only time Beverley would ever hear Annie growl is when a naughty young pup attempts to open a present before Christmas Day!

Annie's most famous trait has been recorded for the archives. Her father, Corrie, was famous for his four feet off the floor leaps - Annie has her own version - a very graceful and elegant variation. She would jump up and down on the spot very slowly and gently if one of her human family left her somewhere she did not want to be - a form of silent protest.

Ch Show B.I.S. 1981

The best in show winner for 1981 was Champion Potterdale Patch of Blue, belonging to Mike and Janet Lewis who also bred him was sired by Champion Orora's Frank, his dam being Champion Blumberg Hadriana at Potterdale.

Patch of Blue, pet name Brian was born in 1980 and as his name suggests was born blue with a full white collar. Brian won three Challenge Certificates altogether, as Mike and Janet were concentrating more on his litter brother Philosopher. Brian was left at home for most of the time, in fact, at one time Mike and Janet nearly sold him, but as he was such a brilliant stud dog and his brother was more of a slow starter, Brian proved his worth and stayed at Potterdale.

Again, like his brother, he only produced black and blue puppies in his many litters.

Ch. Moonhill's Gold Digger

Ch. Potterdale Patch of Blue

Ch. Show B.I.S 1982

1982 Championship show Best in Show winner was Brenda White's homebred dog, Champion Moonhills Goldigger, pet name Digger, he was born 22.2.1979, and was a beautiful rich golden brown. His sire was Broadholme Buccaneer and his dam Brenda's Champion Osmart Black Thorn at Moonhills. Digger won four Challenge Certificates and 3 Reserve Challenge Certificates. He produced both black and brown puppies, sadly no champion offspring, as he had to be withdrawn from stud at a fairly young age, due to an infection causing him to go sterile. Digger came from the first litter bred by Brenda.

She tells me he was a very intelligent dog and always had one eye on the horizon, incase something exciting was about to happen, imagine his delight when suddenly one day, a whole flock of sheep were turned out in the pastures at the back of Brenda's house. Without Brenda realising that Digger had disappeared, he had decided to go and practice what he had been bred for, namely, working those sheep. About ten minutes later Brenda discovered him, hard at it, he had done no damage to the flock and seemed to have worked out how to do formation herding beautifully-round them up, then go through the middle and split them into two bunches, then round them up, then split them, he was having the time of his life. Brenda finally managed to get his attention, call him to her, and take him home, duly put in his place.

Later that day the farmer arrived on the doorstep, confirming that Digger had done no damage to the flock, but making his displeasure clear that Brenda's dog had been in the sheep at all.

Two days later the same farmer was back on the doorstep, shuffling nervously from foot to foot - this time he had come with a request - could Digger go and assist him get three fields of sheep in, as his friend with the border Collie had not turned up. Digger, needless to say, was delighted and within half an hour had successfully rounded all the sheep up.

Ch. Show B.I.S. 1983

1983 was Maureen Betts Pipadene Camio's Best in Show day. Camio, pet name, Millie, was sired by Pepperland Lyric John at Potterdale and her dam was homebred, Pipadene Cassiopeia. Millie was born on the 20th September 1980 and is a very dark slate and white. She is as near to black, without being totally black, as any Beardie I have ever seen. Millie won three C.C.s and two Championship show, best in shows, her other one was at Southern Counties Bearded Collie Club Champion Show. I was judging bitches that day with Tom Horner, one of our top ranking all-rounders, judging dogs. I really fell for Millie's charms and her lovely expressive dark eyes and could not resist giving her bitch C.C. Mr Horner agreed with me to award her Best in Show.

Millie was a most prolific bitch to breed from, as she produced twelve

Ch. Pipadene Camio

puppies in each of her four litters, making a total of forty eight puppies, but the only colours she whelped were black and brown. Out of those litters there were two champions, Pipadene Hosanna and Pipadene High Society.

Millie really took after her mother, Cassie, as she was one of eleven, very even puppies, infact she was a champion that nearly never was. Millie had an identical twin, something I have had fairly frequently in my own litters. Maureen tells me she had fallen in love with Millie as soon as she was born, she doesn't know why, again, something I can fully appreciate, as I have done the same thing with most of the dogs I have kept from my own bitches, there is just something at birth, that shows you a glimpse of future promise, but to go back to Millie and her twin, the twin did have one slight distinguishing mark, inasmuch that she had a small pigment spot on her top lip. It came to the day when the rest of the litter were going to their new homes, and the twins new owner arrived to collect their puppy, Maureen quickly picked out, what she thought was the twin, and popped her on to her new owners knee, where she sat whilst they chatted, prior to leaving.

It wasn't till quite some time later, infact they were just about to go, when Maureen suddenly realised it was Millie who was about to go to a new home, and not the twin. What a relief that the mistake was discovered in time, especially as Millie became Maureens first Champion.

Ch. Show B.I.S. 1984

1983 was Champion Briaridge Lyrical Lords Day. He is owned by Paul and Jean Keith and was bought as a pet with no idea of being shown. Infact he was thirteen months old before he made his debut into the show ring. Briar was bred by Barbara Walker Smith, and when she saw how well he had grown up, she persuaded Paul and Jean to have a go at showing him. They are now completely hooked and have founded the Latchmede Bearded Collies.

Briar was born on the 13th July 1981, his sire is Champion Pepperland Lyric John at Potterdale, dam Briaridge Erin Blue, his colour is a nice mid-slate. As well as his club Best in Show win, he won Birmingham Canine Societies Championship Show Working Group in August 1986, and so far has one Champion offspring, my own Champion Willowmead Plain and Fancy.

Briar is a versatile lad, siring all four colours, mainly slates but with several really dark browns there too, only four blues and one fawn as yet in approximately 130 puppies.

Briar won his third and qualifying Challenge Certificate on 5th May 1985 and ended up a super day by visiting Willowmead en route for home, where he met and fell in love with Willowmead Silver Lace, so he

Ch. Briaridge Lyrical Lord

travelled home a very happy dog.

Due to the somewhat delayed homecoming, as Jean and Paul approached their home, the front window appeared to be boarded up, as they drew nearer, much to their relief and amusement, instead of their first fears being realised that the house had been broken into, to the contrary, the window had been decorated with a banner across saying "Congratulations - Champion Briar" the remainder of the house was festooned with balloons and streamers.

The following Friday John and Barbara Walker Smith, who bred Briar, invited Paul and Jean out for a celebration dinner and arrived at 7.45 to take them there, but instead of arriving at what they thought was their destination, as they were passing Bob and Penny Makins Kennels, John suddenly turned the wheel and drove onto the forecourt.

Paul and Jean will never forget the sight that met their eyes. standing there were approximately 70 guests, made up of family and Beardie friends from North Yorkshire, Lancashire, Nottinghamshire and Derbyshire who had gathered together to give them a surprise party. The main person behind all the planning and secrecy was Annette Taylor, who along with others, had given them the help and encouragement and they were able to celebrate Briar becoming Champion Briaridge Lyrical Lord.

Jean tells me they will both treasure all these wonderful memories, thanks to a seven week old Beardie, bought as a pet and coaxed into the show ring.

Ch. Show B.I.S. 1985

1985 was the day that my own dog, Champion Willowmead Red Admiral went Best in Show. Pet name Addy, he was born 19.2.82 with his sire being my own dog, American Champion Willowmead Red Ruairidh, prior to his export to America and Willowmead Winter Memory.

Addy was born one of the darkest browns I have ever seen, but paled out to almost white as a junior. He returned to his lovely dark brown when his adult coat came in.

Addy won three Challenge Certificates and produced all four colours, including browns with the darkest eyes I have ever seen, and gorgeous happy extrovert temperaments, as I found out when I acquired his daughter Pippin, at seven weeks of age, her main love in life being people.

Addy was one of a litter of eight puppies, Memory had her usual mix of black, brown and blue puppies and I liked the look of Addy at birth. I sold him to a girl called Gail Ridgard, who had asked for a show puppy dog. I remember her saying is he good enough to show, because she was very keen to win well. I said if she did not like him I would keep him myself and made her decide to take him, saying 'he must be good then'. Gail trained and presented Addy very well, and was winning everywhere she took him, including Best Puppy in Show at the Club Championship

Ch. Willowmead Red Admiral

Show, so I was delighted and thought he had a good home for life. Imagine my surprise and dismay to suddenly get a telephone call when Addy was about thirteen to fourteen months old, saying he, and Gail's other two dogs had been dumped in the nearby kennels, and she had gone off with a boyfriend leaving her husband and small boy. I rushed off to the kennels and collected Addy and asked the owners to inform Gail that I had him. So when she got in touch I repaid her all her monies for Addy, and had him transferred back to my name, and started to show him myself.

Time passed, and I decided four stud dogs were too many, as I still had Red Ruairidh, his sire, and decided to let Addy go, in partnership to a friend of many years standing, John Stanbridge, who had just lost his old Champion Benedict Morning Mist, Addy's grandsire, and that is where he has lived ever since. It has been in John's capable hands that Addy has won his championship.

Ch. Show B.I.S. 1986

1986 Best in Show was Champion Potterdale Ptolemy, pet name Tom, who was bred and owned by Mike and Janet Lewis. Tom's sire is Champion Pepperland Lyric John at Potterdale and his dam is Champion Blumberg Hadriana at Potterdale. He was born in 1983 and is a beautiful brown with full white markings.

He won a total of four Challenge Certificates including, as well as his club Show win, Reserve Best in Show at the Scottish Working Breeds Championship Show. He has sired one champion son so far, Champion Coalacre Curiosity and produces slate, brown, blue, fawn and tri-colour puppies, so is a very versatile lad.

I well remember being regularly in the ring with Tom, as he is very near in age, to my own dog, Willowmead Man of the Moment. We regularly competed together. Janet always said how easy Tom was to show as nothing ever bothered him, but every dog has something that can change his usual happy demeanour.

Tom loves to chase things, one day, when Mike and Janet were camping with the dogs, he decided to chase a Deerhound. The Deerhound stood and looked at Tom, who promptly decided it was not such a good idea after all, and turned and ran. The Deerhound pursued him with long easy strides, obviously enjoying the game. Poor Tom, with the tables turned, was terrified.

Tom has another favourite hobby, perhaps a bit safer, he loves collecting things, especially bones. He likes to have all his toys, especially the bones in a nice pile in with him, proving the saying, a dog in the manger, is quite correct to Beardies too.

Ch. Show B.I.S. 1987

1987 Champion Show Best in Show was Althea Richardson's Champion Binbusy Ballade's Day. Pet name "Dee", she was sired by Champion Pepperlands Lyric John at Potterdale out of Charncroft Canticle and bred by Steve and Rosie Haywood. She was born 23rd August 1982, and is typically one of Lyric John's beautiful dark brown puppies. Dee won three Challenge Certificates and three Reserve Challenge Certificates. She also won a Championship show Working Group. Dee has had two litters, her first litter consisted of seven puppies, two browns and five slates including one tri-colour slate. Her second litter had nine puppies, three browns and six slates. Althea tells me she booked a bitch from Dee's dam because she had always been a great fan of the Charncroft line and although she can relate to the Charncroft type through Dee, she most definitely got a Lyric John daughter.

Dee is a very faithful and loyal companion to Althea but she is very capable of thinking and acting for herself. On two occasions when Mac (Champion Swinford Sky Rocket at Macmont, one of Althea's other Beardies) heard thunder and decided to take himself home in the middle of their walk, she ran after him and just ran around him until he sat and waited for Althea. On the second occasion she actually held onto his beard until he got the message and waited for Althea. She has displayed this capability on other occasions and as her instincts take over in this way none of Althea's commands would get through to her. Fortunately she has a very strong sense of what's right and wrong so has never let Althea down.

Ch. Potterdale Privilege

Tambora Points Trophy 1989
Ch. Show B.I.S. 1988

1988 it was once again a dog belonging to Mike and Janet Lewis, who won the Best in Show spot. This time it was Champion Potterdale Privilege, pet name Eric. His sire is Champion Pepperlands Lyric John at Potterdale with his dam being Ch. Potterdale Persuasion.

Eric was born in 1986 and is now a dark slate, after being a very pale silver as a junior dog. At the moment he has fourteen Challenge Certificates but I'm sure he will finish his show career with far more than that. He has done very well with his Best in Show wins, as well as his Club Championship Show win, he has also been Best in Show at National Working Breeds Championship Show, Leeds City Championship Show and a Southern Counties Bearded Collie Club Show.

As he is still relatively young, he has not produced any Champion offspring yet, but he's had black, brown and blue puppies in his litters.

Janet tells me that of all their dogs, Eric is the clown of the group and is a great show off, especially when they have any visitors. He must always be the centre of attention, and will do lots of tricks to make sure he is the one the visitors really notice. His favourite place to lie is on the kitchen floor, trying to imitate a bearskin rug, flat on his tummy, legs outstretched behind.

Ch. Potterdale Premier

Ch. Show B.I.S. 1989

1989 was the year Mike and Janet Lewis's lovely brown dog, Champion Potterdale Premier went best in show. Pet name "Henry", his sire is Potterdale Anderson and his dam Champion Tamevalley Easter Song of Potterdale. Henry was born 12th February 1987, and has three Challenge Certificates so far and three Reserve Challenge Certificates. He only produces slate and brown puppies and as he is still only three years old has as yet no Champion offspring.

Janet tells me he is the Beardie they did not ever think would make a show dog. Henry has always loved jumping, especially on and off anything. Then one day he jumped up onto his crate, and on jumping off he completely tore out one of his claws, it says a lot for his excellent temperament, inasmuch that he still loves his crate, and will, if given the opportunity, still jump onto the top. It seems he will not learn by his mistakes, as another of his favourite tricks is to jump onto the kitchen table and curl up and go to sleep. One day Mike was busy eating his dinner, when suddenly Henry decided he would have his usual nap on the same table, and up he hopped. Straight into Mike's dinner. Needless to say he was removed twice as fast as he went up, and since then has always looked onto the table before he jumps up, just incase there might be a rather annoyed Master eating dinner there.

Tambora Points Trophy Winners

Ch. Bracken Boy of Bothkennar

Tambora Points Trophy 1968

The Tambora Trophy was the first points trophy to be offered in the breed for the top winning Beardie of the year. It was donated by Jackie Tidmarsh of the Tambora Bearded Collies. the first dog to win it in 1968 was Shirley Holmes Champion Bracken Boy of Bothkennar. Bracken Boy was born on 11th November 1962 and died August 1st, 1974. He won fifteen Challenge Certificates and numerous reserve challenge certificates, including Best of Breed at Crufts in 1969. Bracken Boy was a dark slate with a lovely dark eye to match. Shirley tells me he was noted for his soundness and ability to jump!!!

He was the last Bothkennar Champion and the foundation for the Edenborough Beardies. He sired one English Champion, Rowdina Rustler and several overseas champions. His sire Bravo of Bothkennar and dam Champion Blue Bonnie of Bothkennar.

Ch. Edelweiss of Tambora at Crufts

Tambora Points Trophy 1969

1969 saw Jackie Tidmarsh win her own points trophy with homebred Champion Edelweiss of Tambora. Edelweiss, which was her pet name as well as her registered one, was sired by Champion Wishanger Cairnbhan, her dam being Jackie's Burdock of Tambora. She was born on the 6th, April 1967, and died 20th February 1980. Edelweiss was a beautiful dark brown and white. She won a total of six Challenge Certificates, three with Best of Breed, including two Challenge Certificates at Crufts, one with Best of Breed.

Edelweiss proved a very successful dam with several Champion offspring including my own Champion Willowmead Juno of Tambora, Canadian Champion Bronze Javelin of Tambora, Canadian Champion Jeannie of Tambora, South African Champion Willowmead Marguerite of Tambora, Danish Champion Tambora's Peggy Brown and Swedish Champion Tambora's Penny Brown. She had five litters all told, producing thirty one puppies, fifteen black and white and sixteen brown and white. Litter one had seven puppies, five black, two brown, litter two, eight puppies, two black, six brown. Litter three, six puppies, three black three brown, litter four, five puppies, two black three brown, litter five, five puppies, three black two brown.

The following story that Jackie told me about Edelweiss, I can fully appreciate. Edelweiss like most Beardies had a good appetite, she quite often stole food, one night Jackie left a chicken thawing in the front room well out of reach of the dogs, or so she thought. It was on top of the television about four feet from the ground with no chairs to make access easy, and in a deep glass bowl. The next morning Jackie went to get the chicken ready for the oven but it had gone, the bowl was exactly where Jackie had left it, but the bird had flown, so to speak. a search found Edelweiss enjoying a good breakfast. The meat that Sunday was nicely carved before it reached the table, she daren't serve a one winged, half breasted chicken.

I had already found exactly the same trait in Edelweiss myself, she had come to be mated and was staying a few days, the first day, as she was kept in the house for her visit, she devoured a whole box of corn flakes, three quarters of a large loaf, and to finish breakfast properly, half a pound of butter. I think it must have been the butter that put the lid on things, as she was very sick indeed in one of my dog baskets, which I decided to burn rather than try to clean, afterwards everything was placed far to high for even the most agile Beardie to reach.

Edelweiss was a very devoted family dog and when Emily, Jackie's youngest child, came home from hospital after a minor operation, breath still smelling of anaesthetic, they laid her on the settee where she slept allday. Edelweiss refused to leave her side, and kept giving Jackie very reproachful looks because she was doing chores instead of keeping vigil with her. It was time to pick up the eldest two from school, so Jackie asked granddad to keep an eye on Emily for her. No sooner had she gone through the door, Edelweiss started to bark and nothing Granddad could do would stop her. Jackie came home to bedlam, a barking anxious dog, a screaming toddler, and a very frustrated father-in-law.

Edelweiss isn't the only thief in the Tambora clan, her Great Great Granddaughter, Inky, although greedy, is very delicate and ladylike in her methods. Jackie had cooked some pasties, special ones that she'd tried to copy from some they had had in France, friends were coming for supper, Jackie had cooked two each for the men, and one each for the women (sexist, I hear you shout!) Jackie left them cooling on a wire tray, one went missing right from the middle. Jackie immediately blamed husband, John, and shouted to him that as he had pinched a pastie, he would have to make do with one that night . . . Yes, you've guessed, it wasn't John, but little Inky, very carefully she had reached up and taken the one that took her fancy, she was just licking up the last of the crumbs when Jackie found her.

Ch. Wishanger Waterfall

Tambora Points Trophy 1970

1970 was Champion Wishanger Waterfall's year, her sire was Will O'Wisp of Willowmead and her dam, Wishanger River Shirburn. Waterfall was born on the 23rd April, 1968, and was a beautiful silver slate in colour, with full white markings. Waterfall only had two litters of puppies, her first to Wishanger Cairnbhan, which produced the gorgeous rich golden brown Champion Glenwin King Aire Loch, who belonged to Barbro Finkelstein in Sweden, which is where I saw him, when I went over there to judge. There were nine puppies in that litter. Her second and last litter was to Champion Davealex Royle Baron, in which there were five puppies, and although several of her puppies went abroad, apart from King Aire Loch, they went as pets, so did not go in the show ring. Waterfall only produced black and brown puppies, but from her pedigree, I would have been very surprised indeed if she had either blues or fawns.

Waterfall was not a baby puppy when Trish first had her from Mary Partridge, her breeder. Infact, I saw her at Mary's when she was five months old, and she was only put on the lead for the first time that day, so when Trish collected her shortly afterwards, she still had had very little lead training, and no exposure to heavy traffic and noise, as Mary lived in a very small quiet village. Trish, who was used to staid and sensible old family dogs, did not realise all this, and proudly took her beautiful new puppy out for a walk.

Seeing a shop selling ice cream, Trish decided she would buy one, so tied Waterfall up to the ice cream sign, a fairly heavy one, sunk into a concrete base, and went into the shop to make her purchase. Of course, the inevitable happened and a large lorry raced past. Waterfall, who had never seen such a monster in all her short life, just bolted, and took the ice cream sign, complete with concrete base, flying down the road.

Trish raced out of the shop and rapidly caught her very frightened puppy and soon soothed away her fears. Infact, she did such a good job of it, that Waterfall, as well as winning five Challenge Certificates, worked up to test A in obedience, and even competed in working trails, a fantastic achievement after a somewhat inauspicious start to life with Trish. She lived a long and happy life and was the first of the Glenwin Beardies belonging to Trish Gilpin.

Ch. Willomead Juno of Tambora

Tambora Points Trophy 1971

1971 Tambora Points trophy winner was my own Champion Willowmead Juno of Tambora. Her details are under the Championship show winners as she won both. Juno was a dog that always tried to be as brave as a lion. She was always an extreme extrovert, simply loved people, but had very definite ideas as to what constituted good behaviour.

189

As none of my dogs have any contact with small children, apart from when we go out of course, when people come to see the dogs and have any children under five or six, I do usually ask the parents to keep them on the chairs, rather than rushing about in the lounge, which most of them, realising the situation, are only to happy to do. When I had Juno she made quite sure they behaved for me. If any small tot would start to misbehave and rush around, she would immediately leave the nice visitor who was at that moment stroking and fussing her, calmly trot across to the naughty small child and nip it. She would never even mark the skin, just a small pinch, but it always had the effect of very rapid return to parents of miscreant child, and we could all go back to chatting in peace.

But to return to the one and only thing that really petrified Juno, and that was the vet. Up to eleven years old, all she ever had from her friendly vet man, was her yearly boosters and her HD X-ray, apart from being checked over after whelping, which she didn't mind at all, because that was at home. Take her to the surgery and she would become a quivering heap. In the car she was sometimes somewhat too enthusiastic about jumping out as soon as I opened the rear door, but drive up to the vet's, and she would be clinging to the back of the seat, the dog guard, the windows, or anything, legs firmly planted, so that she had to be forcibly dragged out, you couldn't lift her, as all four legs would go in four different directions to grab anything they could to prevent her leaving her safe haven. I remember once taking her into the waiting room, there was only one other dog in there, a huge Irish Wolfhound and he was sitting there, looking extremely doleful and shaking like a leaf, so when I sat down with Juno, it was really quite amusing to see, I'm sure the floor shook, with two very great cowards, sitting there, shivering as if the end of the world was nigh.

Tambora Points Trophy 1972, 73, 74

For all three years of 1972, 1973 and 1974 Champion Edenborough Blue Bracken was the Tambora Points Triophy winner, bred and owned by Shirley Holmes of Edenborough Bearded Collies.

He was sired by Rowdina Grey Fella and his dam was Blue Maggie from Osmart. Blue Bracken who was always affectionately known as Percy was indeed a top dog. His colour was a beautiful blue with full white markings and his record in the show world has never been beaten. He amassed a marvellous total of thirty nine Challenge Certificates and twenty three Reserve Challenge Certificates. He was best of breed at Crufts in both 1973 and 1974 and best opposite sex in 1977.

Percy was also the very first Beardie to ever win Best in Show at an all breed Championship Show. I well remember that day, as my own bitch, Breckdale Pretty Maid was bitch Challenge Certificate winner and best opposite sex. Not content with being the first Beardie, he achieved the same super win no less than on eleven occasions, his last one at ten years of age, just proving how well Beardies last. He was also the very first winner of the title of Veteran of the Year, all breeds.

Percy produced all four colours in his offspring, including eleven English champions, Champions Edenborough Sweet Lady, Edenborough Amazing Grace, Edenborough Kara Kara, Edenborough Grey Shadow, all from the mating to Broadholme Christina, Edenborough Star Turn at Beagold, Edenborough Sweet Lord, Willowmead Perfect Lady, Charncroft Country Maid, Chauntelle Limelight and Mosswood Concorde. Limelight,

Ch. Edenborough Blue Bracken

Grey Shadow and Kara Kara were all exported after gaining their English titles. They won further titles and produced many overseas champions as Percy did himself. His last son, born on Percy's thirteenth birthday, Champion Edenborough Sweet Lord, was to be the last English Champion from Percy. Percy was most certainly a top winner and a top stud dog to the end.

Tambora Points Trophy 1975-76

Both 1975 and 1976 were won by Champion Mignonette of Willowmead at Orora, owned by Bryony Harcourt-Brown, of Orora Beardies and bred by myself. Miggy's sire was Champion Wishanger Cairnbhan, her dam being Champion Broadholme Cindy Sue of Willowmead. Miggy was full sister to my own Champion Willowmead Super Honey, but I did the mating twice, Honey being from the first litter and Miggy from the second. Miggy was born on 29.10.1972 and died in February 1988, in her seventeenth year.

Her show success was outstanding, winning twelve Challenge Certificates, Reserve Best in Show National Working Breeds Championship Show, won the group at Peterborough Championship Show and Reserve in group at Leicester Championship Show. She was also an excellent producer as she had three English Champion offspring, Champions Orora's Frank, Orora's Sugar Plum, Orora's Sugar Bush and Challenge Certificate winner Orora's Demitrius amongst many overseas Champions. In all her puppies she would only produce slates and browns, unlike her sister Honey, who also had fawns and blues. Miggy wasn't just a glamorous showgirl, she had a very naughty streak there too. Bryony tells me that she had a favourite game that would prove infuriating to her human and dog friends. When Bryony took her out for a walk, as she lived mainly in the house, she would disappear off to the Kennels and race up and down outside all the Kennel runs barking, which would set off all the inhabitants to hysterical excitement. Bryony would rush off to catch her and chastise the culprit, only to see Miggy sitting quietly some way away, with the most angelic smile on her face, as if to say "It's absolutely nothing to do with me" type of expression, so she usually got away with it, as Bryony says, how can you be angry with a dog looking like that.

Miggy was a beautiful dog, with a full white collar and a lovely straight silver grey coat. She had the movement I always look for, reachy, smooth and graceful. a dog I was very proud to have bred.

Ch. Osmart Black Thorn of Moonhill, owned by Brenda White

Tambora Point Trophy 1980

1980 Tambora Points Trophy was won by Brenda White's Champion Osmart Black Thorn at Moonhill. Pet name "Tatters", she was a daughter of Champion Osmart Bonnie Blue Braid, her dam being Tambora's Black Petal. Tatters was born on 19th, June 1975, and was a dark slate and white bitch. She won nine Challenge Certificates and eight Reserve Challenge Certificates, two Championship Show Working Groups as well. Tatters produced slate, brown and blue puppies and had three

English Champion offspring, Moonhills Gold Digger, Moonhills Country Gentleman and Moonhills Midnight Treasure. Tatters was the foundation bitch of the Moonhills Beardies.

Brenda tells me she was the Granny for all and every puppy, she was quite unflappable with all their antics, infact as Brenda puts it "bombproof". As well as being so good though, Tatters had the usual Beardie streak of love of food, especially, love of human food. Brenda says she will never forget the Christmas day, they had all eaten the usual Christmas lunch of turkey and Christmas pudding, the remains of which had been left to cool in the kitchen, prior to being placed in the fridge. Brenda went into the kitchen to make a cup of tea to find a rather shamefaced Tatters, who had demolished both wings both legs and half a breast, Brenda says they had only had half a breast for their meal too, so Tatters had really made an excellent lunch. Needless to say Tatters did not get any dinner that night!!!

Ch. Willowmead Star Attraction

Tambora Points Trophy 1981

1981 was Champion Willowmead Star Attraction's year. Owned by Sue and Willie O'Brien and bred by myself, Stanley is a dark slate with full white markings. He was born on 10.11.1978. He has a total of twelve Challenge Certificates, eleven with Best of Breed, and twelve Reserve

Challenge Certificates and was Best in Show twice at Championship Shows. He has, so far, one English Champion daughter, Champion Willowmead A Star is Born and Champion Sammara Star Abide in Denmark, amongst his many other Champion offspring abroad.

Stanley is a dominant black dog, having never produced any other colour to all colours of visiting bitches, which is interesting, as his sire is Pure Magic of Willowmead, who produced black, brown and blue and his dam is Champion Willowmead Juno of Tambora who again produced blacks and blues. Juno was from a blue to brown mating. Touch of Magic, Stanley's litter sister also is dominant for black and blue.

When Sue and Willie approached me to acquire a show quality puppy, I had Juno in whelp to Magic, and had great hopes that it would be a super litter. Previously, Juno mated to Crofter, had produced many champion offspring, and I could see no reason to expect a poor quality litter and as soon as they were born, I knew I had a special litter, nine beautiful, even, puppies. Juno always whelped very small puppies, round about seven to ten ounces at birth, and this was to be her last litter, as she was getting on by now. She was also getting very careless with her babies, she never was particularly careful, even when young, she was inclined to get in with her babies and just plonk down. If a puppy was underneath and squeaked, there were plenty more squeaking elsewhere. She managed in the first twenty four hours to squash four of her nine puppies. If I left her for a second, which of course, I had to do, I would come back to another flattened puppy. After that, the puppies were getting stronger and Juno more careful, so we didn't lose any more. Thank heavens, or one of the best Beardies I have ever known would not have survived to do all the winning he has.

Stanley was not just a pretty face either, as Sue tells me. He went to live with her sister some six miles away and was to be a pet for her, companion for her other Beardie, and hopefully Sue and Willie's show dog. Little did Sue know at that stage, a great show dog. Top puppy, top Junior and a Champion at two years of age, Tambora Points Trophy winner and to their greatest delight, Best of Breed at Crufts in 1982.

Throughout this illustrious career, he continued to live happily as a family pet with Sue's sister and became more and more in demand as a stud dog, due to this successful show career. When his services were required, he was always brought over to Sue and Willie's house by car, the deed carried out and he would be returned to Sue's sister. This situation worked beautifully, until one day when Stanley decided to pack his bags and disappear over the fence and make his way, all on his own, back to Sue and Willie's. This involved travelling six miles and crossing several busy roads, including the main A4 into London. On realising he had disappeared frantic search parties were organised and the Police contacted, as not only was he an adored pet, but a great show dog and the thought of him being hit by a car was too terrible to contemplate.

They need not have worried though, this intelligent dog arrived safely at Sue and Willie's house, some hours later, filthy dirty, but quite confident and happy in his achievement. He was expectantly looking for the lady his thoughts had alluded him into believing he would find there. Stanley was returned back home to Sue's sister, with a flea in his superior ear. To a great show dog though, this had little effect, for a month later, he packed his bags and made the journey again. At this point, Sue's sister, reluctantly, yet relieved, decided that Stanley must permanently reside with Sue and Willie, which he has done ever since and never attempted to go walk-abouts again.

That doesn't mean he hasn't thought about it though, Sue says: "there's many a time she catches sight of that noble gent (now twelve years) sitting in the middle of the garden 'pointing east', with his nose sniffing skywards". Sue says Stanley is the 'thinker' of their doggy family, and she thinks she knows his thoughts.

Ch. Tamevalley Easter Song of Potterdale

Tambora Points Trophy 1982

1982 was the year that Champion Tamevalley Easter Song of Potterdale won the Tambora Points Trophy. Tally, as she was called at home, was bred by Miss Maureen Reader of Tamevalley Beardies, her sire was Mike and Janet Lewis's Champion Pepperland Lyric John at Potterdale and her dam was Maureen's Champion Dutch Bonnet of

Willowmead.

Tally was born in 1978 and is a lovely silver grey, the colour I really love, and she produced it in many of her offpsring too.

Tally was the top bitch Challenge Certificate winner for some time, until she lost that honour to her daughter, Classic. Tally won nineteen Challenge Certificates altogether. She won one other Championship Show Best in Show at the Southern Counties Bearded Collie Club Show and also Reserve Best in Show at both South Wales Kennel Association Show and Driffield Championship Show.

Her champion offspring are really an impressive list for a bitch to produce, proving she really passed on her excellent qualities, even being mated to several different dogs. Her English champion children are Champions Potterdale Prelude, Potterdale Serenade, Potterdale Philanderer, Potterdale Symphony, Potterdale Classic of Moonhill, Potterdale Persuasion, Potterdale Premier.

Tally, as her sire Winston, only produced black and brown puppies. Janet usually handled Tally in the show ring and found it very amusing that she, like my own Juno, knew when she had won, but Tally had an easier habit to deal with, she always loved to bark when being handed her red card. She would also bark when her photo was being taken, a fairly regular event with all her winning. Janet said she will always be remembered by her, for her wow! wow! which she has passed on to many of her children.

Ch. Orora's Frank

Tambora Points Trophy 1983, 84

Champion Orora's Frank bred and owned by Bryony Harcourt-Brown again won both 1983 and 1984 Tambora Point Trophy as Bryony's Miggy had done previously for her mistress. Frank is a son of Miggy, Champion Mignonette of Willowmead at Orora, this time she was mated to champion Osmart Bonnie Blue Braid and Frank was born 26.8.1977 and like his dam is a lovely slate and white.

Frank is another outstanding Beardie as he has won eighteen Challenge Certificates all told, also winning a group at Scottish Kennel Club Championship Show. He has proved an excellent sire, producing all four colours in his offspring and eleven English Champion children including, Champions Potterdale Persuasion, Potterdale Classic of Moonhill, Potterdale Patch of Blue, Potterdale Philosopher, Scapafield True Melody, Mr Bosley of Becktara Diotima Gabriella, Chriscaro Christal, Chriscaro Chianti, Sunkap Bartholomew at Cregagh and Dearbolt Hooray Henry. This is to a variety of bitches of different lines and types which proves what a dominant sire he has proved to be.

He also stayed young in both looks and disposition, as Bryony was still showing and winning well with him up to his twelfth year. He had attended Crufts, a long trip for Frank and Bryony as they live well up in the North of England and Crufts was held in London at that time, down in the South. Well, they went home and Frank had, to his delight, a bitch come to stud, he did his usual rapid mating on the same night that he had travelled home. The next morning Bryony let him out to go his walk and he went the wrong way in his hurry to go. Bryony called him, and rather than go the long way round, he jumped straight over a five barred gate, a good jump for even a young dog. He then realised Bryony was still the other side, so hopped straight back over the gate again, just to prove it was not a fluke going over it once. I think he might have thought his lovely lady friend of the previous night had returned to visit him, or was it just boundless joie de vivre, but it just proves Beardies certainly can stay fit and healthy to a good age.

Tambora Points Trophy 1985

1985 saw Mike and Janet Lewis's Champion Potterdale Philosopher win the top dog spot. I remember I judged him the first time he came out and was very pleased with his beautiful head. He had a lovely easy going temperament and always looked so easy to handle in the show ring.

Philosopher, pet name Angus, was sired by Champion Orora's Frank, his dam being Champion Blumberg Hadriana at Potterdale and was born in 1980. His colour is a mid to dark slate and he produces both slate and blue puppies. Angus has won eleven Challenge Certificates and was Best in Show at the Southern Counties Bearded Collie Club Show, won the Working Group at Darlington Championship Show and Reserve Best

Ch. Potterdale Philosopher

in Show at Ladies Kennel Association Championship Show.

His list of champion offspring is pretty good too, including Champions Potterdale Prelude, Potterdale Serenade, Potterdale Philanderer, Potterdale Symphony, Gillaber Highland Lament, Chriscaro Chantelle, Sunkap Chantilly and Hecatie Hellraiser.

Angus wasn't just a pretty face either. As a junior dog, Mike and Janet took him to a Club Working Test day, held in the orchard at a Club member's home. He passed the Primary Test with no problem and they then decided to have a go at the Junior Test, so in the half hour tea break, Mike and Janet taught Angus to jump, stay and retrieve. What did he retrieve, an apple of course. He passed the test with flying colours, and spent the rest of the afternoon chasing apples.

Tambora Points Trophy 1986, 88

1986 and 1988 the Tambora Points Trophy was won by Brenda White's Champion Classic of Moonhills. Pet name "Cassie" her sire is Champion Orora's Frank and her dam is Champion Tamevalley Easter Song of Potterdale, herself the top Challenge Certificate winner till Cassie beat her. Cassie was born 6th November 1983 and is a beautiful silver slate. She has won 25 Challenge Certificates, the most for any Beardie bitch ever, and 12 reserve Challenge Certificates. Cassie won 5 all breed Championship Show Best in Shows, three Championship Show Reserve Best in Show, eleven Championship Show groups and two reserve Championship Show groups, a really tremendous record and one that I doubt will ever be taken from her. Cassie had produced all four colours in her puppies and has an American and Canadian Champion son, Moonhills Classic Treasure and an English son, Moonhills Midnight Classic who has three reserve Challenge Certificates.

Brenda says the most important day Cassie ever had must be the day she won Best in Show at Crufts in 1988. Brenda knew she had a very special Beardie right from the very first day she collected her from Mike and Janet Lewis, her breeders, Cassie had star appeal even as a small puppy. As a show dog, Cassie always did everything Brenda asked of her, and enjoyed every minute at all the shows she attended. She always had the special sparkle needed to win in all the top spots. When she won the breed and then the Group at Crufts, Brenda started to hope. The morning of the last day of Crufts, Brenda and Cassie went out for their usual early morning jog, one, to calm Brenda's nerves, and two, to loosen Cassie up for her to give of her best when she had to compete with all the other Group winners. Cassie showed to perfection, just as if she knew this was really special and of course, she won through to the ultimate accolade of Best in Show at Crufts, the pinnacle of the dog show world.

Tambora Points Trophy 1987

1987 was once again a dog belonging to Sue and Willie O'Brien of Sammara Beardies. This time it was a homebred dog, English and American Champion Sammara Standing Ovation, pet name Boysie. He was born on 21.9.84, his sire being Potterdale Encore and dam Willowmead Simply Super. Boysie is a mid slate with very little white markings, very useful for the many flashy bitches around these days. Boysie has won eight Challenge Certificates and five Reserve Challenge Certificates, four of his Challenge Certificates with Best of Breed. He also has a group win to his credit at Welsh Kennel Club Championship Show.

So far, Boysie has two champion offspring, Champion Desborough Destiny of Sammara and Champion Desborough Dulcinea of Snowmead. Boysie produces both slate and brown puppies in his litters and is one of the very few Beardies that have both their English and Oversea's Championships. Sue and Willie campaigned him in Great Britain and now he is over in America where he has already his American Championship. He is the only Beardie who will be returning home, all the others have stayed in their new countries. Boysie's stay will be around eighteen months.

Ch. Sammara Standing Ovation

Ch. Swinford Sky Rocket at Maemont

History of the Breed

BEARDED Collies are very special dogs, needing people who will understand and appreciate their many qualities and idiosyncrasies. They are super intelligent, seeming to know what you were thinking, almost before you think it yourself, are the most devoted dog of all time to their owner and family, always liking to have the whole family together, showing the shepherding instinct, so strong in the breed. This description by Alfred Ollivant in his book 'Owd Bob' describes a Beardie to perfection. "No man can mistake the type, a grey dog of Kenmuir is as little indistinct as a Raphael's madonna. Outside a radius of twenty miles from Kenmuir he is never met. Money cannot win one, neither love, for a Moore would as soon as think to sell his child as part with a grey dog. But should you, while wandering the wild sheepland about the twinpikes, happen on Moor or in Market upon a very perfect gentle knight clothed in dark grey habit, splashed here and there with rays of moon; free by right divine of the guild of gentlemen, strenuous as a prince, lithe as a rowan, graceful as a girl, with high King carriage, motions and manners of a fairy queen should he have a noble breadth of brow, an air of still strength, born of right confidence, all unassuming; last and most unfailing test of all, should you look into two snowcloud eyes, calm, wistful, inscrutable, their soft depths

"A GREY DOG AND A BLACK-FACED RAM ENGAGED IN FATEFUL DUEL."

Owd Bob

clothed on with eternal sadness - yearning, it is said for the soul that is not their's - know then, you look upon one of the line of the most illustrious sheepdogs of the North", shows so plainly just what marvellous dogs we still have amongst us. A dog that must live with people, not shut out to be ignored, which really breaks a Beardie's heart.

This following story, which comes down to us from around 1850, was given to me by my brother. The Scotch sheepdog more commonly called the Colley, it is hardly possible to overrate the intelligence of a well taught sheepdog, for if the shepherd were deprived of the help of his dog, his office would be almost impracticable. the memory of the shepherd's dog is simply incredible as may appear from the fact that one of these dogs, when assisting his master for the first time in conducting some sheep from Westmoreland to London, experienced great difficulty in guiding his charges amongst the many crossroads and byeways that intersected their route, but on the next journey, he found no trouble at all, as he was able to remember the points that had bothered him on his former journey and to profit by the experience which he had then gained. These dogs would learn their business so thoroughly, that they will conduct a flock of sheep or herd of cattle to the destined point, and then deliver up its charges to the person who is appointed to receive them. Not the least extraordinary part of its performance is that it will conduct its own flock through the midst of other sheep without permitting a single sheep under its charge to escape, or allow a single stranger to mix with its own flock.

Such abilities as these can be applied to wrong purposes, as well as good ones, and there is a well-known story of a Drover who was accustomed to stealing sheep through the help of his dog. His plan was to indicate by some expressive gesture which the dog well understood, the particular sheep he wished to be added to his own flock and then to send his flock forward under the guardianship of the dog, while he remained with his companions at the public house bar. The clever animal would then so craftily intermingle the two flocks that it contrived to entice the coveted sheep into its own flock and then drive them forwards, carrying off the stolen sheep among the number. If the stratagem were not discovered, the owner of the dog speedily changed the marks on the sheep and so merged them with his own legitimate property. If the fraud were discovered, it was set down as an excusable mistake made by the dog.

Our Beardies still have exactly the same wonderful intelligence, love and devotion today as those Beardies of one hundred years ago, going back to the grey shades of dogs first becoming man's best friend.

The Bearded Collie
Origins and Early History

by James C. Logan

THE safest thing that can be said about the origins of the Bearded Collie is that they are lost in the mists of antiquity. This is a breed which has evolved naturally over the centuries and not one created in the relatively recent past, such as the Golden Retriever and the Dobermann, whose pedigrees can be traced right back to the original stud books. Working dogs with thick shaggy coats and hairy faces had existed in Scotland for centuries, under such names as Scotch Sheepdog, Mountain Collie, Highland Collie or Hairy Mou'ed Collie. Similar hairy-faced pastoral breeds are to be found distributed over the globe from Tibet to the Hebrides (Table 1), generally in mountainous country or in countries subjected to severe winter conditions. Except in one or two cases where the breed is of comparatively recent origin I do not think that any one of these breeds can claim to be the ancestor of any of the others, and I also think it unlikely that all of them had a common ancestor, though those in a particular region, such as Central Europe, the Iberian Peninsula or the British Isles, may have had such an ancestor in the remote past.

Mrs Willison, in her book 'The Bearded Collie', describes how three Polish Sheepdogs were brought to Scotland in 1514. these dogs may just possibly have had some slight influence on the development of the Bearded Collie, though if they were mated at all it would certainly have been to the local dogs. To describe the Polish Lowland Sheepdog as the 'ancestor of the Bearded Collie' is quite unjustified; at the very most it may have contributed a small part to the ancestry of the Beardie. Present day Bearded Collies do bear some resemblance to the Polish Lowland Sheepdog, though in many respects the latter more closely resembles the Old English Sheepdog, but Beardies in the late 19th and early 20th Centuries, such as Panmure Gordon's Jock or the dog drawn by Arthur Wardle to illustrate the breed in Theo Marples 'Show Dogs', look quite different. Interestingly, Hubbard in 'Working Dogs of the World' (1947) suggests that some Russian Owtcharkas may have reached Scotland, where they were crossed with Bearded Collies or similar dogs and used to establish the make-up of the Old English Sheepdog.

All this, however, is sheer speculation, and all that can really be said is that over the years a long-haired, hairy-faced dog developed in Scotland, valued for its hardiness and its ability to work sheep and cattle. Little or no attempt was made to fix type until late in the 19th Century, working ability being the only criterion. As late as 1924 John Buchan, in his novel 'John Macnab', describes the dog Mackenzie as 'A mongrel collie of the old Highland type known as Beardies', and well into the 1970s it was not uncommon to meet farmers or shepherds who owned or who had owned Beardies who were amazed to learn that the breed was recognised by the Kennel Club and becoming popular as a show dog.

There is a strong tradition that Bearded Collies were among the dogs used in the great cattle drives which took place from about the time of the Union of 1707 until the early 1880s. The cattle were driven from the North and West Highlands to the markets, or trysts as they were called, at first at Crieff and latterly at Falkirk. Unfortunately written evidence to support this tradition is completely lacking, and the standard work on droving, A. R. B. Haldane's 'The Drove Roads of Scotland', says little about the drovers' dogs. After the cattle had been sold they would be driven down to England, mostly going to Yorkshire or East Anglia, where they would be fattened before going on to the meat markets in the Midlands or at Smithfield. Beardie like dogs are to be found along this route, such as the Smithfield dogs of South-East England. It is said that these dogs resulted from Rough Collie - Old English crosses, but it seems more than probable that Beardies also played their part. Haldane does tell us how the dogs of drovers who had stayed in the South to work at the harvest or who had returned home by sea made their own way back to Scotland, stopping at the inns or farms at which the drove had stayed on the way south in order to be fed, the drover paying the innkeeper or farmer for the dog's food when he came south in the following year. Paintings and prints of the period show that a number of different breeds were used by the drovers.

Sam Bough's painting of Cattle Crossing the Solway, in Glasgow Art Gallery, shows a sable Rough Collie, and a print of cattle being loaded at Kyleakin in Skye shows a dog which is clearly a Smooth Collie, but a print by an artist called Leitch shows a dog which might be a Beardie. This is not very firm evidence, as all that can really be said is that one can't definitely say that the dog is not a Beardie, and Leitch, who had started his career as a scene painter in the theatre, was in any event inclined to romanticise his work.

Fortunately there are still people alive who were able to hear tales of the droving days first hand from their grandfathers, and all to whom I have spoken confirming that Beardies were used in this trade. This tends to be confirmed by the article by Bailie James Dalgliesh in 'The New Book of the Dog' (1907), in which he states that the Bearded Collie, though less popular with the flockmaster than other collies, is a favourite with the butcher and drover. Beardies are still occasionally to be found today working in Scottish cattle markets. Even quite late in the 18th Century droving was a hazardous trade, and it is significant that drovers were exempted from the Disarming Acts passed after the Jacobite rebellions in 1715 and 1745. One can imagine that Beardies could have been useful in protecting their masters against attack.

One of the earliest paintings depicting a possible Bearded Collie is Gainsborough's portrait of the Duke of Buccleuch with his dog, painted in 1771. A year or two later Reynolds painted a portrait of the Duchess

OLD ENGLISH SHEEP DOG
Oil painting by Philip Reinagle, 1749—1833

Brown Beardie

with what appears to be the same dog. It is difficult in either portrait to determine the actual size of the dog, and the only thing that leads one to suppose that it might be a Beardie is its hairiness. There is a strong tendency amongst researchers to assume that any fairly hairy medium sized dog of this early period must be a Beardie. The temptation to make such an assumption has to be resisted. We are on surer ground when we come to Reinagle's painting of 'The Shepherd's Dog', which appeared in the 'Sportsman's Cabinet' (1804). Although this dog has been called an Old English Sheepdog it much more closely resembles a Bearded Collie, having a long body and unobscured eyes and a brown coat, not found in the English breed. Moreover, the accompanying test states that the breed is preserved in its purest form in the Northern parts of the kingdom, as well as in the Highlands of Scotland. Other paintings or drawings which can be identified as Beardies include Herring's 'Bearded Collie and Hound (1855), a drawing by Rosa Bonheur (1879), and Sir

205

George Pirie's painting 'The Shepherd's Fire', which is in the R.S.A. Diploma Collection.

Jesse's 'Anecdotes of Dogs' was first published in 1847. (In Mrs Willison's book 'The Bearded Collie' he is called Gesse, but Jesse is correct). The engraving of a painting by W. P. Smith entitled 'Scotch Colley' which illustrates the chapter on 'The Colley, or Shepherd's Dog', is quite plainly a Beardie, with typical eyebrows and moustache, a small beard and a rough coat, and drooping ears. But for a lack of hair on the legs it is very similar to photographs of Bearded Collies which started to appear at the end of the 19th Century. Jesse was acquainted with James Hogg, the Ettrick Shepherd, a protege of Sir Walter Scott but a very considerable writer himself, with poems such as 'Kilmeny', 'Lock the Door, Lariston', 'When the Kye Comes Home', and a novel, 'The Confessions of a Justified Sinner', to his credit. Despite his writing activities Hogg remained a shepherd or farmer for most of his life, and he imparted to Jesse several tales of the exploits of his dogs Sirrah and Hector. We do not know definitely that Hogg's dogs were Beardies, but it seems not unlikely that they were. Certainly antics similar to those of his dog Hector are familiar to most Beardie owners. In those days family prayers were held in almost every Scottish household, and it was Hector's invariable habit to leap to his feet and to start barking just before the final prayer ended. At one time Hogg was precentor - leader of the singing, which was unaccompanied - at the local kirk. Hector was always shut in when Hogg left for church, but he invariably escaped and made his way to the kirk, where he would join in the singing heartily as soon as he heard his master's voice. As a result Hogg's tenure of the post was short lived! A portrait of Hector's son Lion was painted by William Nicholson, a well-known painter of the day, and it would be fascinating if this painting were some day to come to light.

So far we have been dealing with the prehistory of the Bearded Collie, but we emerge into history with the publication of 'The Dogs of Scotland' by D. J. Thomson Gray. Gray was the editor of the 'Scottish Fancier and Rural Gazette', for which he wrote under the name of Whinstone, and his book appeared in instalments in this periodical for some months before being published in book form in 1891. Possibly this is the first publication to refer to the Bearded Collie by that name. Gray describes the Beardie as 'A big, rough, "tousy" looking tyke, with a coat not unlike a doormat, the texture of the hair hard and fibry, and the ears hanging close to the head'. Gray quotes extensively from a letter which appeared in the 'Live Stock Journal' of November 15th 1878 from a Mr Gordon James Phillips of Glenlivet, which describes what he calls 'the Rough-coated Collie', rather a confusing name as Gray also applies this title to what we now know as the Rough Collie. The Rough-coated Collie as described by Phillips has a tail which was just a stump, but Gray seems to equate it with the Beardie, rather illogically, as he has previously stated that the only difference between the Bearded Collie and the Old English Sheepdog is the fact that the former possesses a tail. More probably these dogs were Scotch bob-tailed Sheepdogs, and the illustration of one in the 'Live Stock Journal' is so described. Phillips's letter, together with the illustration, also appeared in Vero Shaw's 'Book of the Dog', published in 1881. When I first started to show Beardies in the middle 1960s I was often asked by farmers who had also been exhibitors before the War whether Beardies ever had bob tails, and they seemed surprised when I said that I had not come across any. I saw a dog of this type at Kilmory Knap in the early 1970s, self-coloured grey with a tail about four inches long which its owners assured me was a natural bob, and I have since heard of Beardies which did have naturally bobbed tails. I do not think that these Scotch bob-tailed Sheepdogs can be equated with Beardies, though I think that they undoubtedly contributed to the ancestry of the present day Bearded Collie.

Gray states that although the Bearded Collie is not to be found in plenty anywhere in Scotland he is by no means a scarce animal, and when classes have been provided at Glasgow and some of the other West Country shows they have generally been well filled with specimens of merit. These shows clearly preceded the 1897 Edinburgh Show of the Scottish Kennel Club, often thought to have been the first show at which the breed was classified.

There was, of course, no official standard for the Bearded Collie at that time, nor for very many years afterwards, but Gray gives his own standard, which is as follows:-

The Skull flat, broad, and rather heavy over the eyes, covered with long hair of hard texture.

The Muzzle heavy, of moderate length, tapering slightly to the nose, which is black.

The Eyes, moderately full, vary in colour according to the colour of the dog's coat. A wall or "china" eye is peculiar to the mirled (sic) colour, but a dark brown eye is what is generally seen. Light yellow eyes are objectionable.

The Ears, which droop, are of moderate size, well covered with hair, and carried close to the head.

Neck of medium length, thick, and well covered with hair; chest very deep; shoulders oblique.

Legs - The fore legs straight, with plenty of bone and muscle, heavily covered with rough hair, and hind legs also heavily covered with hair.

Feet oval, toes arched and close, sole well padded.

Body more short and compact than that of the common collie; chest deep and wide, the ribs well sprung. There should be no inclination to droop in hindquarters.

Tail of Moderate length, bushy, and carried low.

Coat very profuse, hard and wiry in the outer coat, with a tendency to waviness or curl; inner coat short, soft, and close.

General Appearance - A big, rough-coated, clumsy-looking dog, with rather large head, sleepy look, and a peculiar action when running.

Much of this would not be out of place in today's standard, though modern fanciers might look askance at the call for a compact body, the call for the coat to be wavy or curled, and the whole of the General Appearance paragraph. No mention at all is made of colour, other than the implication that a merle coat is permissible.

The closing years of the 19th Century saw something of an explosion of interest in the Bearded Collie as a show breed, starting with its classification at the Scottish Kennel Club Edinburgh Show in 1897. The President of the S.K.C. at the time was Mr H. Panmure Gordon, a Beardie enthusiast who was reported always to have representatives of the breed in his kennel. Panmure Gordon was educated at Harrow and at Bonn University and subsequently served in the Army for four years and then spent five years in Shanghai. Returning from the Far East, he became a member of the Stock Exchange, a position he held for thirty years. His duties there do not appear to have been excessive, and he was able to spend much of his time pursuing his interests of fishing, dogs, and managing his estates in England and Scotland. He specialised in Scottish breeds, particularly in Scottish Terriers and Collies. In 1897 he suggested to the S.K.C. Committee that Beardies should be classified at the Edinburgh Show, and that they should be judged by a shepherd. The Committee accepted the first part of this suggestion, but they did not look with favour upon the second and tactfully solved the dilemma by inviting Pamure Gordon himself to judge the classes.Three classes were provided, Open Dog or bitch, which drew five entries, and two classes, Open Dog and Open bitch, confined to bona fide shepherds or drovers, which drew four entries and one entry respectively. In addition, the judge's dog Jock was entered for exhibition only, quite a common practice in those days. The exhibitors evidently valued their dogs, one being priced at £1000, roughly equivalent to £40,000 at today's prices and probably just another way of saying 'Not for Sale'. Other prices were more realistic but still high - two at £100, several at £24, and the lowest priced at £10, a sum which at that time would have been a year's wage for a domestic servant. Not every dog apparently pleased the judge, the single bitch in the Shepherds and Drovers class being awarded only a third prize!

Jock was evidently considered to be a particularly good specimen of the breed. An article in 'Country Life' in January 1898 described him as being of a beautiful dark blue grizzle in colour, with eyes that were dark and a beautiful soft expression. Grizzle - the presence of single white hairs distributed amongst the background colour - is often mentioned in early descriptions, Bailie Dalgliesh's article in the 'New Book of the Dog' (1907), for example, stating that 'the commonest colour is grizzle grey'.

Photograph from around 1900

Many photographs and drawings published during the first decade of the 20th Century are of a similar type to Jock.

1898 saw the publication of two more works relating to Bearded Collies. Arthur Ollivant's novel 'Owd Bob' deals with sheepdogs, sheepdog trials and sheep worrying in Cumberland, and the dogs concerned, notably the hero, Owd Bob, the Grey Dog of Kenmuir, and the villain, Red Wull, are said to be Beardies and are so depicted in the illustrated edition of 1937. Unfortunately when a film of 'Owd Bob' was made in the 1930s the name part was played by a Border Collie, and, worse still, Red Wull had his name changed to Black Wull and was played by a black German Shepherd. It is said that Mrs Cameron Miller's dog Balmacneil Jock had a small part in the film, but this appears uncertain. Owd Bob is described as "A very perfect gentle Knight, clothed in dark grey habit, splashed here and there with rays of moon, free by divine right of the guild of gentlemen, strenuous as a prince, lithe as a rowan, graceful as a girl, with high king carriage, motions and manners of a fairy queen . . ." and so on. Personally I find this all too good to be true, and I much prefer the description of the dog Mackenzie in John Buchan's novel 'John Macnab', already referred to: "He was a mongrel collie of the old Highland type known as 'Beardies', and his towzled head, not unlike an extra-shaggy Dandie Dinmont's, was set upon a body of immense length, girth and muscle. His manners were atrocious to all except his master, and local report accused him of every canine vice except worrying sheep". When 'John Macnab' was serialised by the BBC in 1975 the part of Mackenzie was played by Mr N. M. Broadbridge's Bredon Quarry.

To get back in 1898, the other work published in that year was an article on the breed in Our Dogs by Mrs Hall Walker, which appeared in the issue of 17th December. She was the wife of a Member of Parliament for a Liverpool constituency, and her interests in dogs are said to have been mainly toy Pomeranians and white Collies. She also kept and hunted a pack of 11 inch Beagles. Her article was truly a landmark in the history of the breed. Much of her information came from Panmure Gordon, and the article contained a standard which was to remain, with few alterations, the principal standard for nearly sixty years, and to form the basis of all future standards. Here it is:-

Head: Large, square, with plenty of room for the brain.

Ears: Medium size, drooping, covered with hair.

Eyes: To match the coat in colour, the typical wall eye (otherwise called china or marble), either single or double, suiting the mirl (sic) coat. The eyes should be rather widely apart, big, soft and affectionate, but not protruding. Eyebrows slightly elevated and covered with shaggy hair.

Coat: A Bearded Collie should have a thick skin, with two coats, the under one furry, and the outer hard, strong, shaggy, unkempt, the legs covered right down to the feet, and not bare, as in the better known English (sic) Collie.

Colour: Immaterial, but preference given to slate or reddish fawn. If the coat is varied by a white collar or white on legs, that is no defect.

Nose: Large, square and black, with little hair along bridge, so as to afford contrast to the shaggy "beard" running from each side of the nose and the chin.

Teeth: Large, white, and never overshot or undershot. This is most important.

Tail: Moderately long, must be carried low when walking, and extended when the animal is at high speed.

Measurement: dogs 20in to 24in at shoulder, bitches rather less.

General Appearance: An active dog, with none of the stumpiness of the bobtail, and which, though strongly made, does not look too heavy. The face should have a sharp, inquiring expression.

Faults: Thick, rounded ribs, too round in body, too short in length, meagre, short, bare tail, narrow skull, too long nose.

A photograph of Stella, Mrs Hall Walker's bitch, which illustrated the article, bears a considerable resemblance to one of the dogs in Pirie's painting 'The shepherd's Fire', which was painted in 1911. Like Thomson Gray, Mrs Hall Walker mentions the wall eye as suiting the merle coat, and one of the dogs in Pirie's painting is a blue merle. It is doubtful if blue merle still exists in the registered breed, though Mootie, the dam of Britt of Bothkennar, one of Mrs Willison's dogs, was a merle, as was his much younger full sister, Nell.

Panmure Gordon died in 1902, and during the next decade the leading figure in the breed was Bailie James Dalgliesh, who came from the border town of Galashiels. He not only bred, showed and judged Beardies, but worked them in the stockyards of the South of Scotland. Among his better known dogs was Ellwyn Garrie. Another, Ellwyn Ken, was exported to Canada in 1913. He was not the first Beardie in that country, as the 'Collie Folio' of September 1910 refers to two Beardies being benched at a show at Calgary. Bailie Dalgliesh was the author of the well known article in 'The New Book of the Dog', already referred to. At that time Peebles was a centre of the breed, and he describes judging classes at the Agricultural show there, stating that better filled classes could not be found anywhere. This article was repeated in abridged form in successive editions of 'The New Book of the Dog' and of its successor, 'The Complete Book of the Dog', continuing to appear right up to the 1954 edition. Dalgliesh described Peebles as the 'true home of the Bearded Collie' and this had the somewhat strange effect of leading subsequent writers on the breed, such as Hubbard in 'Working dogs of the World' (1947) and even Glover in 'A Standard Guide to Pure Bred Dogs' (1977) to believe that Beardies were to be found almost nowhere else in Scotland. In fact this was far from being the case. Beardies were regularly being shown, though in small numbers, during the first decade of the century, and not one of the nine dogs which appeared at the SKC Edinburgh shows between 1911 and 1913 came from Peebles, exhibitors

Postcard pre 1914

coming from as far apart as Dundee, Argyll and the Island of Arran. These dogs undoubtedly came from working stock, and it is probable that many of them themselves worked. Another of Dalgliesh's statements, that white Beardies with black or orange markings were often to be seen, apparently made less of an impression, as this colour was omitted when the official standard came to be written.

The Collie Folio, a periodical which existed from 1906 to 1917, contains numerous references to Beardies, the issue of September 1910, quoted above, stating that many specimens of the breed were to be seen benched at almost any Scotch (sic) show. Prominent dogs of the period included Lord Arthur Cecil's Ben and Messrs. Ramsays' Sir Glen, said to have won championship (i.e., best of breed) at Edinburgh in 1909 before his untimely death from blood poisoning. Among the exhibitors at the 1913 Edinburgh show was Dr. J. Russell Greig, who came from Leith. He had written an article in the Scottish Kennel Journal in 1900 stating that a Bearded Collie Club had been formed in Edinburgh under the presidency of Bailie Dalgliesh. This club seems to have come to nothing, but a more promising venture, in which Dr. Greig was the moving spirit, took place about 1912. The outbreak of war in 1914, however, brought these activities to an end before the club had actually proceeded to registration, although at the SKC Edinburgh Show in 1913 a trophy was offered for the best Bearded Collie owned by a member.

Although by 1923 Beardies were again being classified at the SKC shows, and though the breeders and exhibitors included some who had been exhibiting or breeding before the war, no further attempt seems to have been made to form a breed club at that time. Entries were small, with three dogs making five entries at the Edinburgh show in 1923 and six dogs being entered for the single class in 1924. Best of breed at both shows was Ninewells Scottie, and second in 1924 was his dam, Ninewells Nell, who was to become famous as the dam of Mrs Cameron Miller's best known dog, Balmacneil Jock. She was born in 1919 and was bred by I. Stanford by Moss out of Floss.

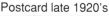
Postcard late 1920's

Balmacneil Jock's sire was Rover an unregistered dog, and he was bred by Andrew

212

Postcard - 3rd August 1927

Scott and born on 27th February 1926. He was originally registered as Vicarsford Scottie, and his transfer to Mrs Cameron Miller in this name appears in the Kennel Gazette of June 1928. In those days a change of name was not, as now, confined to the addition of an affix, and his change of name to Balmacneil Jock appears in the same issue of the Gazette which records his transfer. He was shown all over the United Kingdom, winning many firsts, including one at the LKA in 1930. The judge here was Croxton Smith, later Chairman of the general Committee of the Kennel Club.

In his book 'About Our Dogs' Smith states that none of the other exhibits (presumably in the Beardie classes) could compare with Balmacneil Jock, who was really a delightful dog in every way. The photograph of him in this book does him less than justice, the threequarter view foreshortening his length of body and neck, and it is not helped by the rather awkward stance, as if he was standing on a rather narrow table with his hind legs well under him. A better illustration appears in a Collie Association handbook of the period, as well as in Our Dogs Annual. His son, Balmacneil Rook, out of Findon Beauty, was possibly even more successful in the showring, winning firsts all over the country, from the Orkney Islands to the Kennel Club Show at the Crystal Palace. Mrs Cameron Miller made great efforts to promote the breed.

Between January 1929 and December 1934 she registered 55 dogs and bred ten litters, besides showing throughout the United Kingdom and guaranteeing classes at a number of shows, such as the Scottish Kennel Club, but her efforts did not meet with success. This may have been partly because her dogs were too successful, and partly because she was too reluctant to part with any of her stock, only seven transfers from her being recorded during this period. At the SKC in Edinburgh in 1935 her three dogs were the only entrants for the four classes, and the classification had been discontinued by the 1936 show, although a few Beardies continued to be shown in Scotland up to the outbreak of war in 1939.

After Mrs Cameron Miller's death her dogs seemed to disappear, and no-one knows what happened to her stock. A few years ago Mr Nicolas Broadbridge, of the Sallen affix, discovered an unregistered Beardie whose owner described it as "one of the Lochiel Beardies". Lochiel is, of course, the Chief of Clan Cameron, so this could be very tentative evidence of the survival of the Balmacneil stock. Mr Broadbridge now has descendants of this dog in his kennel. A more tangible memento of Mrs Cameron Miller is the Balmacneil Jock Trophy. She presented this to the Bon Accord Kennel Association, an Aberdeen society, in the 1930s to be awarded to the best Bearded Collie at the society's shows. In 1974 Mr Broadbridge was apprised of the existence of the trophy, which was then being awarded for best Shetland Sheepdog. The Bon Accord Association kindly agreed to let the Scottish Branch of the Bearded Collie Club have the trophy on the provision of a substitute, which the fledgling branch was just able to afford. The trophy is now awarded to the leading stud dog owned by a member of the Branch each year, and is almost certainly the oldest Beardie trophy still extant.

I do not believe that Mrs Cameron Miller has ever received the credit due to her for her efforts to establish the breed. Most recent publications content themselves, if they mention her at all, with a reference to her experiments with the use of Old English Sheepdog bitches, which apparently took place after she had registered her last litter in 1934, although she does not seem to have registered any of these cross-breeds; but she certainly owned a number of typical Beardie bitches, and her stock, as far as one can tell from photographs, compares by no means unfavourably with the early Bothkennars. But for her, there might not have been the judges able to recognise and pass for registration the Beardies of the present dispensation when the time came to do so in 1948.

Mrs Cameron Miller's last registered litter, by Dandy boy out of Balmacneil Nettle, was born in September 1934 and appeared in the Kennel Gazette of December of that year, which also contained the registration of the sire. One Beardie was registered in 1935 and one, by a Mr J. C. Smith, in 1937. The December Gazette of that year notified the transfer of Balmacneil Nettle, then aged eight, to a Mr J. Smith, presumably the same individual, but no registrations or transfers of the breed were recorded in 1938, and only one registration in 1939. This was the last Beardie to be registered for nearly nine years.

Although Bearded Collies had ceased to be registered they had by no means become extinct, nor were they in any danger of doing so. Writing in 'Working Dogs Of The World' (1947) Hubbard describes the breed as almost extinct except (of course!) in Peebleshire. In fact, Beardies were at that time to be found, admittedly in small numbers, all over Scotland, and none of the dogs which were to form the foundation of the modern registered breed actually came from Peebleshire. Hubbard writes that despite the small numbers the best specimens were to be found working with the flocks instead of parading the exhibition rings, and Beardies are still to be found working today which owe absolutely nothing to the registered breed. During the 1970s and early 1980s advertisements regularly appeared in newspapers such as the Oban Times for Beardies to work as 'hunters' (a term now often replaced by the New Zealand term 'huntaways'). (See Table 2). These dogs are required to have 'plenty noise', and they use their voices to drive the sheep up onto the hill grazings. Beardies are, however, quite capable of working in a more orthodox manner. Mr Tommy Muirhead, formerly of Anston Farm, Dunsyre, on the south slopes of the Pentlands, used nothing but Beardies on his hirsel of 1,000 ewes. He is, perhaps, the last shepherd in Scotland to use only Beardies on a large hirsel, although a number of others, though working mainly with Border Collies, keep a Beardie for use as a hunter. Nor are Beardies incapable of the finer work required for sheepdog trials. In 1984 Mr Paul Turnbull's dog blue, working in the North of England but bred in Dumfriesshire, qualified on merit for the International Sheepdog Society Register.

TABLE 1

DISTRIBUTION OF HAIR-FACED PASTORAL BREEDS

Far East
TIBETAN TERRIER   Tibet

European Russia and Middle East
South Russian Owtsharka   Crimea
Ukrainean Sheepdog   Ukraine
Egyptian Sheepdog (Armant)   Upper Egypt

Eastern, central and Southern Europe
KOMONDOR   Hungary
HUNGARIAN PULI   Hungary
Pumi   Hungary
Italian sheepdog (Bergamaschi)   Lombardy
POLISH LOWLAND SHEEPDOG   Northern Poland

Western Europe
Balearic Sheepdog   Balearic Islands
Catalan Sheepdog   Northern Spain
PYRENEAN SHEEPDOG   Southern France
BOUVIER DES FLANDRES   Flanders
BRIARD   Northern France
Schapendoes   Netherlands

British Isles
OLD ENGLISH SHEEPDOG   England
(Dorset Shag)   South-West England
(Smithfield Dog)   South-East England
BEARDED COLLIE   Scotland
(Scotch bob-tailed Sheepdog)   Scotland
Welsh Gray   North Wales

South Pacific
Huntaway Beardie   New Zealand

NOTES: Breeds recognised by the Kennel Club are in capitals. Some of the other breeds are recognised by the FCI.

Breeds which are derivatives from or progenitors of recognised breeds are in brackets.

The Huntaway Beardie is almost certainly derived from the Bearded Collie.

The Schapendoes may be partly derived from the Bearded Collie.

TABLE 2

Typical advertisements from the Oban Times, 1974-1984

Beardie dog, three and a half years, hunt or work at hand, plenty noise.

Beardie dog two and a half years and bitch two years, both good hunting dogs, very noisy.

Beardie dog seven years, done for hill. Might suit drover.

Half-Beardie puppies, eight weeks. Sire good hunter.

Six month Beardie bitch off noisy hunting parents. Keen on sheep and cattle. Used to high ground.

Wanted young hunter, two years or under. Must be noisy. Beardie might suit.

Seven-month-old Cross Beardie Rough Type, started to work, noisy with cattle.

One Cross Beardie pup, off good working hill parents.

Beardie Collie pups, off wide wearing parents. £12 each.

Beardie bitch, hunter, $1^{1}/_{2}$ years old, has plenty noise.

Half Beardie bitch for sale, 8-month-old, good nature.

Collie dog, 18-months, good at hand with sheep. Beardie bitch, 1-year, keen to work.

For sale - Two cross Beardie Collie hunting pups, six-month-old, plenty noise.

For-sale - 8-month-old pure Beardie bitch, off good working strain.

Hunting Collie x Beardie pups, 8-weeks, parents good workers, with plenty noise.

Dogs for sale - 19-month-old Beardy bitch.

Hardy dog pup, off N.Z. Huntaway and noisy cross Beardie bitch. Strong, healthy, £35.

TABLE 3

COMPARISON OF BEARDED COLLIE REGISTRATIONS, 1928-35 AND 1948-55

Figures for registrations by Mrs Cameron Miller (1928-35) and by Mrs Willison (1948-55) are in brackets.

1928	1	(0)	1948	1	(1)
1929	4	(3)	1949	0	(0)
1930	11	(8)	1950	8	(7)
1931	19	(16)	1951	1	(1)
1932	9	(6)	1952	9	(8)
1933	13	(7)	1953	9	(7)
1934	17	(15)	1954	22	(12)
1935	1	(0)	1955	15	(11)
TOTAL	75	(55)	TOTAL	65	(47)

NOTES: The figures relate to the registrations reported in the Kennel Gazette for the years in question. The actual figures for registrations in calendar years may be slightly different.

During the periods covered 8 transfers from Mrs Cameron Miller and 16 transfers from Mrs Willison were notified. In Addition, two dogs bred by Mrs Cameron Miller were registered by the new owners.

73.3% of the registrations during the period 1928-35 were made by Mrs Cameron Miller, and 72.3% of registrations for the period 1948-55 by Mrs Willison.

SCOTCH COLLEY.

Engraving by W. B. Smith
An illustration in Jesse's Anecdotes of Dogs, 1844

Bearded Collies
The Post-War Revival, 1944-1969

Mrs. G. O. Willison, of Bothkennar Grange in Middlesex, was interested in training and working Shetland Sheepdogs. In January 1944 she decided that her next dog would be a Shetland Sheepdog of working stock, so she somewhat optimistically booked one from a farmers' agent in Scotland. Fortunately, but scarcely surprisingly, no such Shetland Sheepdog was available, but the agent, showing commendable initiative, (or perhaps a keen eye to the main chance!), sent her instead a Bearded Collie puppy which his own dog had recently sired from a bitch owned by a Mr. McKie of Killiecrankie. It was upon this happy accident that the revival of the Bearded Collie as a show breed depended, for Mrs. Willison was captivated by the puppy's temperament, intelligence and working instinct, and she was the very person who had the enthusiasm, persistence and opportunity to undertake the revival of the breed.

When the puppy was two months old Mrs. Willison discovered that she was in fact a Bearded Collie. Although she had never previously thought of becoming a dog breeder she felt that she must find a mate for Jeannie, as the puppy had been called. When Jeannie was two years old, and still unregistered, she was mated to a half Beardie who looked, as many of them do, a typical Beardie, and produced a litter of two dogs and eight bitches, all except one of which were typical Beardies. One died and three were put down, and for one reason or another all the remainder were given away without being registered.

Two years later a Collie judge told Mrs. Willison that she could get Jeannie registered, as it was possible in those days for an unregistered dog to be registered if inspected and approved by a judge appointed by the Kennel Club. In 1948 Jeannie was accordingly registered as Jeannie of Bothkennar, the registration appearing in the Kennel Gazette for July of that year, details of parentage and date of birth being stated to be unknown. This was the first Beardie registration to appear since December 1939, and only the fourth since May 1935. Bothkennar, from which Bothkennar Grange took its name and which became Mrs. Willison's affix, is a village in Central Scotland between Stirling and Grangemouth, with which Mr. Willison had family connections.

With Jeannie registered it became more than ever necessary to find a suitable mate. The dog to which she had been previously mated had died, as had the only surviving son in the litter. It is a measure of Mrs. Willison's determination not to be satisfied with second best that in these circumstances she refused the offer of a stud from a dog which she considered to be untypical, bearing too close a resemblance to an undocked Old English Sheepdog. It was shortly after this that there occurred the second of the remarkable changes that attended the revival of the breed. Mrs. Willison had attended a show at Brighton and had gone to the beach at Hove for a swim when she saw in the distance what appeared to be a Bearded Collie. It turned out that not only was he a typical Beardie but his owner was about to emigrate and was looking for a home for him, and Mrs. Willison took him back with her. In the January Kennel Gazette for 1950 his registration as Bailie of Bothkennar appears, his sire being Dandy and his date of birth 28th May 1948.

On 7th April 1950 the longed for litter from Jeannie to Bailie was born. It consisted of three dogs and three bitches, and Mrs. Willison retained the dogs, Bogle, Bravado and Bruce, and a bitch, Buskie. The registration of the litter appeared in the Kennel Gazette for June 1950, the first Beardie litter to be registered since Mrs. Cameron Miller's last litter in December 1934. This was to be Jeannie's last effective litter. In 1951 she had a litter to her son, Bruce, and two of the puppies were in fact registered, but both died before they could be used at stud. In September 1951 Jeannie had been re-registered, her breeding being given as by Baffler out of Mist and her date of birth December 1943.

Later in 1951 Mrs. Willison obtained Bess of Bothkennar, a four year old bitch from Argyll whose parents and grandparents were known. (Her dam's father was called Baldie, hardly an encouraging name for a Beardie!) In December Bess produced a litter to Bogle, Mrs. Willison's first litter by an outcross bitch. This litter included Briery Nan of Bothkennar, a bitch who was to have a profound influence on the breed. A few months later a litter by Buskie to Bailie included another influential bitch, Bra' Tawny of Bothkennar.

In the meantime Beardies had again started to appear in the show ring, Bailie having been first in Not Separately Classified Novice at Crufts in 1951 and first in Open the following year. He was possibly the first Beardie to be shown at Crufts, though Mrs. Cameron Miller's dogs had appeared at the Kennel Club show at the Crystal Palace and at the L.K.A. during the 1930s. One or two individual Beardies were now being registered, though most of these do not seem to have had any registered progeny. An exception was Newtown Blackie, a dog discovered by Capt. C. E. Owen and passed for registration by Mrs. Willison. At the time Briery Nan was in season, and Mrs. Willison allowed Capt. Owen to have her on breeding terms. Two litters were registered in 1953, that by Bess to Bailie including Bond of Bothkennar, who later in the year was transferred to Miss B. Johnson, and by Buskie to Bruce. Also born in 1953, but registered in 1954, was Briery Nan's first litter to Newtown Blackie. Consisting of three dogs, it included Ridgeway Rob, one of the most significant of the early stud dogs. Briery Nan's second litter was born in January 1954. Two puppies, Birkie and Blimber, were registered by Mrs. Willison and the remainder by Capt.Owen, to whom Nan was now transferred. The registration of Bra' Tawny's first litter to Ridgeway Rob, born in May 1954 and including Baidh and Bannoch of Bothkennar, appeared in the August Gazette, and the following month's issue recorded the first Stud Book entry achieved by a Beardie, Bond of Bothkennar having qualified by winning a Junior Working Trail and being allotted the number 1143AM.

By the end of 1954 the number of Beardie registrations had reached 50, still well short of the registrations during a similar period from 1928 to 1934. (See Table 3). There were 16 owners of registered Beardies, but only two of these, Mrs. Willison and Captain Owen, had bred registered litters. It was therefore something of an act of faith to consider the formation of a breed club. Nevertheless, the application for registration of title appeared in the Kennel Gazette for October of that year. Clearly the necessary 25 founder members could not be found from Beardie owners, but fortunately a number of well known breeders, exhibitors and judges of the day, such as James Garrow, Clara Bowring and Frank Williams, gave their support, and the General Committee of the Kennel Club was sufficiently impressed to agree, at their meeting of 16th October 1954, to consider the application. This consideration took place at the meeting of 5th April 1955, and the application to register the title of The Bearded Collie Club was approved. During its early days the Club received considerable support from the London Collie Club, and it was a member of that club, Miss Doris Lowe, who, though she never herself owned a Bearded Collie, became Secretary and Treasurer during the first fourteen years of the new Club's existence. A further step forward came in February 1955 when Beardies were separately classified at Crufts. Twelve dogs made 21 entries, a fairly high proportion of the registered breed. Best of Breed was Baltair of Bothkennar and Best Opposite Sex Bawbee of Bothkennar, the former owned by Mr. and Mrs. W. Ratcliffe and the latter by Mrs. M. Pacey, and both bred by Mrs. Willison.

Britt of Bothkennar

Bra' Tawny of Bothkennar's second litter to Ridgeway Rob was born on 23rd June 1955. It included two puppies which were to have a profound influence on the breed, Barberry of Bothkennar and Barley of Bothkennar. They were to become Ch. Willowmead Barberry of Bothkennar, the foundation bitch of the Willowmead Beardies owned by Miss K. S. Moorhouse, and Ch. Wishanger Barley of Bothkennar, the foundation dog of Miss M. Partridge's Wishanger kennel.

1955 also saw the birth of Britt of Bothkennar on 10th August, though he was not acquired by Mrs. Willison and registered until the following year. He was by Jock, owned by a Mr. Tait, out of Mootie, a blue merle bitch owned by Mr. J. Hutcheon, a Dumfriesshire cattle farmer. He was to become the first C.C. winner in the breed and the most widely used of any of Mrs. Willison's original stud dogs, siring some 15 litters. A few other dogs from unregistered stock continued to be registered by inspection, among them Mr. and Mrs. S. F. Green's Kitty Norton and Mr. T. J. Garrett's Brasenose Bonnie, registered in 1954, both of which were to produce registered progeny.

Mrs. G. O. Willison with Beauty Queen of Bothkennar winning Best of Breed and the first C.C. at Crufts 1959

1956 and 1957 were years of steady progress with 52 Beardies being registered in the former and 67 in the latter and with a corresponding increase in the number of new owners, exhibitors and breeders. Among the dogs of unregistered parentage passed for registration was Jennifer of Multan, obtained by Mr. Keith Hicks in almost identical circumstances to those in which Mrs. Willison obtained Jeannie, a dog of a different breed having been ordered from a farmers' agent in Scotland. She was to become the dam of Ch. Bronze Penny of Bothkennar and also of Wishanger Jessica of Multan. Among the puppies bred by Mrs. Willison was Beauty Queen of Bothkennar, by Bravado of Bothkennar out of Baidh of Bothkennar, who was to become the breed's first champion.

The 1956 Crufts entry comprised 20 entries from 14 dogs, judged by MacDonald Daly. B.O.B. was Bannoch of Bothkennar and B.O.S. Barberry of Bothkennar, who was then only seven months old. The following year 20 dogs made 35 entries, B.O.B. going to Bronze Penny of Bothkennar with Bobby of Bothkennar B.O.S. The judge, Miss Clara Bowring, stated in her critique that the former "galloped very soundly", and the latter "galloped with correct tail carriage", which makes one wonder whether the handlers managed to keep up with them!

In the August Kennel Gazette of 1957 is recorded the issue of an export pedigree to Norway for Ambassador of Bothkennar, who was by Britt out of Bra' Tawny. Possibly he was the first registered Beardie to be exported since those sent by Bailie Dalgliesh to Canada before the First World War. I believe that, apart from Jeannie, he was the only Bothkennar Beardie whose name did not begin with the letter 'B'. The September Gazette records the issue of an export pedigree for Belgium.

Bannock of Bothkennar

Ever since Beardies were first registered towards the end of the last century they appeared in a section at the end of the breed records originally entitled 'Any Other Variety of Foreign, Colonial or British Dog Not Separately Classified', but which by the 1950s had simply become 'Any Other Variety Not Separately Classified'. Besides many now well known breeds this had included such as 'Ethiopian Hairless Terriers' and other equally exotic. By the end of 1957 Beardie registrations had reached the required number of 150, and at its meeting of 21st January 1958 the General Committee considered and approved an application from the Bearded Collie Club for a separate register for the breed. From the publication of the Gazette for February 1958 Bearded Collies took their place in the Non-Sporting section, not yet divided into Utility and Working. Approval was also given for the grant of challenge certificates in 1959.

At Crufts in 1958, the last before C.C.s became available, the entry was slightly down at 27 from 17 dogs. The result was a repeat of 1956, B.O.S. going to Bannoch of Bothkennar and B.O.B. to Willowmead Barberry of Bothkennar. The judge, Mr. Bill Siggers, described each of them as being 'pigeon blue', a colour that I don't recall seeing in the breed records in recent years! In the following year the Dog C.C. went to Britt of Bothkennar and B.O.B. to Beauty Queen of Bothkennar, who went on to gain her title at the next two shows.

Only four sets of C.C.s were available in 1959, and over the next ten years the number fluctuated between six and ten. An interesting feature is that in one year the London Collie Club, which had regularly classified Beardies at its shows, was granted C.C.s for the breed, but these were withdrawn the next year. Judges were invariably all-rounders, often Collie or Shetland Sheepdog specialists.

Besides the granting of C.C.s two other notable events took place in 1959. The Bearded Collie Club produced its first newsletter and held its first open show. There were still insufficient Beardies being shown to provide a reasonable entry for a show, so classes were also provided for Rough and Smooth Collies. This is the reason why the trophy list for the Club's open shows contains trophies both for Best in Show and for Best of Breed. For many years now they have, of course, gone to the same dog, but this was not always the case and in the early days it was the exception rather than the rule for the B.I.S. trophy to be won by a Beardie.

The 1960s was a period of steady but slow development, as may be seen from the following table:-

TABLE 4 - Bearded Collie Registrations 1959-67

1959	65	1962	93	1965	148
1960	77	1963	59	1966	134
1961	48	1964	121	1967	163

Show entries and the number of C.C.s on offer reflected these figures. As late as 1967 the four classes at the Scottish Kennel Club Representative Show drew an entry of only 22 from 14 dogs, and in 1970 only 11 sets of C.C.s were available.

Besides the dogs already mentioned some of the outstanding dogs of the period were Ch. Benjie of Bothkennar, Ch. Wishanger Cairnbhan, Ch. Willowmead My Honey and Ch. Edelweiss of Tambora, to name only a few. In 1964 Mrs. Willison had to give up breeding owing to ill health, and her two youngest champions, Ch. Bravo of Bothkennar and Ch. Blue Bonnie of Bothkennar, went to Mr. and Mrs. K. Osborne where, together with Bluebelle of Bothkennar they formed the foundation of the Osmart Beardies, their son, Ch. Osmart Bonnie Blue Braid, becoming one of the leading stud dogs of the period. A litter brother of Bluebelle's, Bracken Boy of Bothkennar, was acquired by Miss Shirley Holmes of the Edenborough Kennel, where he became, in his day, the breed record holder. On the Obedience side, Ob. Ch. Scapa, owned by Miss Jeni Cooke (now Mrs. Wiggins) became the breed's first, and so far only, Obedience Champion.

Two other important events besides the retirement of Mrs. Willison took place in 1964. One was the birth of the Bearded Collie Club's magazine, Bearded News, under the editorship of Mrs. Betty Foster. Starting as an unpretentious duplicated foolscap affair, by its eighth issue in November 1969 it had already progressed to including a

Ch. Bengie of Bothkennar

photograph (of Glendonald Silver Braid) on the cover. It has continued to thrive over the years, and November 1990 sees the production of its 50th issue.

The other event was the revision of the breed standard. No official standard was in existence before 1955, and the standard adopted then was drawn up from that used by the abortive club formed before the First World War. The main innovation in the 1964 standard concerned height. The previous standard had given a height range of 20 to 24 inches for dogs, with bitches rather less, but in the new standard an ideal height of 21 to 22 inches for dogs and 20 to 21 inches for bitches was substituted for the height range. This did not find favour with Mrs. Willison, who was afraid that it might lead to the breed becoming too small, though in recent years the main fear seems to have been that heights in excess of the ideal will become too common.

1966 saw the formation of the first overseas Bearded Collie Club, that of the Netherlands, which thus became the world's second oldest club for the breed. Less pleasantly, it also saw the arrival of Hip Dysplasia in the breed. Articles in Bearded News urged owners to x-ray their dogs under the KC/BVA Scheme, and many responded. Hip Dysplasia has been a continuing source of concern ever since, and generally speaking breeders have adopted a responsible attitude.

Ch. Bravo of Bothkennar

In 1969 we were at last granted a specialist judge to award C.C.s when Jenny Osborne judged the breed at Blackpool. Few breeds can have served a lengthier apprenticeship than Bearded Collies. More than 60 years elapsed between the time when Beardies were first shown and the granting of a separate breed register, and almost as long before the formation of a registered breed club. The club was not to hold a Breed Championship Show until seventeen years after its registration, and a specialist judge was not appointed to award C.C.s until ten years after Certificates were first awarded. Progress had been slow indeed, but the next twenty years were to show a remarkable change.

The Bearded Collie
Years of Expansion, 1970-1990

IN almost every respect the years from 1970 to 1990 were years of steady expansion of the breed, both in the United Kingdom and Overseas. As far as registrations are concerned this growth had started during the late 1960s. Standing at 163 in 1967 they had climbed to 565 by 1972. As can be seen from Table 6 progress thereafter has been regular, avoiding the great leaps shown by some other breeds which have sprung to popularity but climbing continuously. By 1988 Beardies had reached 21st place in the list of leading breeds. In the following year the two tier system of registration previously in force was replaced by a single tier system. As an exceptionally high proportion of Beardies recorded under the old system - more than 70% - had been registered, this caused the breed to drop to a more realistic 29th place, even though the number of registrations showed, as was to be expected, a considerable increase.

Increasing numbers of registrations meant increasing numbers of owners, and a good proportion of these joined the breed clubs. In May 1969 the paid-up membership of the Bearded Collie Club stood at 94. By 1976 it had reached 712 (including 126 Overseas members), and by 1979 it had passed the 1,000 mark. Despite the increasing number of clubs it continued to grow, and by 1988 was over 1,500, a figure which it maintained in the following year. The first of the regional clubs, the Southern Counties Bearded Collie Club, gained its registration of title in 1977, and in only ten years from its formation its membership too had reached 1,000 and continues to increase. Table 7 shows the growth in the number of clubs in the United Kingdom and the parallel growth in the number of branches of the Parent Club. The Annual General Meeting of the Bearded Collie Club in 1971 gave approval to a suggestion by Barry Diamond that regions should be empowered to appoint Area Representatives, and the first of these, for the Midlands and for Scotland, were appointed in the autumn of that year. At its A.G.M. in 1973 the Bearded Collie Club gave approval for the formation of the Scottish Branch, which gained its registration of title later that year, to be followed the next year by the Southern Branch. In following years branches were formed in the Midlands, the North of England, The West of England and South Wales, and the North-East of England. On the formation of the Southern Counties Bearded Collie Club the name of the Southern Branch was changed to the East Anglia and South-East Branch, which more accurately reflected its sphere of activities. Today the branches run the Club's open shows, which circulate throughout the country, and hold matches, primary shows, obedience and agility shows, working tests and social events, while the Club Committee is responsible for overall policy and the championship show.

Branches cannot hold breed shows above Primary level, and with

Tommy Muirhead's Working Beardies

Balmacneil Jock - The property of Mrs. Cameron Miller, Balmacneil,
Ballinluig, Perthshire

increasing entries and the availability of more sets of Challenge Certificates the desire naturally arose to form regional clubs so that more breed club Open and Championship shows could be held. The Southern Counties Bearded Collie Club in 1977 was followed by the Bearded Collie Club of Scotland the following year, and 1984 and 1986 saw the registration of the Eastern Bearded Collie Association and the North of England Bearded Collie Club respectively. The Southern Counties B.C.C. gained championship status in 1980, the B.C.C. of Scotland in 1982, and the Eastern B.C.A. in 1988. The North of England B.C.C. has been allotted certificates for 1991. All these clubs, like the branches of the national club, hold events such as Obedience, working tests, Agility, social events and seminars as well as their shows.

Overseas there has been a similar development, with the Bearded Collie Club of America being formed in 1969 and that of Canada in 1970, although Beardies were recognised as a show breed in the latter country before they were in the States, where they did not achieve full recognition until 1976. The Swedish Bearded Collie Gruppen was founded in 1971, and by 1985 had attained a membership of about 1,200. In both the U.S.A. and Canada there are also a number of regional clubs. Regional is a relative term, as some of these clubs cater for an area larger than the United Kingdom. Other clubs now exist in the Scandinavian countries, France, Australia, and in other European countries.

In the early 1970s the system of allocation of Challenge Certificates in the United Kingdom was changed. Previously it had depended upon the number of registrations, but the new criterion was the number of entries at championship shows during the previous three years. The new system was to the advantage of our breed, as a relatively high proportion of those registered were shown. Table 5 shows the growth in the allotment of Challenge Certificates during the period. By 1981 certificates were available at all except one of the General Championship Shows, and three years later they were allotted to the remaining show, Belfast. The following year the grant of Championship status to the Scottish Breeds Canine Club saw the number of sets of certificates allotted to Beardies at General Championship Shows rise to 27, the maximum number at present possible. With the grant of certificates to the National Working Breeds in 1973, the Working Breeds Association of Scotland in 1979 and the Working Breeds Association of Wales in 1985 a further three sets became available, and with the North of England B.C.C. gaining status in 1991 the number of sets of C.C.s available to the breed in that year will be 35. In fact, the Beardie entry at championship shows in recent years would entitle the breed to several more sets of certificates, but there are at present no more championship shows to which they could be allotted. At about a third of championship shows in recent years the Beardie entry has exceeded 200 dogs, and more than 300 dogs have been entered at the Bearded Collie Club Championship Show on several occasions, reaching 358 dogs in 1989.

Though the period was to be one of steady expansion there were two inauspicious events near its start. In 1970 the Kennel Club decreed that from the next year registration by inspection would cease to exist and that only the progeny of registered dogs could themselves be registered. The revival of the breed had depended entirely on the registration of the progeny of unregistered dogs from working stock, and it was felt to be essential that this facility should continue to exist, both because the gene pool of the registered breed was still a comparatively narrow one and in order to retain the ability to introduce bloodlines from working stock if the breed should seem to be losing its working characteristics. The Bearded Collie Club therefore wrote to the Kennel Club to request that the facility should be retained by the breed, at least for a limited period. The Kennel Club gave an undertaking that it would consider the registration of dogs from unregistered parents if proof of pure breeding, such as pedigrees or photographs, could be presented, and two Beardies, each with one unregistered parent, were in fact registered in 1971. By 1976, however, when a number of matings between registered and unregistered Beardies had taken place in Scotland, the Kennel Club refused to register two dogs descended from such matings, even though the evidence presented was of precisely the type for which it had asked, and it became apparent that it had unilaterally abrogated its undertaking. One of these dogs had three registered grandparents, and its only unregistered grandparent was proved to be a younger full sister of Britt of Bothkennar, so that this valuable second line to Jock and Mootie was tragically lost to the registered breed, except on the Obedience and Working Trails Register. A further development came in 1984, when Paul Turnbull's dog Blue, bred in Dumfriesshire from pure working stock, gained entry on merit to the International Sheepdog Society's register. As the Kennel Club had accepted for registration Border Collies which were on this register it could not logically deny the same facility to Beardies, and a number of Blue's litters from registered bitches have since been registered. The last Beardie to be registered both of whose parents came from working stock, however, remains Jenny Osborne's Osmart Black-Eyed Susie, registered at the end of the 1960s.

The second potentially damaging event was the withdrawal by the Kennel Club of permission for clubs catering for Rough and Smooth Collies to classify Beardies at their shows. This brought to an end the close connection between the London Collie Club and the Bearded Collie Club. The cups for the Beardie classes were returned to the Bearded Collie Club, and were allotted to the newly formed branches, that for the Best of Breed, the Bothkennar Trophy, going to the Scottish Branch, where it is awarded to the best exhibit from the Scottish Owned classes at the Club's open shows held in Scotland. The cup for Best of Breed at the Scottish Collie Club show was also returned to the Scottish Branch, and is now the Best of Breed trophy at the Working Breeds Association of Scotland Championship Show. In the event, the withdrawal of classes at Collie club shows, coming at a time when more and more shows were starting to classify Beardies, did not cause undue damage, and the Kennel Club seems to have chosen the right time to withdraw their permission.

Though the standard approved in 1964 satisfied many breeders, exhibitors and judges, there were others who considered that in certain respects it was insufficiently specific; and it contained comparisons to other breeds, which it was known that the Kennel Club considered to be undesirable. The Annual General Meeting of the Bearded Collie Club in 1975 therefore set up a committee to consider the revision of the standard. This committee reported to a special meeting held immediately before the 1976 A.G.M., but the draft standard which it had produced did not in some respects find favour with the meeting, and it was decided that a further draft should be considered at an open meeting to be chaired by a nominee appointed by the Kennel Club. The meeting, chaired by Judge Michael Argyle, took place in the autumn of 1976, and an agreed draft was forwarded to the Kennel Club. One of the most controversial clauses in the new standard concerned the white markings, which had simply been described in the 1964 standard as "white collie markings". The new standard defined these markings very precisely, which was not to everyone's liking, and it is noticeable that when, shortly afterwards, the Rough and Smooth Collie standards were revised a very much less rigorous definition was adopted. When the Kennel Club's draft was submitted to the Bearded Collie Club and to the newly formed Southern Counties Bearded Collie Club in the middle of 1977 it was discovered that the clause concerning the muzzle had been altered to make the muzzle slightly longer than, instead of equal in length to, the skull. Both clubs protested that this was incorrect, but when the revised standard appeared in the Kennel Gazette in February 1978 it contained the Kennel Club's version. Prolonged correspondence and intensive lobbying throughout 1978 finally caused the Kennel Club to yield, and the amendment giving effect to the breed clubs' version appeared in the December Kennel Gazette.

The new standard was not to remain in force for long. As a result of the World Congresses in London and Edinburgh the Kennel Club decided to revise all breed standards in order to bring them into a common format and at the same time to remove any clauses which might result in abnormalities in a breed. A draft was circulated to breed clubs for comment in 1985, and the revised standard was promulgated in the following year. The main differences concerned the shoulder, where the attempt to define the angle between the scapula and the humerus, which had been incorrect in the previous standard, was abandoned, and in the mouth, where a scissor bite was merely tolerated instead of accepted. Thus the breed, which had managed without an offficial standard for its first sixty years, was to have four in its next thirty.

An important event in 1977 was the appearance of a Bearded Collie Club Yearbook for the previous year. This publication was entirely the result of the enterprise of Jenny Osborne, who produced it virtually single-handed. It was a mine of information and proved highly popular. Jenny continued to produce the Yearbook until the special edition for the Club's silver jubilee in 1980, after which she felt unable to continue. There was a year's hiatus, after which the Yearbook appeared in a new hardback form under the editorship of Marita Bott, who was succeeded by Garth Nicholls and then by Graham Atkins. Today the Yearbook is a thoroughly professional publication and an essential tool for anyone with a real interest in the breed.

There has always been a number of Beardies working in Obedience, and in 1976 the Bearded Collie Club for the first time put on Obedience classes at its Open Show. Today most of the clubs and several of the parent club's branches hold Obedience classes, either in conjunction with their open shows or as separate events. Entries have been as high as in the eighties, though around forty to fifty is more common. No Beardie has as yet scaled the heights reached by Ob. Ch. Scapa, though a number have worked in Class C and Frances Cross's Liath Morach Bho Mointeach represented Scotland in the Crufts Regional Obedience Competition, which at that time was confined to Class C.

Ever since Bond of Bothkennar became the first Beardie to gain a Stud Book entry in 1954 there have been a few dedicated owners taking part in the extremely severe discipline of Working Trials, and in 1987 Elizabeth Yeld's Tam o' Shagg's Bluff gained his title as Working Trials Champion. In the late 1970s and early 1980s a new outlet for those who wished to work their dogs arose in the sport of Agility, and here too Elizabeth Yeld was one of the first Beardie handlers to make a mark, reaching the semi-final of the competition held in conjunction with the horse show at Olympia. A number of the clubs and branches now feature Agility, and in 1986 a team organised by the Scottish Branch of the Bearded Collie Club won the competition held by the Scottish Kennel Club at the Royal Highland Show, beating into third place the Dundee team which had been runners-up at Crufts that year and which was to win there in the two succeeding years. For some years the Scottish Branch has run an Open Agility Show, the 1990 event drawing an entry of about 650 and requiring the use of three rings and three judges. The Bearded Collie Club of Scotland also runs an Open Agility Show in conjunction with the annual City of Glasgow Show.

Towards the end of the 1970s Denise Barley started training her Beardies for mountain rescue work, possibly the most arduous task that a dog can be asked to perform, with dog and handler liable to be called out at any time and in any weather conditions. Three dogs were trained, Strathourn Swinging Gael, Sallen Rhum and Quinbury Stormdrifter at Runival. The first named passed the higher assessment, and the last showed his versitility by qualifying C.D.Ex. in working trials and by winning Best of Breed at Crufts in 1985.

As Beardie entries at shows increased and more classes were provided more judges came to recognise the qualities of the breed and it started to make a mark at Group level. The breakthrough came in 1974 when Andrew Drake's Ch. Andrake Persephone won the Working Group at Blackpool. She went on to become, in her day, the bitch record holder for the breed. At the very next show, Windsor, Shirley Holmes's Ch. Edenborough Blue Bracken won the Working Group and went on to take Best in Show, the first Beardie to achieve this honour at a championship show. This dog dominated the breed during the first half of the 1970s, winning 38 C.C.s between 1972 and 1979, a record which still stands. He also had a great career as a veteran, being the only Beardie so far to win Veteran of the Year, All Breeds. Later in 1974 Phyl Bailey's Charncroft Crusader won Best in Show at the Scottish Kennel Club August Show. The latter part of the 1970s was dominated by Janet and Mike Lewis's Ch. Pepperland Lyric John at Potterdale, who won 30 C.C.s between 1976 and 1981. He proved to be an outstanding sire, and with their foundation bitches Ch. Blumberg Hadriana at Potterdale and Ch. Tamevalley Easter Song at Potterdale, who became the bitch record holder, the Lewises built up the Potterdale kennel which exercised a powerful influence on the breed during the 1980s. During 1975 and 1976 the leading Beardie in the show ring was Bryony Harcourt-Brown's Ch. Mignonette of Willowmead of Orora, one of the foundation bitches of the Orora Beardies. Her son to Ch. Osmart Bonnie Blue Braid, Ch. Orora's Frank, became another very potent sire. Mated to Ch. Tamevalley Easter Song of Potterdale (Ch. Pepperland Lyric John at Potterdale out of Ch. Dutch Bonnet of Willowmead) he sired Brenda White's Ch. Potterdale Classic of Moonhill. In 1988 this bitch won 11 C.C.s, taking her dam's bitch record in the process and including three Best in Shows at General Championship Shows, a Reserve Best in Show and two other Group wins, and best in Show at a Group Championship Show. The following February she became the first Beardie to win Best in Show at Crufts.

At the start of the 1990s it is almost commonplace for the Best of Breed Beardie to be pulled out into the final selection in the Working Group, and Group or Best in Show wins come as no great surprise. Beardies regularly appear in such competitions as the Champion and Veteran Stakes Finals and in the Pup of the Year Final. Clearly, if the main object of breeders is to produce stock which is capable of winning at Group or Best in Show level they have been outstandingly successful. Whether they have been equally successful in maintaining the true breed type as defined by the standard is, to say the least, open to question.

TABLE 5 - Allotment of C.C.s, 1971 to 1991

Year	General Shows	Group Shows	Breed Club Shows	Total
1971	12	-	-	12
1972	14	-	1	15
1973	16	1	1	18
1974	16	1	1	18
1975	21	1	1	23
1976	22	1	-	23
1977	22	1	1	24
1978	24	1	1	26
1979	24	2	1	27
1980	24	2	2	28
1981	25	2	2	29
1982	25	2	3	30
1983	25	2	3	30
1984	26	2	3	31
1985	27	3	3	33
1986	27	3	3	33
1987	27	3	3	33
1988	27	3	4	34
1989	27	3	3	33
1990	27	3	4	34
1991	27	3	5	35

Table 6 - Bearded Collie Registrations, 1972 to 1989

1972	565	1978	757	1984	1487
1973	661	1979	1082	1985	1443
1974	651	1980	1345	1986	1487
1975	677	1981	1179	1987	1496
1976	393*	1982	1179	1988	1524
1977	373*	1983	1371	1989	1945**

*　　During this period a three tier registration system was in operation.
Only active registrations were published
**　During 1989 a single tier registration system, replacing the previous two tier system, was introduced.

Table 7 - Growth of U.K. Bearded Collie Clubs

Year	No. of Clubs	No. of Branches of B.C.C.
1971	1	-
1973	1	1
1974	1	2
1976	1	3
1977	2	3
1978	3	4
1982	3	5
1984	4	5
1986	5	5
1987	5	6

Useful Names and Addresses

The Bearded Collie Club.
Hon. Secretary.
Mrs. Denise Atkins.
"Labooshar".
13, Ferry Street. Stapenhill.
Burton-on-Trent.
Staffordshire. DE15 9EU.

Southern Counties Bearded Collie Club.
Hon. Secretary.
Mrs. Anne Waldron.
11 Silverdale Drive.
Sunbury on Thames. Middlesex. TW16 6HE.

Eastern Bearded Collie Association
Hon. Secretary.
Mrs. Joyce Collis.
"Peewit House".
Astwick Road.
Stotfold. Hitchin. Herts.

Northern Bearded Collie Club.
Hon. Secretary.
Mrs. Joanne Pickford.
29. Delph Lane.
Oldham. Lancs. OL3 5HX.

Bearded Collie Club of Scotland.
Hon. Secretary.
Mrs. L Sichi.
2 Back Street.
Tarbolton. Ayrshire.
Scotland.

The Kennel Club.
1, Clarges Street,
Piccadilly.
London. W1Y 8AB.

Tailpiece

IN thinking back to all the Beardies I have owned, I like to think they are all similar to the lovely description of "Owd Bob", but if one is honest, no dog quite fulfills the ultimate accolade. I definitely have some that are 80 per cent like Owd Bob, with the last 20 per cent like MacKensie from John MacNab, and again, some, luckily in the minority, 80 per cent like "Bloody MacKensie" and only 20 per cent like Owd Bob. I suppose the ultimate would be to aim for 50 per cent of both, but Beardies are extremely adaptable dogs and you will find, more often than not, that they will adjust to your life style and temperament, so which ever suits you best, Owd Bobs "Gentle Knight", or MacKensie's "mischievous roustabout" that is what he will grow up to be, because he is a dog that tries to the very best of his ability to devote his life to pleasing his owners wishes.

Please, when you acquire a beardie, do not abuse his trust and devotion, appreciate his sterling attributes and always, always give him masses of love.

You don't need to talk to give an opinion!